"Dempster makes biblical theology come alive in this engaging book. A trusted guide, he takes readers through the Bible's dramatic, true story of the restoration of God's perfect rule over creation with human beings as his vicegerents and priests. As Dempster points out, this kingdom often appears to be upside-down in comparison to the kingdoms of this world. Insightful and accessible, this book both instructs us about God's kingdom and rightly exhorts us to live in light of its consummation."

Kevin S. Chen, professor of Old Testament at Christian Witness Theological Seminary and author of *The Messianic Vision of the Pentateuch*

"Stephen G. Dempster has gifted the untutored Christian with an understanding of the story line of the Bible and how all its parts contribute to that story, succinctly captured in the book's title, *The Return of the Kingdom*. It's a magisterial presentation. But his gift is also for those most educated in that story. Rarely do I want to pick up a book again after having read it. I will pick up *The Return of the Kingdom* many times. I enthusiastically commend it to all who hope for Christ's return or are without hope."

Bruce K. Waltke, professor emeritus of biblical studies, Regent College, Vancouver, and distinguished professor emeritus at Knox Theological Seminary

"In this wonderful book, Stephen Dempster summarizes and renarrates the biblical narratives from Genesis to Revelation showing how they all interlace with one another looking forward to the first and second coming of Christ the Servant-King. Through a comprehensive survey of kingdom allusions in the Scriptures, he demonstrates the will of God to establish his gracious and compassionate rule and reign on the earth and Jesus as the One who fulfills this will. In addition, Dempster brings many, many years of scholarship and pastoral wisdom into his readings that bring fresh and welcome insights into well-known stories. This should be compulsory reading for all students of the Scriptures."

Lucy Peppiatt, principal of Westminster Theological Centre and author of *Rediscovering Scripture's Vision for Women*

THE RETURN OF
THE KINGDOM
A Biblical Theology
of God's Reign

STEPHEN G. DEMPSTER

An imprint of InterVarsity Press
Downers Grove, Illinois

InterVarsity Press
P.O. Box 1400 | Downers Grove, IL 60515-1426
ivpress.com | email@ivpress.com

©2024 by Stephen G. Dempster

InterVarsity Press® is the publishing division of InterVarsity Christian Fellowship/USA®. For more information, visit intervarsity.org.

All Scripture quotations, unless otherwise indicated, are translated by the author.

While any stories in this book are true, some names and identifying information may have been changed to protect the privacy of individuals.

The publisher cannot verify the accuracy or functionality of website URLs used in this book beyond the date of publication.

Cover design: Brad Joiner
Interior design: Daniel van Loon
Cover image credit: © lasagnaforone / Getty Images

ISBN 978-0-8308-4291-9 (print) | ISBN 978-0-8308-4293-3 (digital)

Printed in the United States of America ♾

Library of Congress Cataloging-in-Publication Data

Names: Dempster, Stephen G., author.
Title: The return of the kingdom : a biblical theology of God's reign / Stephen G. Dempster.
Description: Downers Grove, IL : IVP Academic, [2024] | Series: Essential studies in biblical theology | Includes bibliographical references and index.
Identifiers: LCCN 2023039511 (print) | LCCN 2023039512 (ebook) | ISBN 9780830842919 (print) | ISBN 9780830842933 (digital)
Subjects: LCSH: Kingdom of God–Biblical teaching. | Bible. Genesis–Criticism, interpretation, etc. | Bible. Revelation–Criticism, interpretation, etc. | Jesus Christ–Royal office.
Classification: LCC BT94 .D455 2024 (print) | LCC BT94 (ebook) | DDC 231.7/2–dc23/eng/20231026
LC record available at https://lccn.loc.gov/2023039511
LC ebook record available at https://lccn.loc.gov/2023039512

30 29 28 27 26 25 24 | 13 12 11 10 9 8 7 6 5 4 3 2 1

I would like to dedicate this book to my daughter, Joanna Ruth,

whose name represents the coming of the kingdom in both testaments.

The birth of this book coincides with the far more amazing birth of

Armaan, the son of Joanna Ruth and her husband, Anwaz.

The meaning of Armaan—hope—constitutes

an essential feature of kingdom life in the present.

Reading the Bible as Scripture is never a matter of handling texts
and the relationships between texts. It is above all a matter of being
in the presence and open to the handling of the One who, in some sense,
is the final "author" of its message, because he is the one whose story it tells,
and it is as we know him, as we dwell in his presence, and as he dwells in us
that we see and hear what he is saying and showing to us through it.

TREVOR HART

CONTENTS

SERIES PREFACE

BENJAMIN L. GLADD

THE ESSENTIAL STUDIES IN BIBLICAL THEOLOGY is patterned after the highly esteemed series New Studies in Biblical Theology, edited by D. A. Carson. Like the NSBT, this series is devoted to unpacking the various strands of biblical theology. The field of biblical theology has grown exponentially in recent years, showing no sign of abating. At the heart of biblical theology is the unfolding nature of God's plan of redemption as set forth in the Bible.

With an influx of so many books on biblical theology, why generate yet another series? A few reasons. The ESBT is dedicated to the fundamental or "essential" broad themes of the grand story line of the Bible. Stated succinctly, the goal of the ESBT series is to explore the *central* biblical-theological themes of the Bible. Several existing series on biblical theology are generally open-ended, whereas the ESBT will be limited to ten or so volumes. By restricting the entire series, the scope of the project is established from the beginning. The ESBT project functions as a whole in that each theme is intentional, and each volume does not stand solely on its own merits. The individual volumes interlock with one another and, taken together, form a complete and cohesive unit.

Another unique dimension of the series is a robust emphasis on biblical theology, spanning the entire sweep of the history of redemption. Each volume

traces a particular theme throughout the Bible, from Genesis 1–3 to
Revelation 21–22, and is organically connected to the person of Christ and
the church in the New Testament. To avoid a flat biblical theology, these
projects are mindful of how the New Testament develops their topics in fresh
or unexpected ways. For example, the New Testament sheds new light on
the nature of the kingdom and messiah. Though these twin themes are
rooted and explored in the Old Testament, both flow through the person of
Christ in unique ways. Biblical theology should include how Old Testament
themes are held in continuity and discontinuity with the New Testament.

The audience of the series includes beginning students of theology, church
leaders, and laypeople. The ESBT is intended to be an accessible introduction
to core biblical-theological themes of the Bible. This series is not designed
to overturn every biblical-theological rock and investigate the finer details
of biblical passages. Each volume is intentionally brief, serving as a primer
of sorts that introduces the reader to a particular theme. These works also
attempt to apply their respective biblical-theological themes to Christian
living, ministry, and worldview. Good biblical theology warms the heart and
motivates us to grow in our knowledge and adoration of the triune God.

ACKNOWLEDGMENTS

NO BOOK LIKE THIS occurs in a vacuum. My parents instilled in me a love not only for the Bible but also its Author, the great King, without whom this book would never have been written. Past mentors such as Raymond Dillard, Richard Gaffin, and Palmer Robertson created a love for biblical theology, and others like John Revell and John Wevers did the same for biblical Hebrew. I am also indebted to those who have served with me over the years in the Biblical Theology Study Group for the Evangelical Theological Society: Scott Hafemann, Paul House, Mark Dubis, Jim Hamilton, Bob Yarborough, Dan Timmer, and most recently, Ched Spellman. This is not to mention my many students from whom I have learned so much, as well as my spiritual advisors and mentors: Ted Newell, Rick Thomas, Mark Smith, and Ron Albinet. Benjamin Gladd, the series editor, and Rachel Hastings and her team at IVP have definitely improved the delivery of the content of the book. Their enthusiasm has greatly encouraged me. Finally, I am in great debt to the great company of writers in the field of biblical theology.

THE RETURN OF
THE KINGDOM

THE BIBLICAL THEOLOGY OF GOD'S REIGN

WHEN CONTEMPORARY CHRISTIANS SPEAK of the Return of the King, they are referring to the second coming of Jesus Christ, who came the first time in the middle of history to bring about salvation for the penitent through his life, death and resurrection, and who will come again to finish his mission at the end of history to usher in the new heavens and new earth wherein dwell righteousness and justice. Christians have called this second coming "the blessed hope" (Titus 2:13) and it has been more or less emphasized and deemphasized at various points in the last two millennia. For example, at the end of the first millennium AD there was a great expectation of such an event,[1] and at different times in the second millennium and into the third, there has been a flourishing of cults and individuals who target the credulous with their claims about knowing the precise date of an impending apocalypse.[2]

[1]Tom Holland, *Millennium: The End of the World and the Forging of Christendom* (New York: Little, Brown, 2011). See especially his first chapter, titled "The Return of the King."

[2]John M. Court, *Approaching the Apocalypse: A Short History of Christian Millenarianism* (London: Bloomsbury Academic, 2008). See also contemporary works by evangelical authors: Hal Lindsey,

But the phrase "Return of the King" when used by Jews in the postexilic period and into the period of the first century AD meant the return of David, or more accurately the coming of a Davidic descendant. In this understanding David was eventually going to have a descendant who would rule the world and bring all of Israel's enemies into subjection, slaying them with the breath of his mouth, and vindicating the righteous.[3]

But the way I am using this phrase is slightly different. I am arguing that the phrase is a way of comprehending the entire biblical message. The biblical story begins with the creation of the universe by a sovereign King, who creates human beings to be the vicegerents of his creation and to have dominion over the world, to subdue it in such a way that their work brings glory to their Sovereign. They are royal representatives, called as God's image bearers to extend the divine rule in his vast creation, to have dominion over it for the glory of God. Or to use another image, they are to be priests leading the congregation of creation in one great song to their Creator.

In Psalm 148, the elements of creation are called on to praise the Lord, starting with the high heavens and the angels and working down from the heavenly inanimate elements such as the stars and sun and moon to the earth with its sea creatures, and land animals, to human beings—kings and princes, and men and women, both young and old. Finally, there is mention of Israel, a people close to God's heart. As James Luther Mays mentions,

> How are sun and moon, heavens and water, storms and mountains, animals and birds, to answer the call to praise? How can they fulfill their obligation? One might attribute the call to them to poetic license, but that would miss the theological seriousness behind the hymnic joy. Perhaps there is the hint of an answer in verses 5-6 and 8. The celestial lights and firmament and the waters are the work of the Lord's command, and they are maintained in their place and purpose by his power. The stormy wind fulfills his command by being a stormy wind.[4]

The Late Great Planet Earth (Grand Rapids, MI: Zondervan, 1970); Tim LaHaye and Jerry B. Jenkins, *Left Behind: A Novel of the Earth's Last Days* (Wheaton, IL: Tyndale House, 1998).

[3]Michael Snearly, among others, insightfully points this out in his excellent monograph on the fifth book of the Psalter: *The Return of the King: Messianic Expectation in Book V of the Psalter* (New York: Bloomsbury, 2015).

[4]James Luther Mays, *Psalms*, Interpretation (Louisville, KY: John Knox, 1994), 445.

Israel, however, is mentioned last since it alone knows the exalted name of the Lord, and "they are given the voice to express the unspoken voice of all creation. . . . In the praise of the people of the LORD, the name that is the truth about the entire universe is spoken on behalf of all the rest of creation."[5] Thus humanity is not only regal but priestly since they have a mediatorial role toward the rest of creation, not only ruling it but mediating God to it and articulating its praise to the Lord.

Humanity is made to be a royal priesthood, a thought that coheres aptly with the call of Israel in Exodus 19:5-6 and blends well with the idea that Genesis 1 is the writing of someone with priestly concerns, and of course with the thought that permeates the Bible and the ancient world of the temple being a microcosm of the cosmos, the preeminent place of the divine presence.

This can be seen in numerous places in Scripture. When Isaiah has his vision in the temple after his earthly monarch, Uzziah, dies, he sees the heavenly king, surrounded by the chanting heavenly beings, seated on a throne, robed in a royal garment whose train fills the temple. The micro-universe (the temple on earth) filled with the train of the divine robe is a striking analogy of the macro-universe (the temple of creation) filled with the glory of God, as the heavenly beings recognize resoundingly in their chant: "Holy, Holy, Holy is the LORD of Hosts; the entire earth is filled with his glory" (Is 6:3). This is a vision of the kingdom of God in its fullness as the true King of the universe is sitting on a throne!

A similar evocation of praise happens when Israelites perceive the glory of God in the thunderstorm, and "in his temple all cry, 'Glory!'" (Ps 29:9). The temple in this context is the world, as it is in the holy chant of the seraphic angels. In both cases it is the enthronement of Yahweh as King and his divine glory throughout the world that is being praised (Ps 29:10). This is in fact also the case when God's future reign over the earth is celebrated. The created elements of his universe break out in song praising his kingship. No longer is it enough for worshipers to sing in the physical sanctuary—the inhabitants of the cosmic temple must cry out:

---

[5]Mays, *Psalms*, 445.

Let the sea roar and its fullness, the world and all its inhabitants! Let the
rivers clap their hands; together with them let the mountains sing for joy.
Before Yahweh, for he comes to judge the earth. He will judge the earth in
righteousness and the peoples in equity. (Ps 98:7-9)

I have used as the title of this book *The Return of the Kingdom*, because it
captures in one succinct phrase the storyline of the Bible. Instead of human
beings fulfilling their royal calling to rule the creation on behalf of their Sovereign,
they decided to rebel and live for themselves, plunging the world into enslavement under the rule of a dark, serpentine Lord. Human beings became
his miniature despots, tyrannizing and destroying their relationships and their
environment. Instead of the world being filled with the glory of Yahweh it became
replete with violence, sin, and death (Gen 6:5-6, 11-12). At the same time God,
the sovereign King, promised through a human being to restore the rightful
rule of humanity over creation by defeating the dark Lord and sin and death,
establishing a world where peace and justice would reign, where the lion would
lie down with the lamb, where a little child would lead them, and every serpent
would shed its harmful nature (Gen 3:15; Is 11:1-10, 65:17-25). The Isaianic passages recall the pristine beginnings of creation and the Edenic imagery prominent there. They make known that God's final intent for human beings not
only echoes but even surpasses his original intention. The biblical narrative is
an "enormous rescue plan,"[6] and the world awaits the return of the kingdom of
God, and its rightful heirs—human beings crowned with glory and honor!

DISCUSSION QUESTIONS

1. How does viewing the world around you as a sacred temple change
   the way you think about it?

2. What are some practical applications about your view of the natural
   environment, the use of natural resources, the treatment of animals?

3. The English poet George Herbert wrote ("Providence") that if humans
   as the royal priests of God refuse praise they "doth commit a world of
   sinne in one." What do you think he means?

---

[6]Sandra L. Richter, *The Epic of Eden: A Christian Entry into the Old Testament* (Downers Grove, IL:
IVP Academic, 2008), 137.

Chapter One

THE BIG PICTURE

THE BIBLE'S BOOKENDS

ALTHOUGH THE BIBLE IS a collection of books, it is remarkable that it constitutes a coherent story. In fact, there are signs of this in its various collections.[1] Even in the early church there was the idea of a plotline to the biblical story: the analogy of faith. Irenaeus spoke of how heretics would rearrange the Scriptures to suit their needs and thus create the image of a fox or dog instead of a king.[2] But one way to make sense of a book is to study its beginning and its end. The beginning sets the stage and introduces major themes, and the end provides closure for the story. In the Bible the first few chapters provide an introduction not only to the book but to the world, and the last two chapters provide a conclusion for both. So in a sense in this book the world and the story are intimately woven together; some scholars would say that the Bible contains the true story of the whole world.[3]

[1]W. Edward Glenny and Darian R. Lockett, eds., *Canon Formation: Tracing the Role of Sub-collections in the Biblical Canon* (London: T&T Clark, 2023).
[2]Irenaeus, *Against Heresies* 1:8.
[3]Craig G. Bartholomew and Michael W. Goheen, *The True Story of the Whole World: Finding Your Place in the Biblical Drama* (Grand Rapids, MI: Brazos, 2009).

In the first chapters there is a world that is created by a transcendent God, a world of life and beauty, wild and wonderful, and in it human beings are placed as rulers to have obedient dominion over the creation (Gen 1:26-28). They are God's image bearers in the earth. As those image bearers they are priest-like to represent God to the rest of his creation, and to represent creation to God. They have a mediatorial role.

At the end of the Bible, Jesus, the Ruler of the kings of the earth, by his salvation has constituted Christians to be a kingdom, to be priests for God, to reign on the earth (Rev 1:6; 5:10). When the new heavens and new earth finally arrive, Christians reign with Christ, and like the high priest in the ancient temple, they each have the divine name on their foreheads (Rev 22:3-5). The last chapters of the Christian Bible emphasize the beginning to show not only the repetition of the beginning but the superiority of the ending. In fact, the end is not just a return to the beginning but a greater and more wonderful new start. Several scholars have highlighted some of the correspondences between the beginning of the story in Genesis 1–3 and its culmination in Revelation 21–22.[4] Yet, a dire situation occupies the middle and throws into relief the fundamental difference between the beginning and the end. The end not only forcefully echoes the beginning but resolves the peril in between.

Table 1.1. The biblical story from beginning to end

BEGINNING GENESIS 1–2	IN BETWEEN GENESIS 3– REVELATION 20	END REVELATION 21–22
Creation of heavens and earth (Gen 1:1)	Sin, death, oppression	New creation of heavens and earth (Rev 21:1)
Creation of seas (Gen 1:2, 9-10)	Seas are often wild and unruly (cf. Ps 93)	No sea (Rev 21:1)
No human death (Gen 1:31; 2:17)	Death pervades	No death (Rev 21:4)
No pain and tears (Gen 1:1–2:25)	Pain and tears	No pain and tears (Rev 21:4)

---

[4]W. J. Dumbrell, *The End of the Beginning: Revelation 21–22 and the Old Testament* (Eugene, OR: Wipf and Stock, 2001); Bruce K. Waltke, *An Old Testament Theology: An Exegetical, Canonical, and Thematic Approach* (Grand Rapids, MI: Zondervan, 2007), 169.

BEGINNING GENESIS 1-2	IN BETWEEN GENESIS 3– REVELATION 20	END REVELATION 21-22
Creation of sun and moon (Gen 1:14-19)	Presence of sun and moon	No sun and moon (Rev 21:23)
All is darkness (Gen 1:2) and then darkness is restricted (Gen 1:3-5)	Darkness (restricted) and spiritual darkness pervades	No darkness (Rev 21:25)
River of life with one tree of life (Gen 2:8-14)	Tabernacle/temple (in which there is water and garden imagery)	River of life with trees of life (Rev 22:1-4)
No curse (Gen 2:17)	Curse everywhere (except tabernacle/ temple)	No curse (Rev 22:3)
No sin (Gen 2:17)	Sin everywhere (except tabernacle/ temple)	No sin
Divine rule (Gen 1–2)	No divine rule except in tabernacle/temple and in covenants	Divine rule (no temple)
Humans as divine image bearers and as co-rulers (Gen 1:26-28)	Humans as distorted image bearers, redeemed to image God	Humans as image bearers and as co-rulers (Rev 22:4)

There is thus a description of the old creation, the heavens and the earth at the beginning and a new creation of the heavens and earth at the end. At the beginning humans rule as the image of God, and at the end they rule as well. The exact phrase "image of God" is not used of humans in Revelation 22:4 but they are described as having the name of God on their foreheads, which means that they in effect reflect the character of God, and they reign forever.[5] There is no sin and death at the beginning and end, no pain and tears. The rule of God over the universe, which began in Genesis, finally returns to earth through his imagers but in a more glorious manner.

But it is clear that in the major part of the book—the great "in between"—something drastic has happened—a horrific disaster. This world collapsed

---

[5]They also represent the high priest for he was the only one who wore the name of God on his forehead (Ex 28:36-38).

downward into a place of darkness and death. Some parts of the Bible refer to this period as an epoch of death and sin (Eccles 1–12; Rom 5:12-17). No longer the place where everything is very good (Gen 1:31), this world has become filled with violence (Gen 6:5-7, 11-12; 8:21). Human beings, once alive with the Spirit of God, are now dead in trespasses and sins, inspired by a dark Lord, who holds them captive to evil lusts and desires (Eph 2:1-3).

CREATION, FALL, RESTORATION

Many scholars use a *U* shape representing creation, fall, and restoration,[6] or in similar terms as a grand rescue project,[7] to diagram the message of the Bible.

Figure 1.1. The traditionally understood
U-shaped message of the Bible

In the words of F. Buechner, the novelist, "God creates the world; the world gets lost; God seeks to restore the world to the glory for which he created it."[8] Thus "eschatology is like protology," the end like the beginning.[9] The second world, however, at the end is superior to the first creation as the second has

---

[6]Northrop Frye, *The Great Code: The Bible and Literature* (Toronto: University of Toronto Press, 2006), 190-219.

[7]Sandra L. Richter, *The Epic of Eden: A Christian Entry into the Old Testament* (Downers Grove, IL: IVP Academic, 2008).

[8]Frederick Buechner, *The Clown in the Belfry: Writings on Faith and Fiction* (San Francisco: Harper-SanFrancisco, 1992), 44.

[9]Jon D. Levenson, "The Temple and the World," *The Journal of Religion* 64 (1984): 298.

no sea, no darkness, and has many trees of life as opposed to only one—and significantly, there is no tree of knowledge of good and evil. It is a grander creation—better than the original. So rather than a *U* shape, the message of the Bible should be drawn as a checkmark, with the second line higher than the first.

Figure 1.2. The superiority of the restoration in the message of the Bible

One of the crucial points in these depictions of the beginning and the end is that in the first world before the collapse, humans were made to rule the world *on God's behalf.* Thus, this was a place of divine kingship. It was the place where the kingdom of God was to be prominent. And at the end humans are ruling *with God* forever and ever.

Moreover, the "in between" exhibits clear adumbrations of the beginning and the end. For example, the tabernacle and temple, designed to be the location of God's rule, were miniature worlds in contracted space and were meant to reflect the cosmos.[10] A similar universal thrust is also found in the call of Abraham. Through his seed the entire world would one day be blessed and restored. The covenants God makes with the people of Israel, the seed of Abraham, establish a holy nation and a priestly kingdom, offering a glimpse of the future for the entire world, a world again brought under God's rule.

---

[10]See, e.g., the parallelism between the creation of the world in Genesis 1:1–2:3 and the creation of the tabernacle in Exodus 25–31, 35–40. Stephen G. Dempster, *Dominion and Dynasty: A Biblical Theology of The Hebrew Bible* (Downers Grove, IL: IVP Academic, 2003), 102-3.

Thus, there is in the "in between" the beginning of the end, the pathway from tragedy to glorious destiny. That pathway marked through the Bible is not straight ahead but more like a long winding road that goes forward, curving off to the side, tracking backward, zigzagging in another direction before advancing again.

There is no better place to start reading a book than at the beginning. The beginning of a story often lays out the key framework for understanding the book. The key players, the key scenes, the key elements of the plot—all essential for understanding the development of the story—are found here. It is certainly the case with the Bible. Here are introduced God and his image, and an anti-God/anti-human enemy, key players in the biblical narrative. The stage on which this drama is played is the earth.

DISCUSSION QUESTIONS

1. What do you think the impact on your understanding of Scripture is by not reading it as a story, with a beginning, a middle, and an end?

2. Jesus criticized some of the religious leaders of his time for treating all the details of the law (tithing the smallest herbs, justice, mercy, and faith) all on the same level. How can an understanding of the complete Story—the big picture—help rectify this error?

Chapter Two

THE KINGDOM BEGUN

GENESIS AND KINGSHIP

THE BEGINNING OF THE BIBLE IS THE TORAH and it consists of five books: Genesis, Exodus, Leviticus, Numbers and Deuteronomy. But it can also be subdivided into two divisions: Genesis 1–11 and Genesis 12–Deuteronomy 34. The first section is often called the Primeval History, and the second can be termed a National History. The Primeval History deals with universal concerns, such as creation and fall, and all peoples as shown by the Table of Nations in Genesis 10. The National History concentrates on one family and its evolution and growth into the nation of Israel. The universal problems and curses encountered in the Primeval History are going to be addressed by the National History. Indeed, the mission of Israel is to begin the process of reestablishing God's kingdom begun in Genesis 1–2 but thwarted in Genesis 3. As has been aptly described by one scholar: "God so loved the world that he chose Abraham and called Israel."[1]

---

[1]Christopher J. H. Wright, *The Mission of God: Unlocking the Bible's Grand Narrative* (Downers Grove, IL: InterVarsity Press, 2006), 263.

IN THE BEGINNING

An overview of the beginning of Genesis shows that it is structured in the
form of a genealogical tree, stressing the importance of human descent and
lineage. One of the purposes of a genealogical structure within the Bible is
not just a tracing backward but a pushing forward to a divine goal. There are
essentially ten of these branches to the genealogical tree in Genesis, which
start in Genesis 2:4 and continue. Each one emerges out of a previous section
(Gen 2:4; 5:1; 6:9; 10:1; 11:10, 27; 25:12, 19; 36:1; 37:2).[2]

The beginning of Genesis 1:1–2:3 functions as a prologue to the whole,
introducing some of the main themes to follow, almost providing a type
of overture for a musical performance. It is distinguished by being written
in a distinctive style of elevated prose narrative. It is almost poetic prose,
a *proem*. Its symmetrical structure and precise wording compose a majestic
introduction to the book of Genesis and the Bible. Every word counts.[3]
The sequence using the number seven is stressed throughout: the initial
verse consists of seven words, creation occurs over seven days, God sees
the goodness of creation seven times (Gen 1:4, 10, 12, 18, 21, 25, 31), the
title of God appears thirty-five times, and thirty-five words describe the
events of the seventh day, which also contains three sentences consisting
of seven words each (Gen 2:2 and the first part of Gen 2:3). This sevenfold
emphasis in this liturgical production can hardly be fortuitous, along
with the tenfold repetition of the creative word (Gen 1:3, 6, 9, 11, 14, 20,
24, 26, 28, 29), the climactic creation of the divine image, and the "Sabbath"
day conclusion.

In a series of actions described as a human work week of seven days, God
creates the universe. The world is created for the flourishing of its creatures,
ruled by human beings under the divine rule. After creating the universe,
the focus shifts to the earth as a place of order and harmony, shaped from
unformed matter described as an abyss of water enveloped in darkness. Two
triads of organization occur, where a habitat is formed, and then filled with
inhabitants. The first triad (days 1-3) consists of light, the heavens separating

---

[2]There is an additional genealogy of Esau in Gen 36:9.
[3]"Nothing is here by chance; everything must be considered carefully, deliberately, and precisely."
Gerhard von Rad, *Genesis: A Commentary* (Philadelphia: Westminster John Knox, 1973), 47.

waters above from waters below, then the land emerging from the waters below, complete with vegetation (Gen 1:3-13). The second triad (days 4-6) comprises the inhabitants of these habitats: the sun and moon rule the sphere of light, the fowl the sky and the fish the water, and finally animals and humans live on the earth and humans rule the whole (Gen 1:14-31).

Significantly, only darkness and water occupy the beginning. This is totally uninhabitable space, and both the darkness and the water are preserved in the creation. The darkness is separated from the light and is preserved as a recurring period—day and night—in which light alternates with darkness. The waters are then separated into seas and oceans and partially subside as dry ground appears, making space for future plants, animals, and human habitation. Both darkness and water are restricted and serve as reminders of the very beginning and reflect God's grace in providing light and land. Each day, in a sense, is a reminder of the original creation.

CREATION, ENTHRONEMENT, AND HUMAN DOMINION

But there are three more salient points to consider about this world. First, the entire account reflects the sovereign power of the Creator. Unrivaled, his word is sovereign. The command-response sequence is automatic. From ancient Near Eastern creation accounts we learn that creation means enthronement.[4] Other creation texts in the Bible highlight this: "The Lord has become king; he is robed in grandeur; the world stands firm, it cannot be shaken" (Ps 93:1); "For the Lord is a great God, a great king above all gods. In his hand are the depths of the earth, the peaks of the mountains are his. His is the sea, He made it, and the land which his hands have fashioned" (Ps 95:3-5). Creation is a function of the reign of God.[5]

Second, despite the vast plethora of creation during this sequence of seven days, there is a climactic buildup to the creation of humanity on the sixth day. Some of the key differences between the creation of humans and the other creations are as follows. First, every other animal creation is created

---

[4]Moshe Weinfeld, "Sabbath, Temple and the Enthronement of the Lord," in *Mélanges Bibliques et Orientaux En l'honneur de M. Henri Cazelles,* ed. A. Caquot and M. Delcor (Kevelaer: Butzon und Bercker, 1981), 501-12.

[5]John Gray, *The Biblical Doctrine of the Reign of God* (Edinburgh: T&T Clark, 1979), 48.

en masse, but humanity is created as male and female. Second, this creation of humanity is set apart since there is a pregnant pause before the creation of human beings as God ponders and reflects before their creation. As von Rad clarifies, the previous creations happen from a distance as there is a bond between the creatures and their environment, as they are brought forth from the earth or the seas in a simple command-consequence sequence. But human beings originate "from above, from God, in absolute immediacy." Thus "God participates in this creation more intimately and intensively than in the other works of creation."[6] Third, where all previous creations emerge from the earth or water and produce after *their kind*, this creation emerges from God, is patterned after *God's kind*, and is therefore in God's image. Finally, because humans are made in God's image, they have a different relation to the rest of creation and a different relation to God. They rule the rest of creation and have an immediate relation to God.

The terms that capture this unique relationship are *image* and *likeness*. It used to be thought that these were essentially synonyms, a distinct theological vocabulary found only in the Bible. But a recently discovered bilingual inscription in Akkadian and Aramaic in northern Syria, dating to the ninth century BC, uses these terms in a way that helpfully expresses their distinct nuances. The inscription appears on the back and front of a large statue of a governor named Hadad-yithi,[7] indicating that he ruled in a certain place, and *his image proclaims his rule and his likeness his homage to his god*. In a sense he faces outward to the world in his image while he faces inward to his god in his likeness. While the words in the Hebrew texts do overlap in meaning, this nuance of rule and dominion of the world (facing the world as his image) on God's behalf as his obedient servant (facing God as his likeness) provides some insight. Put another way, "As the human creatures faced God in communion, they can now face the world in dominion."[8] This way of putting the matter is crucial, for if they do not face God in communion, their dominion will be distorted into domination.

---

[6]Von Rad, *Genesis*, 57.

[7]W. Randall Garr, "'Image' and 'Likeness' in the Inscription from Tell Fakhariyeh," *Israel Exploration Journal* 50 (2000): 227-34.

[8]I owe this description to Jacob Leeming in an unpublished paper on Genesis 1-2.

There is unmistakably a royal dimension to humanity, as it now is called to rule the world on God's behalf. One could say that in their distinct role they are to image the divine rule over all creation. Peter Gentry and Steven Wellum draw this very conclusion about the ancient Near Eastern idea of the image of God:

> To sum up, the term "image of god" in the culture and language of the ancient Near East in the fifteenth century B.C. would have communicated two main ideas: (1) rulership and (2) sonship. The king is the image of god because he has a relationship to the deity as the son of god and a relationship to the world as a ruler for the god.[9]

The third salient distinctive of Genesis 1 is the absence of death or curse. Animal predation may be present, but the text is silent about this (cf. Ps 104:20-21). There is a sense of everything being good, fulfilling the divine purpose and intention. This cannot be overemphasized since the word *good* is repeated seven times, concluding with the emphatic verdict "very good" (Gen 1:31).

Before leaving this chapter, it is worth noting two other texts where the terms *image* and/or *likeness* are used to describe human beings, as well as a passage from the Psalms that reflects on humanity's role in Genesis 1. Genesis 5:1-3 repeats Genesis 1:26 where the terms describe the creation of humanity in the divine likeness, after the divine image. The terms here are found in reverse order with different prepositions, which suggest semantic overlap.

Table 2.1. *Image* and *likeness* in Genesis 1 and Genesis 5

GENESIS 1:26	GENESIS 5:3
God said, "Let us make humanity in our image (*bəṣalmēnû*), according to our likeness (*kidmûtēnû*)."	When Adam had lived 130 years, he had a son in his own likeness (*bidmûtô*), according to his own image (*kəṣalmô*).

What is crucial is that Adam has a son in his own image and according to his own likeness. This text deals with the transmission of the image. The English

---

[9]Peter Gentry and Steven Wellum, *Kingdom Through Covenant: A Biblical-Theological Understanding of the Covenants*, 2nd ed. (Wheaton, IL: Crossway, 2018), 192; Catherine McDowell, *The Image of God in the Garden of Eden* (Winona Lake, IN: Eisenbrauns, 2015), 117-77.

phrase, "like father like son," essentially captures the import of the meaning. This is like the English expressions that a child is a "chip off the old block" or is the "spittin' image" of their parent. A clear physical resemblance is meant as well as a character likeness. The son presents to the world the image of his father as he faces the world, and the likeness of his father as he faces him. However understood, as long as the child is alive, the father in a sense is not dead. His image lives on. But the son most effectively communicates his father's image to the world if he not only shows the physical likeness but displays the father's character as well. The latter, of course, depends on the son's relationship with his father.

The other example is found in Genesis 9:6 after the flood. God implements laws that will restrict the rampant violence of humanity, instituting a death penalty for murder.[10] Humans are now given license to kill, responsibly, members of the animal kingdom to procure food, but they must not eat the blood (Gen 9:1-5). In a sense the flesh of the animal belongs to humans, and they can take control of it but not its life source—the blood—since it belongs to God. But humans are prohibited from killing each other because they are made in the image of God. Indeed, if a human sheds the blood of another human, the blood of the killer must be shed because humans are made in God's image (Gen 9:6). It is interesting that the specific word *image* is used here and not *likeness*. This is probably due to two reasons. First it is as God's image that human beings represent God to the world as dominion bearers and rulers. Homicide is an assault on the divine rule. Second, only God's representative, God's ruler, has the authority to execute the death penalty on another human being. Thus, the term *dəmût* ("likeness") is avoided here since it places the emphasis on the relationship between God and the human being—communion, rather than dominion.[11]

These two texts support the strong bond between the deity and humanity. The relationship resembles that of a father and son, almost like a blood bond between the creature and the Creator. In effect, the bond between the Creator

---

[10]P. J. Harland, *The Value of Human Life: A Study of the Story of the Flood* (Leiden: Brill Academic, 1996).

[11]The term may be implied by the frequent reference to blood (*dām*), which sounds similar in Hebrew to the word *likeness* (*dəmût*).

and his image is a matter of kinship, and it is incumbent on the relative of a homicide victim to avenge the death. God is a kinship redeemer![12]

Psalm 8 is essentially an exegesis of Genesis 1:26-28 that highlights several features. First, it is a hymn in which God's name is displayed throughout the earth and in the heavens, and then indicates that human beings are especially the locus of this revelation.

After first considering the divine glory set above the heavens, the psalmist shifts attention to the earth and witnesses the revelation of the glory in the babbling of infants. Infants—humanity in its weakest state—reveal God's glory, and God uses this weakness to stymie his adversaries (Ps 8:2). In the second movement from the heavens to the earth, the psalmist expresses wonder at the vastness of the heavens: "When I consider the heavens, the works of your fingers, the moon and the stars that you have made . . ." (Ps 8:3). In a series of rhetorical questions, the psalmist then praises God for his astonishing concern for insignificant humans who, in the vast scheme of things, seem nothing but dust in the wind: "What is frail humanity that you have made him? What is weak humankind that you visited him?" (Ps 8:4). Rather than being overwhelmed by his insignificance in the cosmos, the psalmist responds with the revelation of Genesis 1: God made him a little less than God (literally) (Ps 8:5). Although this reference ("less than God") can refer to angels—divine-like beings—its primary reference is probably to the creation of humanity in the divine image. One scholar interprets the phrase as humanity lacks "little of God."[13] The glory of God, the supreme manifestation of God's name, is not found in all the magnificent wonders of the heavens and earth but in God's creation of humanity as the vicegerent over all creation. Humanity's royal status is further emphasized by the regal language: "You . . . crowned him with glory and majesty!" (Ps 8:5). The consequence of this royal enthronement is that "you have made him rule over all the works of your hands," which is further interpreted as "You have placed all things under his feet" (Ps 8:6). This is evidently the language and imagery

[12]Catherine L. McDowell, *The Image of God in the Garden of Eden: The Creation of Humankind in Genesis 2:5–3:24 in Light of the mīs pî, pīt pî, and wpt-r Rituals of Mesopotamia and Ancient Egypt*, Siphrut 15 (Winona Lake, IN: Eisenbrauns, 2015), 120-23.

[13]J. J. Stewart Perowne, *The Book of Psalms*, 4th ed. (London: George Bell and Sons, 1878), 155.

of dominion as there are many depictions of ancient kings in the ancient world with their hostile enemies placed under their feet.[14] Thus this text is essentially an exegesis of Genesis 1:26-28 in which human beings are commanded to have dominion over the birds of the air, the animals on the ground, and the fish in the sea. The psalmist repeats the adjective *all* and uses the conjunction *also* to describe the comprehensiveness of human dominion over the animals (Ps 8:7-9).

The seventh day brings the creation account in Genesis to a conclusion. There is an extraordinary emphasis on the cessation of God's labor, with the seventh day mentioned three times in Gen 2:2-3. It is remarkably distinguished from the other days as it alone is blessed and sanctified. It is the only day without a conclusion since it has no "morning and evening." In ancient Near Eastern sources, the goal of creation was for the god to be enthroned in his temple.[15] The seventh day highlights the "rest" of God not as something impassive, but as taking up residence on his throne over which he surveys his creation as a vast temple. He has finished his creative work in a sense, placed his image in his temple, and now the human rule of history can begin.[16]

It is clear from this overture to the book of Genesis, the Torah, the Old Testament, and the entire Bible, that God is the sovereign King of the world, over which he has established human beings as his royal image bearers to rule his good creation on his behalf. There is much kingdom work to do, to fill the world with his images, to assert dominion over the creation in the name of God and for the glory of God. This is a great beginning.

---

[14]See the Nine Bows in Egyptian art and iconography in which nine bows, representing the Pharaoh's enemies, would be placed under his feet. See also Othmar Keel, *The Symbolism of the Biblical World: Ancient Near Eastern Iconography and the Book of Psalms* (Winona Lake, IN: Eisenbrauns, 1997), 48-60.

[15]Weinfeld, "Sabbath, Temple and the Enthronement of the Lord." Note also, "In the Genesis prologue the creator appears as a workman who performs his task and then takes his rest—or more specifically he is portrayed as a king who builds himself a palace, and then occupies the throne." Meredith G. Kline, *God, Heaven and Har Magedon: A Covenantal Tale of Cosmos and Telos* (Eugene, OR: Wipf and Stock, 2006), 38.

[16]J. Richard Middleton, "Creation Founded in Love: Breaking Rhetorical Expectations in Genesis 1:1–2:3," in *Sacred Text, Secular Times: The Hebrew Bible in the Modern World*, ed. Leonard J. Greenspoon and Bryan F. LeBeau, Studies in Jewish Civilization 10 (Omaha, NE: Creighton University Press, 2000), 47-85, esp 65.

DISCUSSION QUESTIONS

1. In contemporary Western culture there is an identity crisis. People are preoccupied with self-image and with becoming someone significant. How could the understanding of humanity found in Genesis contribute to self-understanding?

2. Look at the ministry of Jesus and the way he viewed people as compared to things (Mt 6:25-34; Lk 12:4-7)? Where did he get such an understanding?

3. Think of five implications of seeing yourself and other people as made in the image of God.

Chapter Three

KINGDOM COME

AFTER THE DRAMATIC OVERTURE OF CREATION, the story of the Bible begins with a genealogy: "These are the generations of the heavens and the earth" (Gen 2:4 NRSV). The genealogies in Genesis always emerge from a previous account, and here at the beginning there is no exception. This is the only account in the Bible with a genealogy of the heavens and earth because the biblical story continues from the previous prologue where they were created. Now the story tells of what happens in the heavens and the earth, specifically the history of human beings who have been entrusted with the rule of creation.

The text of this story uses a different style and terminology and presents a different order of creation, yet by its position after the liturgical introduction the editor or author ensures this story complements the overture. This text is more thematic than chronological, as it begins the story of humanity. It moves from the more panoramic view of the heavens and the earth, climaxing with the creation of the image of God in Genesis 1, to a more close-up version that zeros in on this climactic creation so that everything is related to it, even the reason for the creation of the earth. For example, the text mentions at the beginning that no rain fell and no vegetation grew on the earth was because humanity did not exist to work the ground (Gen 2:5). If the previous text spoke of humanity made in the image of God, this one speaks of humanity made from the earth yet infused with the divine breath. If the preceding text divided humanity into two genders, this text indicates how this happens. If the earlier text stressed the purpose of the gender complement to be procreation, this one accentuates communion.

COVENANT IN THE GARDEN

There are several features that point to the profound significance of this passage, and the special—even covenantal—relationship that exists between the Creator and his creation. First, this passage is unique in the Bible with its use of the divine name Yahweh juxtaposed to the title God.[1] In English translations the words LORD God are used for the Hebrew, Yahweh Elohim. Nowhere else in the Hebrew Bible is there such a pervasive and consistent use of this name for two entire chapters. The writer is indicating that the transcendent God of Genesis 1 has a name, revealed in the covenant later made with the people of Israel before the greatest act of salvation that occurs in the Old Testament, the exodus from Egypt (Ex 3:15). In fact in the only other significant occurrence of this double divine name, namely the account of the seventh plague of hail and thunder (Ex 9:30), the Pharaoh is compelled to see that the earth belongs to Yahweh, that he is in fact the God of the entire world. And yet Moses knew that Pharaoh and his servants would not yet worship Yahweh God.[2] In Egypt God revealed his identity as the God who was present to save and to deliver: Yahweh. Here in Genesis 2 the Creator God is seen to be the same God, the God who draws near to human beings and enters an intimate relation with them on a first name basis. He is in covenant with his creatures.[3]

---

[1]The only time in Genesis 2–3 where the name Yahweh does not appear with God is when the Serpent (Gen 3:1, 5) and the woman (Gen 3:3) speak of God. Both instances are telling.

[2]J. L'Hour, "Yahweh Elohim," *Revue Biblique* 81 (1984): 524-56. See also Craig Bartholomew, "Covenant and Creation: Covenantal Overload or Covenantal Deconstruction," *Calvin Theological Journal* 30 (1995): 29, who makes the same point about covenant.

[3]Without getting involved in a lengthy discussion over whether there was a covenant in Genesis 1–3, I point to the close relationship between humanity and God at the beginning. Of all the creatures, humans enjoy the closest relationship with God and are called to present his image to the world in a way that embodies the divine rule. After the fall, this relationship is renewed in the covenant

Next, the text describes the conditions on the earth before there was any rain, vegetation, and humanity to care for the environment. Consequently, the earth comes into being as a home for humanity in which the latter are tasked with a specific role to work the ground. Then God creates the man in an intimate way. The text depicts God as a potter molding the clay from the *adamah* (the ground) to form the *Adam* (man). This illustrates the sovereignty of God, as the potter forms the clay. An English translation which could capture the play on words here would be something like, God made a *human* from the *humus*. But the man is inert until Yahweh Elohim lifts him up, as it were, to his face and blows into his nostrils the breath of life and the man becomes a living creature. The Hebrew word translated as "the breath of life" is uniquely used of human beings who are alive (Gen 2:7).[4] They have been specially inspired by Yahweh and owe, in a distinctive way, their life breath to Yahweh. As Derek Kidner comments, the creation while showing the transcendence of the Creator also shows his immanence as he is portrayed with "the face-to-face intimacy of a kiss."[5]

The Adam is then placed in a Garden, which begins to yield an abundance of fruit trees. But this Garden is also unique. It represents a place that has two special trees, one the tree of life and the other a tree of knowledge of good and evil. The Garden is further described as the source for the major rivers of the world: it stands at the head from which four rivers emerge to provide water for the world.[6] Thus it is the source of abundant life. Here the man is placed to work and to preserve or guard it.

---

with creation in language reverberating from Genesis 1 (Gen 6:18; 9:2-7). Thus, the kingdom is present through a covenantal relationship. Some would argue that because the word *covenant* does not appear, it is illegitimate to import it into the text. For a fair presentation of both sides see John H. Stek, "'Covenant' Overload in Reformed Theology," *Calvin Theological Journal* 29 (1994): 12-41, and the response in Craig Bartholomew, "Covenant and Creation."

[4]The word *našāmâ* occurs twenty-four times in the Hebrew Bible and is used of divine and human breath. It may be used of the wind of God (2 Sam 22:16; Job 4:9; Is 30:33), but it has more particular reference to God imparting breath to human beings (Job 27:3; 33:4; 34:14; Is 2:22; 42:5). There are texts that may imply God's animating breath in all living creatures (cf. Gen 7:22; Deut 20:16; Josh 11:11, 14; Ps 150:6), but in my judgment these texts refer to human beings. When there is no breath, humanity is dead (1 Kings 17:17).

[5]Derek Kidner, *Genesis* (Downers Grove, IL: InterVarsity Press, 2016), 65.

[6]Since the Garden is in Eden, it may be that Eden is a mountain or hillock from which the water flows down into the Garden, then dividing into the four rivers (cf. Ezek 28:11-15). The point is clear, however, that the source of life is nearby.

Although the exact terms *image* and *likeness* are not used here, this text is more concrete and shows how these terms function, particularly in illustrating the task of humanity in having dominion over the creation. The man is called to have a vocation of "working" and "keeping" the Garden, which indicates his is the distinct task of stewardship, cultivating and conserving the creation to enhance its development (Gen 2:15). These words also suggest priestly service as they are later used in the Torah to describe the work of Levites in the sanctuary of God. In their practice of trimming the lamp, cleaning the sanctuary, preparing sacrifices, protecting the sanctuary, and so on, they were helping the people of God worship (Num 3:7-8; 8:26; 18:3-7). So these words on the one hand suggest royalty and dominion but also worship and liturgical service.

It is interesting that in the ancient Near East one of the tasks of kings was to be a gardener. Not only were kings to exercise their power by military conquest but also by farming and cultivation near their palaces so that by "planting and cultivating gardens, these kings may have been imitating their divine counterparts, creating their own 'heavens' on earth."[7] Early translators understood this. The Septuagint translates the Garden of Eden as the "paradise" of Eden (*paradeison en Edem*), a Persian loanword for a cultivated park.

Besides working and taking care of God's creation, humanity must freely eat from all the trees in the Garden. God is no miser, and his generosity is boundless as humanity is called on—indeed commanded—to enjoy the creation thoroughly. God gives the man an emphatic command: "You must surely eat from all the trees in the garden" (Gen 2:16). The Hebrew is insistent. The creation is good and to be enjoyed in all its vastness and variety! At the same time, however, God forbids only one activity in this kingdom: eating from the tree of knowledge of good and evil. The penalty is certain death (Gen 2:17).

LIFE AND DEATH IN THE GARDEN

Scholars have long debated what this tree signifies but the most reasonable solution is that of moral autonomy. "Man would determine himself what was

---

[7]Francesca Stavrakopoulou, "Exploring the Garden of Uzza: Death, Burial and Ideologies of Kingship," *Biblica* 87 (2006): 6.

good and what was not—a divine prerogative."[8] There is nothing inherently wrong with this tree, but its symbolic importance is paramount: by eating from this tree human beings are defining for themselves good and evil. In contrast, by obeying this command they are completely trusting in the divine Word and the divine character and must assume that God is good and has their best interests at heart. To eat from this tree is to die. Again, the Hebrew expression is categorical: "In the day you eat from it you will surely die" (Gen 2:17). The writer is surely aware of the meaning of death. There may be a hint in the creation of man as he is made from the dust. To die in later biblical terminology is to return to the dust (Eccles 3:20; 12:7; Ps 22:15; 104:29). So biological death is surely present here, but the biblical idea of death is much more comprehensive. Biological death is but the tip of the iceberg.[9] In Hebrew thought all the forces against human flourishing are dynamic and are representative of death. Disease, sickness, persecution, exile, loneliness, old age, enemies, sin, unforgiveness, war, and strife—these forces are antagonistic and antithetical to life.[10]

The most powerful forces are those that would bar the individual from the presence of God. The psalmist says, "If you remain silent, I will be like those who go down to the pit" (Ps 28:1); "Do not hide your face from me or I will die" (Ps 143:7).

The key to living in the kingdom of God is obedience to the King and a simple formula can describe the result:

Table 3.1. Life and death in the kingdom of God

LIFE	DEATH
Human Existence + Divine Word = Divine Rule (Kingdom of God)	Human Existence - Divine Word = Human Autonomy and Slavery

We will return to this formula later. Suffice it to say that Jesus' teaching on prayer to his disciples makes this very point synonymous with the kingdom.

---

[8]W. Malcolm Clark, "A Legal Background to the Yahwist's Use of Good and Evil in Genesis 2–3," *Journal of Biblical Literature* 88 (1969): 278. A good parallel to this account are the corrupt judges in Isaiah's day, calling evil good and good evil (Is 5:20).

[9]See, e.g., Byron Wheaton, "As It Is Written: Old Testament Foundations for Jesus' Expectation of Resurrection," *Westminster Theological Journal* 70 (2008): 245-67.

[10]Othmar Keel, *The Symbolism of the Biblical World: Ancient Near Eastern Iconography and the Book of Psalms* (Winona Lake, IN: Eisenbrauns, 1997), 62-77.

They are to pray "Your kingdom come, your will be done on earth as it is in heaven" (Mt 6:10). Similarly, when Jesus is anointed for his mission by his heavenly Father, he is driven into the wilderness where he fasts and prays and prepares for his encounter with the ruler of the earth, whose will is done on the earth—Satan (Mt 4:1-11). As the Serpent tempted Eve in the Garden, Satan tempts Jesus to eat, essentially testing him to use his own power to satisfy his hunger. Jesus responds that the true kingdom way first understands human identity. The ultimate priority for a human being is not to meet physical need, but rather to satisfy a much more fundamental spiritual necessity for life: a relationship with God. Thus, Jesus cites Deuteronomy 8:3 that humans do not depend on bread alone but on every word that proceeds from the mouth of God. The context for that statement is Israel's wandering in the wilderness where they had to learn each day to depend on God for their daily sustenance, the manna from heaven. They learned the lesson that even the provision of daily food depends on the divine will, and they were to look beyond it to the Provider.

THE ONE "NOT GOOD" IN CREATION

So a picture of the kingdom is emerging with humanity living in obedience to the divine command and integrated into the world. But the creation is not complete as there remains a fundamental lack: a companion for the man. The man's solitary existence is regarded as "not good" (Gen 2:18). In fact the use of this phrase to describe human existence in the Garden up to this point resoundingly clashes with the overture in the proem of Genesis 1, where each of the created works of God was pronounced good. In the prologue, there rings an endorsement of the creation six times, and a seventh crowns the final creation with a "very good." In the second chapter, with a more topical arrangement, the writer proceeds to describe the creation of animals for the benefit of relieving human loneliness. First, the animals are brought to the man for the purpose of identification and classification. By naming the animals, the man exercises dominion, defining reality in the same way that God defined reality in the first three days, naming the day and night, the sky, the land, and the seas (Gen 1:5, 8, 10). But the divine creation of animals and the human description of reality are not enough to alleviate human loneliness because this action only exacerbates the man's social isolation, making him more acutely aware of his lack.

Second, the writer is obviously aware of the importance of sexual differentiation for procreation among the animals. But the gender complement for humanity means much more than procreation: it is about companionship and communion. Accordingly, when God induces a deep sleep for the man, the divine surgeon takes a bone from his side and forms it into a woman. This may be a covenantal act because the word *tardēmâ* denoting the man's deep sleep is later used to describe Abraham's condition when God makes a covenant with him (Gen 2:21-22; 15:12, 18).

When the man sees the woman, he instantly experiences the solution to the problem of his loneliness. He instinctively names the woman in a beautiful poem which puns on the difference between the man and the woman: "She shall be called *'iššâ* ('woman') for she was taken out of *'îš* ('man')" (Gen 2:23). The act of dominion is not emphasized here by the action of naming, but rather the act of discernment, because the man sees a companion and partner in the creation of woman, not a servant. Moreover, the narrator uses the story to make a point about his contemporary social order: "That is why a man leaves his father and mother and is united to his wife, and they become one flesh" (Gen 2:24). It is as if he is saying, "By the way if you had not noticed, this explains the current practice of marriage in our society where the man leaves his parents and cleaves to his wife and they become one flesh." And so marriage is explained as the rejoining of what was once an original whole but was separated, in order to alleviate loneliness.[11]

---

[11]Various interpretations have arisen that seek to explain the first man as androgynous, and that this "earth creature" becomes sexually differentiated after the divine operation. See, e.g., Phyllis Trible: "Hence the first act in Genesis 2 is the creation of androgyny (2:7) and the last is the creation of sexuality (2:23)." Phyllis Trible, "Eve and Adam: Genesis 2–3 Reread," *Andover Newton Quarterly* 13 (1973): 74-81. This interpretation observes correctly that *'ādām* can include both genders as a generic noun much like "humanity" in English. The specifically gendered word for *male* in Hebrew, *'îš*, is not used until after the separation of the male from the female. But the Achilles heel of such an interpretation is the conclusion to the story, which states that the man (*hā'ādām*) and his wife were naked and not ashamed. While it is true that the noun *'ādām* can be used for both genders, it is clear in this context that the word is being used for the male alone, and it is later used as a proper name for the first man (Gen 5:3).

So here in essence is the kingdom of God in seminal form in Genesis 2. God rules the world through his human representatives, who are to till and preserve the land of the Garden, exercise dominion over the animal kingdom and live as one flesh in a transparent relationship with each other and with their Creator. The general mandate for humanity is given in Genesis 1, which presents a panoramic picture of God as sovereign King over his creation, and especially the climax of his creation, and its goal in the Sabbath. Genesis 2 presents this being realized in a particular way in a covenantal relationship with God and fulfilling the calling to exercise dominion over creation by working and preserving a specific piece of real estate, the Garden, in the vast world of creation, and living a life of obedience.

Therefore, in many ways the picture in Genesis 2 is a microcosm of the macroscopic picture in Genesis 1 and provides a more concrete application of the general picture in one specific place. Genesis 2 constitutes the seminal expression of the general command in chapter 1. Here is the beginning of human history, a history focused on human beings in relation to God, to each other, and to their natural environment. Their task of exercising dominion over the creation will have its beginnings in looking after a particular Garden, but this task will mirror their task in creation in general as they spread out and bring God's image to the rest of the world outside the Garden.[12] In covenantal relation with each other, and with their God they will build a human community centered around God, where they will honor him in enjoying and developing the natural world, and filling it with his images. Graeme Goldsworthy has described the kingdom of God laconically: God's people living in God's place under God's rule.[13] This is what other writers have called the vocation of humanity.

The result of this integration and harmony is often described in the Hebrew Bible with the word *shalom*, which is usually translated "peace." But shalom is much more than the absence of hostilities or tension. It is the presence of health, harmony, joy, and life. Shalom is what was present in creation at the

---

[12]For detailed development of this idea see Gregory K. Beale, *The Temple and the Church's Mission: A Biblical Theology of the Dwelling Place of God* (Leicester, UK: Apollos, 2004).

[13]Graeme Goldsworthy, *According to Plan: The Unfolding Revelation of God in the Bible* (Downers Grove, IL: IVP Academic, 2002), 99.

beginning, and it is preserved by obedience to the divine word regarding the tree of knowledge of good and evil. And human beings are regarded as the mediators of this shalom to the rest of creation. When they are rightly related to God and fulfilling their appointed task, the creation will flourish. When they fail in their task there are universal repercussions—the unraveling of creation.

RETURN TO COVENANT

There is a covenant with humans and the creation in Genesis 1. Much has been written about such a covenant or lack of such in this text. Covenant presupposes a relationship of mutual support wherever it occurs in the Old Testament, whether ratifying an existing relationship or initiating a new relationship. "Secular" covenants nearly always imply an oath that seals the deal, and these covenants indicate a mutual commitment of the parties involved. When a divine partner is involved, the deity always initiates the covenant, with benefits and responsibilities for both parties. Although the word *covenant* is not used in Genesis 1–2, many covenantal characteristics are present: parties in relationship, terms dictated, and consequences for fulfillment or violations of the obligations. The fact that this special relationship is later strongly echoed after the flood as a reset of the original situation in Genesis 1 strongly suggests the presence of an original covenant (Gen 9:1-17). As mentioned before, the use of the divine name, which was the covenantal name revealed to Israel in the exodus, also contributes to the covenantal relationship between God and humanity and creation in Genesis 2.

Later covenants include ratifying signs: the rainbow for the creation covenant after the flood (Gen 9:12-17), circumcision for the Abrahamic covenant (Gen 17), the Sabbath for Sinai (Ex 31:12-18), and so on. But what would be the covenantal sign for this creation covenant in Genesis? It is most likely the seventh day, which is the only day that is not distinguished by a concluding time formula marking the day and night. It is uniquely marked for sanctity among the days of creation, it is the only day that is blessed, it is the final day of creation, and it is highlighted strongly by the repetition of key phrases and the number of words used. It represents the day when the images of God cease from their work in imitating the divine rule and glorify their King in worship and adoration. God defines their lives. As their sovereign King, they formally recognize the divine majesty.

In later Israelite history, the Sabbath command is given as the last of the specifically Godward commands (Ex 20:1-17; Deut 5:7-21).[14] Israel is to pause from its activity of imaging God in its work to reflect on God and his likeness in order to find its location once again in a world which would seek to dislocate it. Rest is not only required for humans but also their animals. What Robert Webber says about worship can be equally said about the Sabbath: "Worship finds us in our dislocation and relocates us in God."[15] Similarly, Deuteronomy urges the remembrance of Sabbath by reminding the Israelites not of creation but of their redemption from slavery. Every week Israel must pause to remember freedom so that they do not become a slave to their work. Therefore, the Sabbath, as Abraham Heschel observes, is a type of sanctuary in time, a place for reaffirming the divine rule and honoring the divine presence.[16] It is no accident that the Israelites are functioning as *priest*-kings particularly in their later observance of the Sabbath (Ex 19:5-6; cf. Gen 1:26-28).

Thus, the Sabbath functions as a sign of the goal of creation: the world in harmony under the divine rule—the kingdom of God.[17] By resting, humanity offers the fruit and service of its work to the King of creation as a gift. It is thus no accident that humanity's first full day in the creation over which it is to rule, is to recognize the divine rule by ceasing the human activity of work. Later, Israel would celebrate the end of each week in its calendar, by cessation of royal labor to worship the Supreme King and offer him the fruits of their regal endeavors. In so doing they would imitate their God, working

---

[14]The commands are often divided into two groups: directives toward God (1-4) and directives toward neighbor (5-10).

[15]Cited in Kevin Drudge, "Living by the Sign of the Sabbath," *Vision: A Journal for Church and Theology* (Fall 2005): 8.

[16]Abraham J. Heschel, *The Sabbath: Its Meaning for Modern Man* (New York: Farrar, Straus and Giroux, 1951).

[17]Gerhard Hasel aptly remarks about the Sabbath's later function as a sign: "Its 'sign' signification is *commemorative* of God as Creator and Redeemer where the sabbath-keeping community confesses its continuing relationship to its covenant Lord; it is also *prospective* in signification in that it is a 'sign' of the covenant history moving forward to its appointed goal; it is at the same time a 'sign' signifying the believer's *present* posture vis-á-vis God with physical, mental, and spiritual renewal taking place in each sabbath celebration." Gerhard Hasel, "Sabbath," in *The Anchor Bible Dictionary*, ed. David Noel Freedman (New York: Doubleday, 1992) 5:852.

for six days and resting for one. The goal of *homo faber* is *homo religiosus* (The goal of humanity the worker is humanity the worshiper).

DISCUSSION QUESTIONS

1. We are often given a definition of what it means to be human in the contemporary world: born to shop, born to party, life is simple: eat, sleep, play sports, repeat. . . . What brief phrase could you use to describe this chapter's view of human nature?

2. Jesus summarized the biblical view of humanity in terms of two great commands: love God with all your being and love neighbor as yourself. How might these two commands be traced back to the Garden? If the greatest command is to love God with all your being, what might the greatest sin be?

Chapter Four

THE LOSS OF THE KINGDOM

ENEMY IN THE GARDEN

GENESIS 3 IS ONE OF THE MOST IMPORTANT chapters in the entire Bible as it locates in time the tragedy of what many theologians call "the fall." Here the kingdom, the rule of God, begun in the Garden on the earth ends abruptly. Communion with God disintegrates, humans become alienated from one another, and their relationship to the natural world is profoundly damaged. Humans, made to rule the earth, will now be buried beneath it. The cosmic effects of disobedience suggest not only death for humanity but death for the natural world. But it is worth spending some time on this chapter to get a general overview of how the kingdom of God is lost and replaced by another kingdom ruled by another power.

SERPENTINE STRATEGY

Genesis 3 opens with an ominous wordplay. The last verse of Genesis 2 stressed the nakedness of the first couple as completely transparent to God and to each other, without any sense of shame. But now a new character appears in the Garden paradise: the cunning Serpent. It is as if he is a known entity by the author since the definite article is used to describe him. He is portrayed as shrewder than all the created animals (Gen 3:1). In the Hebrew, the word *cunning* or *crafty* (*ārûm*) rhymes with *nakedness* (*ārôm*) and foreshadows what will happen to the primal unity of the couple symbolized by their state of complete transparency. The Serpent's shrewdness will bring an end to their *nudeness*.

In a bizarre development, the Serpent begins to engage the woman in conversation. Something is obviously wrong for this will be the first of two times in the Old Testament that an animal will speak. In the other example a donkey is given supernatural inspiration (Num 22:28-30). Likewise, what the Serpent says is just as bizarre as its act of speaking. The syntax of the Serpent's statement is unique in that its opening words are *'ap kî*. In Hebrew, this expression never appears at the absolute beginning of a discourse, except here. Normally it makes a comparison to a previous statement:

> Death and Destruction lie open before the LORD—*how much more* do human hearts! (Prov 15:11; cf. 1 Sam 14:29-30)

It appears, then, that the audience in Genesis 3 is transported right into the middle of an ongoing dialogue between the snake and the woman. While the snake and the woman have been discussing the divine prohibition in the Garden, the Serpent has been casting doubt on the previous divine speech (Gen 2:16-17). In order to view the comparison correctly, it is probably best to interpret the Serpent's speech as follows: "[Yes that speech of God. There are problems with it . . . and much more.] Did he really mean to say that you should not eat from any tree in the Garden?" Here he is trying to smuggle in a bald-faced lie by using some of Yahweh God's words.

His speech is crafted in such a way that it plants doubts in the woman's mind and as many commentators note, these doubts virtually ensure success. First, not only does the Serpent flatly distort the divine word, which was in fact incredibly generous, commanding humanity to eat from all the trees in the Garden except one, but he also does not use the divine name. And this is the first time the divine name, Yahweh, is not used in this text. The Serpent only knows God from a distance, not in a personal, covenantal way.

Second the woman does not use the divine name either but just the title "God" in her response (Gen 3:2-3). Her response corrects the Serpent's interpretation but in such a way that she downplays her personal relationship with God, subtracts from the divine word, and also adds to it: "The woman said to the serpent, 'We may eat fruit from the trees in the garden, but God did say, 'You must not eat fruit from the tree that is in the middle of the garden, and you must not touch it, or you will die'" (Gen 3:2-3 NIV). She subtracts from the generosity of the divine command when God commanded to *surely* eat from *all* of the trees in the Garden, that is, the command to emphatically enjoy all the fruit. She also subtracts from the punishment, which stated that they would *surely* die *on the day* the prohibition was violated. By not including the name, Yahweh, she assimilates into her consciousness the Serpent's impersonal understanding of God and diminishes the certainty and the immediacy of death. But she also adds to the command, stating that the fruit was not to be touched. God's command is far more restrictive in her new estimation. These changes increase the likelihood that the Serpent with his shrewdness will be able to end her *nudeness* and therefore her transparent openness to her husband and to God.

The Serpent then sharply contradicts the word of God in his response, "You will not certainly die . . . for God knows that when you eat from it your eyes will be opened, and you will be like God, knowing good and evil" (Gen 3:4-5 NIV). Here, another syntactical anomaly reinforces the Serpent's lie. In Hebrew, a forceful negative statement, such as "You will not certainly die," uses two verb forms, the first an infinitive absolute and the second the finite verb. The first verb emphasizes the verbal idea and so translators use the adverb *certainly* or *surely*. Normally the negative is placed before the finite verb form, but in this case it is placed before the infinitive form, thus emphasizing the categorical, absolute denial of the Serpent: "No! You will not surely die" or "There is no possible way you will die!"

The Serpent gives further rationale to support its claim. God is jealous and he wants to keep the human pair in a subservient state, so that they cannot become like him, knowing good and evil. By blindly submitting to an authoritarian appeal, the man and woman cannot realize their full potential.

THE FALL OF THE KINGDOM

By this time the Serpent has all but succeeded in his efforts to entice the woman to disobey God. The woman, then, sees three things: the fruit looks good to eat, is very sensuous to the eyes, and is coveted for understanding or gaining insight (Gen 3:6). This progression suggests a gradual yielding to the temptation so that the last step is a rationalization of the act. This is how temptation often works: once one's mind becomes made up, reason is used to rationalize. Martin Luther describes this process as the prostitution of the will.[1]

The woman subsequently gives the fruit to her husband who, blithely standing nearby, also eats. This point needs to be underscored. He was with her and did not object or intervene, or even seek to protect her from the Serpent's lies, but simply accepted his wife's capitulation to the Serpent's twisted logic. His immediate response led to instant consequences (Gen 3:6-7). As the Serpent said, their eyes would be opened, and they were. But instead of the previous vision of a world completely integrated under the divine rule around the love of God, each other, and their natural environment, they have a radically new vision. In the first cover up in history, they use their creative powers to make clothes to hide from each other, they use their intelligence to hide from their Creator, and they use the trees of the Garden made for their enjoyment to provide a hideaway. There is an instantaneous loss of transparency and openness to God, to each other, and to their natural environment. When God in grace comes looking for them, the rupture of their relationships is illumined even more. The man shifts the responsibility to his female partner, and the woman shifts the blame to the Serpent. Cover up and irresponsibility become the first marks of the post-fallen human psyche in this new kingdom.

But the kingdom will bear the marks of divine judgment (Gen 3:14-15). First the triumph of the Serpent is relativized. As it deceived the woman, it will forever bear the mark of its subjugation by being condemned to slither on the ground, eating the dust for food. The Serpent's posture acquires a new meaning. It will not literally eat the dust, it is simply a figure of speech, like

---

[1]For an insightful essay on this aspect of Luther's thought see Jeffrey K Mann, "Luther on Reason: What Makes a Whore a Whore," *Seminary Ridge Review* 18 (2015): 1-17.

the English "bite the dust." Its locomotion is a sign in this new kingdom of its eventual demise.

Second, this demise will be accomplished by an enmity placed between the woman's descendants and those of the Serpent. In a profound theological text, this is hardly predicting an antipathy between the female gender and reptiles. Rather, it signals a titanic battle between two powers, which leads to the conquest of the Serpent's seed by that of the woman: the Serpent's seed will wound the heel of the woman's seed, but in so doing it will sustain a lethal blow to the head. The battle thus indicates a victory that needs to be won, a victory that will eliminate the Serpent's influence and rule from the world. A new kingdom needs to be destroyed and the previous kingdom restored by a new Adam. As King Herod knew too well millennia later when hearing about the birth of a new king, one kingdom cannot have two kings (Mt 2:1-18). One must be eliminated. This promise to the woman thus indicates that her progeny will eventually win a battle that will restore the world to the primeval conditions of Genesis 1–2, where humanity can rule together and expand God's dominion over the rest of creation under God's authority. The fact that the triumph will happen because of the seed of *the woman* means the return of human beings to their rightful rule over the world, the return of the kingdom. This is nothing less than the return of Adam, or what Adam and Eve were intended to be. Thus, it is no accident that the book of Genesis focuses on descendants using genealogies. Genealogies in Genesis not only look back, they also point forward to a coming liberator, a ruler, who will establish the kingdom of God.

While the first word of judgment on the Serpent contains a sign and prediction of its demise—and thus a victory for humanity, the second judgment on the woman reveals the costly nature of that demise for her as she experiences much pain in giving birth to a line of descendants and estrangement from her husband (Gen 3:16). There are echoes here of the tree (ʿēṣ) that led to her demise becoming part of her "birth pain" (ʿeṣeb). Similarly, the earlier ecstatic union between "her" (ʾiššâ) and her "husband" (ʾîš) is now fraught with friction: each will seek to dominate the other: "To love and to cherish [now] becomes 'To desire and dominate.'"[2]

---

[2]Derek Kidner, *Genesis* (Downers Grove, IL: InterVarsity Press, 2016), 76.

Finally, the relationship between the "man" (*ʾādām*) and the "ground" (*ădāmâ*), now becomes fractured as the ground does not yield its produce easily but only as the result of extreme effort (Gen 3:17-19). Because he ate from the "tree" (*ʿēṣ*) the man will also experience "pain" (*ʿiṣṣābôn*) when he eats from the ground. Thorns and thistles now spring up from the ground as well, frustrating his farming. And as a final blow, the ground, which should have been under the foot of humanity, is now placed over humanity as the man returns to the ground when he dies. Death—indeed biological death for humanity—now becomes a reality. Death rules rather than humanity.

These primal unities are shattered: God and humanity, man and woman, humanity and the natural environment. The last word of the three judgments is telling. "To the dust you will return" (Gen 3:19). Death. Decay. Disintegration. This pronouncement can be read over chapter 3. The pristine world teeming with life awaiting the dominion and rule of humanity is now blighted with death under the rule of an anti-god figure. Humanity has been not only dethroned but enslaved.

SIGNS OF HOPE

The first act of the man after the judgment is to name his wife, Eve (Gen 3:20). Some have suggested that this is a selfish act because she is named for what she can produce: she is the mother of all human life. She is a means to an end and not an end in herself. Perhaps, but it is more likely that this naming is a sign of hope. The man has heard the pronouncement on the Serpent and views his wife's birth pains as a sign of future victory. In the midst of death, she will birth life, and life that will eventually destroy the Serpent.

As the second act after the judgment, God provides much more suitable clothing for the human pair with garments made from animal skins (Gen 3:21). This action assumes the first act of violence in the Bible as animals would have been slain to provide such clothing. As some commentators have mentioned, this is the first step in that long trajectory that will result in a final act of violence to which God will subject himself on the cross, to provide covering for the sins of humanity.[3]

---

[3]J. C. K. von Hofman, cited in John H. Sailhamer, *The Meaning of the Pentateuch: Revelation, Composition and Interpretation* (Downers Grove, IL: InterVarsity Press, 2010), 230.

But the final act of hope is to save humanity from itself, from eating of the second tree in the middle of the Garden, the tree of life (Gen 3:22-24). To eat from this tree implies the gift of immortality, and to gain immortality without a change in heart would be disaster. To determine for oneself good and evil and to live forever would be horrific as the world would collapse into complete chaos. So, the Lord God banishes the couple from the Garden where the tree of life is located so that they cannot be immortal without a change in character. Angelic beings, cherubim, take their stand at the border of the Garden as guards to block the pathway to life. Humans will not be able to enter here on their own. It will be up to God to bring about a return. But they are exiled not only as judgment but as grace. Humanity will have to wait for another tree of life, and the eating of a different fare, for the opportunity for immortality, and this will come complete with a newly converted heart indwelt by God himself! This will result in open eyes in which they will see the divine face (Lk 24:30-32; Rev 22:4).

THE FALL RECONSIDERED

This text narrating these events is often viewed by Christian theologians as the fall. Many biblical scholars object to this loaded theological term, because such a doctrine cannot bear the theological weight placed on it by the biblical text.[4] There is hardly any reference to this particular account in the rest of the Old Testament and it seems like later Christian interpretation developed by the apostle Paul has contributed to the development of this doctrine. Yet there are rudiments of this interpretation found in the traditions of intertestamental Judaism as well (Wis 2:23-24; Sir 25:24; 2 Esdr 3:4-11; 2 Bar 54:15; Josephus, *Antiquities* 1.2.3). In addition, the primacy of this story at the beginning of the canon,[5] and the avalanche of sin that follows,[6] as well as the outbreak of sin in strategic places in Scripture,[7] indicate the significance of this text as a deliberate reflection on the human

---

[4]For example, Brueggemann writes: "Nothing could be more remote from the narrative itself." Walter Brueggemann, *Genesis*, Interpretation (Atlanta: John Knox Press, 1982), 41.

[5]Terence E Fretheim, "Is Genesis 3 a Fall Story?," *Word & World* 14 (1994): 146.

[6]Gerhard von Rad, *Genesis: A Commentary* (Philadelphia: Westminster John Knox, 1973), 108-17.

[7]Gary A. Anderson, *Christian Doctrine and the Old Testament: Theology in the Service of Biblical Exegesis* (Grand Rapids, MI: Baker Academic, 2017), 59-73.

ondition. It is in fact, as Gerhard von Rad has remarked, the etiology of
all etiologies.[8]

If some scholars think that the sin in Genesis 3 seems trivial when compared to the later horrific violence that caused the flood, they miss the
mundane observation that the slightest act can have huge ramifications. A
small spark can lead to a massive explosion, one tiny cancer cell can lead to
innumerable multiplication and death, a look of anger can lead to murder.[9]
Genesis 3 begins the trajectory that leads to fratricide (Gen 4:1-16), unlimited
vengeance (Gen 4:17-18), the pervasiveness of evil and sin before and after
the flood (Gen 6:5; 8:21), slavery (Gen 9:25-26), and titanic pride (Gen 11:1-9).
The reason is clear: there is a new king in charge of the world and human
beings, while being slaves to this new king, have used their God-given onto-
logical status as divine image bearers for tyranny instead of servant-rule
reflecting their Creator.

Luther once described sin as *homo incurvatus in se* (humanity curved
in upon itself). Augustine before him in his great treatise spoke of the inhabitants of the two cities, the city of man and the city of God. What marks
the first is the love of self and the use of God and other things, and what
characterizes the second is the love of God and the use of things.[10] Of course,
the result is that instead of being a servant-king and bearing the image of
a loving God, one becomes a king who demands service, distorting the
image of God.

A major consequence of human rebellion is the ecological implication.
Thorns and thistles spring up from the ground as well the struggle to eke out
an existence in the world. The gift of labor now becomes an oppressive burden.
Human beings, rejecting their royal mediatorial and stewardship roles toward
creation, have brought about alienation and a curse on the earth. This is
under the control of that serpentine figure who rules in such a way that each
human being has become a law unto his or her own self—each a mini-tyrant.
In her book *The Epic of Eden*, Sandra Richter describes what happens in the
fall as a reversal of the days of creation, the seven days turned upside down:

---

[8]Von Rad, *Genesis*, 24.
[9]Cf. Jesus' statements about anger and lust in the Sermon on the Mount in Matt 5:21-30.
[10]Saint Augustine, *City of God* (London: Penguin, 2003), XIV, 13, 28.

What we've seen in the curses of Genesis 3 is not merely the spewing of random penalties in response to a bad decision, but the reversal of intended benefits. Those made in the image of God and designed to live eternally will now die like the animals; the earth, which was designed to serve, will now devour; the bringing forth of life will now produce death. In other words, the perfect seven-day structure of Eden has been turned upside down, thrown into a tailspin by the treason of God's stewards.[11]

The reality is that the only way there can be a return to the conditions of Genesis 1–2 is to defeat the Serpent.

THE SPREAD OF SIN

The conclusion of this fall narrative of the Bible is sketched out in two revealing acts, one committed at the beginning of Genesis 4 and one committed seven generations later at the end of that same chapter. By the end of the passage, civilization has undergone rapid progress: the first city, domestication of agriculture and animals, development of technology and the arts. But this progress has been accompanied by an equally rapid moral devolution. The first act is fratricide, the murder of Abel by his brother Cain, in a fit of jealous rage over a religious matter. After the murder, Cain meets the divine interrogator, questioning him regarding the whereabouts of his brother, with a cynical response, "Am I my brother's keeper?" (Gen 4:9). Note that this rhetorical question, which expects a negative answer, is now the cold response of a killer with no brotherly concern whatsoever. Here we gain insight into living in the kingdom of God versus the kingdom of the Serpent. Before the fall, if this question could have been posed hypothetically to Cain, it also would have been a rhetorical question but with the implied affirmative answer.

God's answer to Cain is unequivocal. His first rhetorical question is gentle and merciful since it was calculated to elicit confession and repentance. But now God responds with the importance of justice: "The blood of your brother cries out to me from the ground (pleading for justice)" (Gen 4:10). The shedding of innocent blood will require payment. This is the assumption

---

[11]Sandra L. Richter, *The Epic of Eden: A Christian Entry into the Old Testament* (Downers Grove, IL: IVP Academic, 2008), 112.

behind the cry of blood. It demands justice. But God is merciful and only condemns Cain to a life of wandering: the ground for him will be further cursed because he shed innocent blood on it (Gen 4:12). God provides him with a mark of protection so that his life will be spared wherever he goes, as members of the race will see what he has done and be reminded of God's grace. God personally vouches for the protection of the world's first murderer: "I will avenge the death of Cain seven times" (Gen 4:15), which suggests a complete vindication. Perhaps God is thinking ahead to the day when the blood of Christ will speak better things than that of Abel (Heb 12:24).

Cain's genealogy then becomes the focus as he builds a city in direct contradiction to his condemnation. The origin of the city in the Bible is birthed by a murderer. It will find its climax in Babel and Rome, cities that greedily devoured their populace, the cities that were capitals of empires of seduction and destruction and their contrast will be the city of God, Jerusalem, the city of shalom under the divine rule.

Cain's genealogy moves swiftly from Adam through the generations to the seventh, Lamech, who has four children, noted for the cultural and technological achievements of the early human race. Human society has rapidly progressed in these ancient times. But cultural progress has coincided with moral regress. Lamech is the only member of the genealogy who is given a platform to speak, and his first and only words reveal the character of this entire line of descendants. He is the first explicit polygamist whose wives, Adah and Zillah, each bear two children, noted for the advance of civilization and culture: Adah has two sons, Jabal, responsible for domestication of agriculture and animals and settlements, and Jubal, the originator of the arts, especially music; Zillah has one son noted for metallurgy, Tubal-Cain, and a daughter, Naamah, whose name implies pleasantness and beauty.

Lamech's speech is a superb specimen of Hebrew poetry, in which the second line intensifies the meaning of the first:

Adah and Zillah, listen to me;
    wives of Lamech, hear my words.
I have killed a man for wounding me,
    a young lad for injuring me.

> If Cain is avenged seven times,
>> then Lamech seventy-seven times. (Gen 4:23-24)

Here his polygamy is showcased to his wives, summoned to applaud his bloodthirsty prowess. Whereas before, his distant ancestor had tried to cover up the murder of his brother, Lamech now boasts about the bloodletting of even a young lad. Whereas God would specifically avenge any injury to Cain with a sevenfold limit, Lamech will have none of this; his personal vengeance knows no bounds. How things have changed! Here we have the kingdom of the Serpent in which there is great progress in some areas but now men treat women like sexual objects—trophies—and these sexual objects become the audience for a spectacle of blood.

WHAT ABOUT THE PROMISE?

The question then remains, What about the promise regarding the crushing of the Serpent's head? This prospect seems jettisoned by the death of Abel. But this episode is not finished. As often in Hebrew narrative style, a particular storyline must be completed before an earlier point in the story is resumed. Thus, the narrator returns six generations to the death of Abel, where Eve conceives another son, Seth, who is viewed as a replacement for the murdered Abel. His description as another "seed" echoes the promise of the seed who would strike the Serpent (Gen 4:25; cf. Gen 3:15). And thus with the birth of Seth's son, Enosh, humans begin to call on the name of Yahweh, the first occurrence of this act of worship in the Bible (Gen 4:26). This new line of humans is not noted for its economic, technological, and artistic progress but for worshiping Yahweh. This is the first use of the divine name by a person in the narrative and suggests the covenantal God is pursuing his kingdom goal in the world. That goal will eventually lead to people giving up their swords for plowshares and their spears for pruning hooks (Is 2:1-5) and announcing forgiveness seventy times seven to repentant sinners (Mt 18:21-35). And instead of evaluating people as objects to be used, people of the kingdom will elevate people and see them as the image of God, in need of service and love (Mk 10:35-45).

DISCUSSION QUESTIONS

1. The genealogy of Cain is replete with relevance for understanding cultural evolution. What parallels do you see between Genesis 4 and the evolution of culture in your society over a long period of time?

2. Think about the worldview of Adam and Eve living before the fall and after the fall. What explicit points of contrast between these two periods of human history can you draw out from the text?

3. After Jesus told a questioning young man that the ethic demanded for the eternal life of the kingdom was to love one's neighbor as oneself, the young man responded with a question, "Who is my neighbor?" How is that question like and unlike Cain's, "Am I my brother's keeper?"

Chapter Five

KINGDOM RESTORATION BEGINS

ADAM TO ABRAHAM

THE TIME FROM ADAM TO ABRAHAM develops the theme of kingdom restoration and is sketched in broad strokes because the narrator is anxious to arrive at the story of Abraham. In fact, thousands of years are covered in Genesis 5–11 while most of the Abrahamic story (Gen 12–22) constitutes about twenty-five years.

TWO DIVERGING GENEALOGIES; TWO DIVERGING KINGDOMS

In Genesis 5 the genealogy of Seth parallels the genealogy of Cain. There are striking similarities between the genealogies, including similar and identical names, the importance of the number seven, and the conclusion of each genealogy with a speaker named Lamech. Whatever their original sources, these genealogies are evidently to be read together as studies in contrast. They develop the theme of the seed of the woman and the seed of the Serpent in Genesis 3:15, and a hope for the future.

Cain's genealogy focuses on human achievements, the building of a city, and the birth of civilization. Human progress and moral regress—technology, the economy, the arts, unbridled sexuality, and murderous vengeance—dominate Cain's line. Cain's distant descendant has magnified the sin of his ancestor. Lamech is a king in reverse, a cruel tyrant in love with himself and his power.[1]

In contrast, Seth's genealogy focuses on humans as the image of God and deliverance from death. This is the most important characteristic of transmission.[2] Adam, who bears the image of God, has a son in his own image, which not only demonstrates the transmission of this characteristic, which defines this line, but suggests that sonship is linked to the image. What is important then about this line is that these descendants of Adam and Eve are royal sons of God. And the Lamech at the end of this line is preoccupied not with killing and vengeance, but with the birth of a son who will bring relief from God's curse of the earth. While Cain's genealogy is a dead end as no one in it survives the future deluge, Seth's genealogy has a future as its distant descendant (Noah) survives the flood and enters a new world. While the passing of generations occurs without flourish in Cain's genealogy, each generation in Seth's line shows signs of blessing in the birth of many children (sons and daughters) and long age of the progenitor before death, with one exception. Thus, the reality of the curse of death persists despite longevity, and its drumbeat repetition sounds like a *cantus firmus* in a fugue throughout the text. The lone exception to the curse of death is Enoch, who walked with God (Gen 5:24), a trait that will later describe someone in right relationship with God. Evidently it is because of this relationship that Enoch escapes the grim reality of death. He fulfills the human vocation of living as the image of God and becomes an early signpost of the possibility of overcoming the universal curse.

Whereas Cain's genealogy through Lamech ends on a note of horrific violence in the brutal "Song of the Sword" (Gen 4:23-24), the Sethite Lamech

---

[1]Some have suggested that Lamech is an anagram of the word for king in Hebrew (Melech). See Y. T. Radday, "Humour in Names," *On Humour and the Comic in the Hebrew Bible*, ed. Y. T. Radday and Adele Brenner, JSOT Supplement 92 (Sheffield, UK: Almond, 1990), 78.

[2]In the modern context, Lesslie Newbegin remarks that if humans were created for an eternal relationship with their Creator, then surely this should be part of the core curriculum of any school whose beliefs accept this understanding. Lesslie Newbigin, *Foolishness to the Greeks: The Gospel and Western Culture* (Grand Rapids, MI: Eerdmans, 1986), 67.

concludes the genealogy in Genesis 5 with a desire to be relieved from God's curse of the earth, and envisions this as arriving through the birth of his son, whom he names "Relief," that is, Noah (Gen 5:29). Thus in these two lines which in their present literary context intentionally parallel one another, there is a line of human beings who represent the seed of the Serpent and the seed of the woman:

Table 5.1. The genealogies of Cain and Seth in Genesis

CAINITE GENEALOGY		SETHITE GENEALOGY
Adam		Adam (image of God)
Cain (murders brother)		Seth (image of God)
Enoch (city named after him)		Enosh (calls on Yahweh)
Irad		Kenan
Mehujael		Mehalalel
Methusael		Jared
Lamech (Speaker—focus on sevens, polygamist, violent killer)		Enoch (escapes death)
		Methusaleh
Jabal, Jubal (by Ada)	Tubal-Cain, Naamah (by Zillah)	Lamech (speaker—focus on sevens, focus on hope)
		Noah (relief from the curse)
		Shem Ham Japeth

As Augustine insightfully observed, here are the two cities, the city of man and the city of God, or two kingdoms, one of the Serpent and one of the woman.[3]

PRELUDE TO THE FLOOD

These two kingdoms develop alongside one another. One seems more dominant (Gen 4) than the other (Gen 5), which seems much less influential from a human perspective. In the latter there are no noted cultural achievements, but rather a concern for life and blessing amid a world of death. Suddenly as if out of nowhere, appears a text, which jars with the context (Gen 6:1-4).

---

[3]Saint Augustine, *City of God* (London: Penguin, 2003), XIV, 13, 28.

There now appears a reference to the multiplication of human beings on the earth, and the marriages of individuals called the sons of God to beautiful females, resulting in divine displeasure, a divine judgment of a 120-year period, and an explanatory comment about individuals called the Nephilim. This all seems to contribute to the proliferation of evil in the world to such an extent that it infects the thought of every human being all the time. Consequently, God decides to destroy the world that he crafted to his exquisite delight. But one man finds grace, that is Lamech's son, Noah (Gen 6:5-8).

While this text, particularly Genesis 6:1-4, is considered an interpretive crux, spawning multiple interpretations, the overall context is often ignored, in which two lines of humanity are contrasted. Throughout the second line there has been a constant reference to the multiplication of human beings (sons and daughters). Genesis 6:1 ("When humanity began to multiply on the earth and daughters were born to them") uses a grammatical construction that can function as a flashback to the previous text, and this is exactly what is happening. The reference to the sons of God in the literary context suggests the line of Seth, which is concerned for the transmission of the image of God. As Adam is a son of God, Seth his son is the same. They are the line specifically concerned with walking with God. But what happens is that they experience "a fall" with language that echoes the temptation in the Garden. They see beautiful women and take for themselves wives from whomever they choose. These women are probably Cainites, and thus these royal sons of God are becoming like the Cainite Lamech. What makes for the divine displeasure is the capitulation of a believing line, and the dissolution of the whole notion of the importance of walking with God. Thus, there is the decision to reduce the long-life spans to 120 years.[4] This is followed by an explanatory comment about Nephilim, individuals in the land in those days and even after that time. These were famous warrior-like men, notorious for violence and evil, before and after these intermarriages. Probably the loss of any consciousness of God and his image in humanity, caused by these intermarriages, contributed to greater acts of violence, which led to acts of

---

[4]An alternative interpretation regards this time span as a period of grace before the flood, but the text explicitly says, "his days will be 120 years." A gradual but noticeable reduction in longevity characterizes the generations after the flood.

outrageous evil.[5] The royal sons of God have become tyrants, which led to widespread barbarity.

The end result is the total corruption of the human race. God can no longer stand to look at his creation, which once evoked wonder and delight, and he decides to wipe out his own handiwork. This is a case of suffering love, by someone who loved his masterpiece but now sees it torn to shreds. Further description elaborates on the catastrophe. All flesh had corrupted its way, and the earth was filled with violence instead of the glory of God. Clearly the image of God is not reflected in the earth but instead the image of the Serpent. The use of the Hebrew interjection sometimes translated "behold" (*hinnê*) often provides new information that is a surprise, and it also gives the audience the opportunity to see through the eye of the subject in the text. The difference between the world of Genesis 1 and that of Genesis 6 is stark:

> God saw all that he had made and *behold* it was very good. (Gen 1:31)

> God saw the world and *behold* it was corrupt, for all flesh had corrupted its way upon the earth. (Gen 6:12)

There is no redeeming virtue. What has happened to the promise in Genesis 3:15? Why has there been such a complete meltdown of any line of promise? There has been a mixture of the lines that has resulted in the near loss of identity of humans as the image of God. Violence is ubiquitous, which explains the prominence of a penalty for capital punishment after the flood for the crime of murder (Gen 9:5-6).

The world is now a house of horrors where human life has been objectified and cheapened. This is a world where the words of the last man in Cain's line serve as a motto:

> I have killed a man for wounding me, a young lad for hurting me. If Cain is avenged seven times then Lamech will be avenged seventy-seven times. (Gen 4:23-24)

---

[5]A number of interpretations understand the "sons of God" as angels or human kings claiming divinity. There are strengths to each understanding. For a robust defense of the Sethite interpretation, see Rita Cefalu, "Royal Priestly Heirs to the Restoration Promise of Genesis 3:15: A Biblical Theological Perspective on the Sons of God in Genesis 6," *Westminster Theological Journal* 76 (2014): 351-70. For the defense of the angelic view, see Michael S. Heiser, *The Unseen Realm: Recovering the Supernatural Worldview of the Bible* (Bellingham, WA: Lexham, 2015), 101-9.

GRACE AMID CURSE

Yet in the midst of this violence and mayhem appears a short contrastive sentence. All is not lost, because of God's grace: "Noah found grace in the eyes of Yahweh" (Gen 6:8). God responded to the heart cry of the Lamech in Seth's line that his son might help relieve the curse imposed on the earth. The Hebrew has a beautiful wordplay to highlight this grace: And "Noah" (*nōaḥ*) found "grace" (*ḥēn*) in the eyes of Yahweh. God is going to turn things upside down with his grace and not make a clean sweep of the world but provide a salvation for this man and his family and the animal kingdom, not because he is more righteous, but because God is more gracious.[6] It will be through Seth and his line, concluding with Noah, that the world will be saved and not through the line of Cain which comes to a dead end.

The flood story found in Genesis 6–9 is God's determination as the king of the world to regulate his world in the absence of a fifth column. As the just judge of the world, the administration of the world through the kingdom of the Serpent has become so corrupt and so depraved, and the other kingdom, the kingdom of God, has become so assimilated into it as to be indistinguishable. God must start over. But instead of making a completely new beginning, he extends grace to one family, and this family becomes like a new Adam and Eve. In fact, when the years of the genealogy are tabulated, Adam is the first patriarch to die, and Noah is the only one to survive the flood.[7] As a result of God's grace Noah rules over the new kingdom of the ark. The kingdom under the Serpent's power would resist this. Other scriptural texts give every indication of Noah's persecution (2 Pet 2:5). But Noah believes in the word of the Lord and this word is underscored in the text. In fact, Noah does not utter one word in the entire flood narrative and even afterward he has only one speech. He is a model of obedience.[8] He obeys the divine word and preserves human and animal life. The rest of humanity in its defiance of the divine word would end up killing itself in brutality and violence, so God mercifully brings an end to this kingdom.

---

[6]Carol M. Kaminski, *Was Noah Good? Finding Favour in the Flood Narrative* (London: Bloomsbury T&T Clark, 2014).

[7]Adam dies 126 years before the birth of Noah.

[8]Gordon J Wenham, *Genesis 1–15*, Word Biblical Commentary (Waco, TX: Word, 1987), 205-7.

Thus, there are two kingdoms, the kingdom of God in which Noah rules over the world in God's stead, preserving a future for the world, and the rest of humanity, living in chaos and violence, everyone doing what is right in their own eyes.

A NEW WORLD AND THE LOGIC OF GRACE

The story of the flood is about an old creation being destroyed and purged and a new one being born. The new, of course, is part of the old. The first act of Noah after he emerges from the ark is an act of worship (Gen 8:18-22). He builds an altar and offers sacrifices. Because of the divine acceptance of the offering, the order of creation is secured. Though the human heart is evil from its youth, never again will a flood destroy the world. There is the guarantee of world order despite the fact that the human heart has not changed.[9] It was the heart of humanity in its persistent depravity that had caused the flood, but now as a result of the sacrifice of Noah, there has been a change in God's logic: "Were it not for the changed logic of God, in that he now cites man's depravity as a ground for his mercy rather than for his judgment, the descendants of Noah would be heading for extinction in another deluge."[10] Consequently a new world will not only come about because of God's mercy but this implies that someday the human heart must be transformed. For the present, however, for God's kingdom to return to the world, the world must be preserved. Eventually there can be the return of the King, where his rule is acknowledged and the earth, rather than filled with violence, is filled with divine glory. But we are not there yet.

The content of a new creation covenant is specified after the flood and, in many ways, it is a reset of the original covenant at creation. The command in Genesis 1 to be fruitful and multiply is repeated (Gen 9:1-6). But now the command comes to eight members of humanity instead of two. Second, they are given dominion over all the animals but there are two new elements: the animals will be alienated from humanity, as fear and terror mar their

---

[9]There is a slight change between the preflood view and the postflood view. Preflood, every thought of the heart is only evil throughout the day (Gen 6:5), whereas postflood the thought of people's hearts is evil from their youth (Gen 8:21).
[10]Wenham, *Genesis 1–15*, 206.

relationship; moreover, humans can now consume animal flesh as they previously ate vegetation.

Finally, there are two major prohibitions. Although animals can be killed for food, their blood must not be consumed. Moreover, except for capital punishment, human blood must not be shed. Then, in a direct echo of Genesis 1, a more extensive prohibition of killing a human life is given complete with a motive:

> One who sheds the blood of man will have his own blood shed by man,
> (šōpēk dam hā ʾādām bā ʾādām dāmô yiššāpēk)
> for in the image of God he made man.
> (kî baṣelem ʾělōhîm ʿāśâ ʾet-hā ʾādām) (Gen 9:6)

The wordplay associating blood (dām) and humanity (hā ʾādām) underlines the prohibition against killing a human. The basis for this command of capital punishment is the fact that humans are made in the image of God. Because human beings represent God, their lives are sacred; homicide is tantamount to deicide. Second, only someone who represents God as his royal representative can perform the execution. This command safeguards the value of a human life.

There is now a sense in which humans "own" animals and can kill them for food. But they cannot kill fellow humans because they alone are made in the image of God and therefore are "owned" by God. The image stamps them with God's signature.

All these commands after the flood indicate both continuity and discontinuity with Genesis 1. The continuity is found in the blessing to have dominion over the world and to be fruitful and multiply, as well as the reminder that all humanity is made in the image of God. The discontinuity prevails in the alienation between the animals and humans, and the divine license for humanity to eat meat. But humanity also requires protection from not only animals but from itself. The reason for this protection probably has to do with the rampant violence and carnage that existed before the flood.[11]

---

[11]Peter Harland, "The Value of Human Life in the Story of the Flood in Genesis 6–9" (PhD diss., University of Durham, 1992).

Then a covenant is made with Noah and all flesh (Gen 9:8-17). It is clearly a covenant with creation. The sign of the covenant, the rainbow, is given to the first human community as the divine pledge not to destroy the world ever again by a deluge. The sign is not only for human benefit but for God to be reminded of his sacred word to uphold the order of the world. The order and stability of the world is guaranteed by the divine word of promise. Thus, the kingdom of the Serpent perished in the waters of the flood and the kingdom of God preserving the seed of the woman continues. But it is not long before the kingdom of the Serpent reappears.

THE BLESSING OF SHEM AND THE CURSE OF CANAAN

As has been mentioned, the heart of humanity after the deluge is still evil, and God's change of heart in which this evil becomes a ground for mercy rather than judgment has coincided with sacrifice and atonement. But now the issue of the corruption of the human heart and its consequences for humanity re-emerge. After the flood, Noah and his family settle down and he plants a vineyard, from which he makes wine, leading to his intoxication and nakedness (Gen 9:20-27). Here again are shades of the temptation in the Garden of Eden. In the tent one of his sons, Ham, sees him naked while he is asleep and tells his brothers. After his brothers cover his nakedness with a garment, their father awakens, remembers what Ham did to him, and pronounces a curse on a future son of Ham, named Canaan, condemning him to a life of servitude. The other two sons are blessed, particularly Shem, who is identified with the covenant God—Yahweh, the God of Shem—and in whose tents Japheth may come to dwell and experience blessing.

In this text, a strategy is unfolding for the kingdom of God. Somehow the kingdom is linked with the tents of Shem and divine blessing. To be linked with Shem is to experience this blessing. Moreover, a future descendant of Ham is cursed because his ancestor violated an ancient taboo.

What was this taboo? There are many theories about this episode but the most probable indicates an act of incest.[12] To uncover the nakedness of someone in ancient Israel could mean maternal incest (Deut 22:30 [Heb. 23:1];

---

[12]John S. Bergsma and Scott W. Hahn, "Noah's Nakedness and the Curse on Canaan," *Journal of Biblical Literature* 124 (2005): 25-40.

27:20).[13] In other words, Ham attempted to usurp the authority of his father by sleeping with his mother (cf. Gen 35:22; 2 Sam 3:6-8; 16:20-22; 1 Kings 2:13-23). Noah, speaking prophetically, curses Canaan because he sees Canaan as the result of incest.

This strange story shows, among other things, that evil remains in the human heart, and that acts of evil transcend their original context. Even Noah, a paragon of moral virtue, becomes intoxicated as human culture begins to develop again, and his youngest son takes advantage of this moral lapse, to grab power for himself by sleeping with his mother. This cancer of sin, lodged deep in the human heart, will burgeon once again in society. Later in Genesis 11, the entire human community revolts against God, a revolt that can only be quelled by divine judgment in the form of linguistic confusion (Gen 11:1-9). But here in Noah's pronouncements of both a curse and a blessing, we have a roadmap for the future of the biblical narrative. The line of Shem is blessed, and the line of Japheth will profit from this blessing, but the line of Ham brings on itself God's curse, which will eventually result in judgment during the future conquest of Canaan (Gen 15:16, Josh 1–12). The kingdom of God will be found in Shem's line.

The next passage clarifies this orientation by providing a list or table of nations in which seventy are listed, suggesting comprehensiveness for this ancient world map (Gen 10:1-32). According to the end of this list, these nations were spread abroad after the flood (Gen 10:32). What is clear from the map and from its place in the biblical narrative is that the dispersal of the nations was caused by humanity's failure to heed the command of God to scatter over the earth. The map is the result of divine judgment. Yet despite the judgment the map highlights the line of Shem both geographically and in its literary structure since Shem will be the son through whom the blessing of Noah will be transmitted.

In this world map, the various nations are oriented toward the line of Shem. Japheth is mentioned first to the north of Shem (Asia), Ham mainly to the south (Africa), and Shem is in the center of the map, in Mesopotamia and Palestine. But second, the literary presentation highlights Shem as it

---

[13]See also Corrine Blackmer, "No-Name Woman: Noah's Wife and Heterosexual Incestuous Relations in Genesis 9:18-29," *Judaica Ukrainica* 1 (2012): 29-46.

concludes with Shem down through the line of the two sons of Eber, Joktan, and Peleg, and follows the line of Joktan. Then it resumes with the line of Peleg after its interruption by a vignette (Gen 11:1-9) that explains the dispersal of the nations to their geographical positions.

WHAT'S IN A NAME?

This vignette of Genesis 11:1-9 relays how God dispersed the nations because they were seeking en masse to erect a city and tower that would reach the heavens. In biblical terminology this is a project of gargantuan hubris, an effort to eliminate the distinction between the divine and the human, a project that had failed at the beginning. But this time it is not just the determination of one couple representing humanity but the entire human community! And the place is aptly named Babel. Its building was under the leadership of someone known, much like the Nephilim, as a mighty warrior, specializing in power and violence and rebellion against God. In fact the *kingdom*—and this is the first explicit mention of this word in the Bible—was first established here by Nimrod, before he moved to other locations (Gen 10:8-12). But the project was an abysmal failure. Instead, Babel, meaning a "gateway to the gods" (its original meaning in Babylonian), becomes the place of linguistic confusion, as the author links the name with the Hebrew word for "babble" (*bālal*). Numerous other significant wordplays in the text highlight the failure of this kingdom building project. The construction of this tower and city takes place in "Shinar" (*šin'ār*), where the people seek to make a "name" (*šēm*) for themselves "there" (*šām*) by building the "tower" (*migdāl*) so high it will reach the "heavens" (*šāmayim*). They call the name of the place *Babel* but its tower is so massive that God needs to come down from heaven to see it! There he "confuses" (*bālal*) the language so that this kingdom is divided and scattered across the face of the earth, the situation already described in Genesis 10.

But God envisions a different type of kingdom, to cover the earth, one in which he will call out someone by his grace and magnify his "name" (*šēm*). God will create a way to unite heaven and earth through his own tower and ramp, and he will do it through the building of a family. A seed will bless the entire earth, not just eight individuals, with a new tree of life, which will bring about the transformation of human hearts.

It is no accident, then, that after the tower of Babel episode, the genealogy of "Shem" (*šēm*) resumes, this time with the second son of Eber, Peleg, whose name suggests the events of Genesis 11:1-9, the division of the peoples of the earth (Gen 10:25). Shem's genealogy is a ten-generation sequence paralleling the preflood ten-generation series (Gen 5:1-32). This also is no coincidence as each sequence ends with an individual who is critical for rescuing the world: Lamech fathers Noah, and Terah fathers Abraham. God makes a covenant with each and each one is brought into right relationship with God. This postdiluvian genealogy emphasizes Shem, the "name," highlighting the resumption of the line of the woman whose seed will bring about the return of the King, whose name will one day be above every name, to which every knee will bow, in heaven and on earth, in an everlasting kingdom (Phil 2:9-10).

DISCUSSION QUESTIONS

1. Compare Genesis 6:5 and Genesis 8:21. What has changed?

2. What do you think was the main point of the story of the flood?

3. How is Noah a new Adam?

Chapter Six

THE PATRIARCHAL NARRATIVES AND THE KINGDOM OF GOD, PART 1

ABRAHAM AND LIFE OVER DEATH

AS SOCIETY BEGINS TO GROW, the nature of the kingdom not only begins to change, but God's plan for reestablishing his reign and rule begins to take shape. There will be an inauspicious beginning with the calling of a seventy-five-year-old man, with his barren wife, ten years his junior. They will eventually produce a son against all odds, and this family line will be followed throughout Genesis in three cycles of stories about Abraham, Jacob, and Joseph. These are called cycles since they are loose collections of episodes cycling around a major figure. At the same time, each cycle begins with programmatic texts that set the agenda for each account: Genesis 12:1-3; 25:23; 37:7-9, 11-12. These strategic statements are about kingdom and rule. First, God chooses Abram to become a great nation and to bless the entire world. Second, the election of Jacob focuses on an unlikely carrier of this universal blessing. Third, the choice of Joseph results in an Israelite literally blessing and saving the world through his wisdom and provides a preview of a future world ruler at the end of history.

Throughout these ancestral narratives, in keeping with the idea of the birth of a human who will triumph over the Serpent, descendants are often the focus of attention. There are many obstacles to these descendants reaching even a modicum of success, whether they are natural obstacles, such as infertility, or sinful propensities among the descendants themselves. Patriarchs place their wives in danger several times, and some try to domesticate the promise. There are foreign armies, enemies who pose as friends, seductresses, and even family members that seek to kill the bearer of the promise. And at times it may seem that God himself is the enemy. But the point is that by the end of the book of Genesis someone will be blessed among the sons of Israel who will emerge as a royal figure to rule the nations. As the creation of a new world happened at the beginning, this person will arise at the end of history to establish a new world order (Gen 1:1; 49:1).[1] And it will be through this person that the Serpent will be defeated, and the promise of universal blessing will come.

THE PIVOTAL PLAN FOR KINGDOM BLESSING

The ancestral narratives are distinguished by being an introduction to Israel's history, and the rest of the Bible. Genesis 3–11 has documented the spread of sin like a cancer and the judgment of God. God has reestablished the creation covenant with a reset in the flood story, when he called Noah to save humanity and the animal kingdom from the judgment. But this reset could not alter the fundamental state of the human heart (Gen 6:5; 8:21) so that humanity may represent God's image faithfully in the world, that the world would be filled with the glory of God, and that the divine verdict could once again be pronounced over the world: "Very good!" The postflood genealogy of Shem suggests a continuation of the story and the certainty of God's plan. Just as the end of the preflood genealogy concluded

---

[1]For further reflection see Stephen G. Dempster, "'At the End of the Days' (בְּאַחֲרִית הַיָּמִים)—An Eschatological Technical Term? The Intersection of Context, Linguistics and Theology," in *The Unfolding of Your Words Gives Light: Studies on Biblical Hebrew in Honor of George L. Klein*, ed. Ethan C. Jones (University Park, PA: Eisenbrauns, 2018), 118-41.

with Noah, with whom a covenant was made to save the world (eight people plus representatives of the animal kingdom), a postflood genealogy concludes with another man with whom a covenant will be made and through whom *the entire world* will be blessed. If Noah was a new Adam, Abram will be a greater Adam. From this perspective the covenant with Noah is a foundation for the covenant with Abraham, a type of damage control to preserve the world's continuation for the worldwide blessing of the Abrahamic covenant.

The story has an inauspicious beginning (Gen 11:27-32). We are introduced to the death of Haran in Mesopotamia after he fathers a son named Lot. Haran is one of the sons of Abram's father, Terah. His two other brothers marry: Abram marrying Sarai, and Nahor marrying Milcah. But Sarai is barren—another sign of death. Then Terah takes his son Abram and Sarai, as well as his grandson, Lot, and heads for Canaan, but they stop short of their goal and remain in northwestern Mesopotamia, Haran, where they settle until Terah dies.

This looks very much like the arbitrary migration of a forlorn group of people. Most people moved in the ancient world in search of survival and prosperity. Here this group headed for a destination, but they aborted the trip, and after one son dies, and the wife of another son proves barren, the father finally dies.

If this is the resumption of the course for the future kingdom of God, it seems like a dead end. Death not life, curse not blessing, pervades the beginning. But the next three verses, Genesis 12:1-3, function as the answer not only to this dead end but to the entire prehistory of thousands of years beginning in Genesis 3.

These verses also function as an explicit divine plan to return to God's primal intentions for humanity reflected in Genesis 1-2. Yahweh speaks and he decisively intervenes just as much as God definitively intervened in creation, with the flood, and at the tower of Babel. The entire text needs to be considered. The structure is transparent: two sections, each beginning with an imperative followed by three imperfect (future) verbs. Each section develops a theme: (1) personal blessing and (2) universal blessing.

The LORD said to Abram,

"Go from your country, your people and your father's household to the land
I will show you:

I will make you into a great nation
and I will bless you
and I will make your name great.

Be a blessing:

I will bless those who bless you,
    and whoever curses you I will curse;
and all peoples on earth will be blessed through you." (Gen 12:1-3)

The first sequence begins with an imperative to Abram to depart from a place designated by three descriptors, each becoming more and more personal: your country, your birthplace (town), and your father's house. It continues by stating an unspecified destination: "a land I will show you." This is followed by three verbs emphasizing nationhood, divine blessing, and fame.

In these verses the concept of kingdom emerges, and it is one that is established by God through Abram. This man who is married without children is told to leave his own home and extended family to become a great nation. The writer could have used various terms for the word *nation*. He could have *chosen* a word that implies "kinship" (*'am*) and one that implies "many people" (*lə'ōm*) but the chosen word (*gôy*) emphasizes more the political and social rather than kinship bonds and usually requires a common language, a defined territory, a sizable population, and an institutional authority.[2] It is very rarely used of the land of Israel, but rather for other nations.

Many commentators make the point that the promise is threefold here: blessing of Abram (Israel) through a divine-human relationship, posterity, and land.[3] That clearly has kingdom ramifications. But the second command shows the purpose of national blessing for Abram: universal blessing.

---

[2]See, e.g., its use in the table of the nations: Gen 10:5, 20, 31, 32.
[3]For example, David J. A. Clines, *The Theme of the Pentateuch* (Sheffield, UK: Sheffield Academic Press, 1997), 30.

Everyone aiding this mission will be blessed and everyone hindering will be cursed, until the mission of global blessing is finally accomplished.[4] This climactic text will occur four more times in the subsequent narrative (Gen 18:18, 22:18, 26:4, 28:14). All the families of the "land" (*ădāmâ*), which has been cursed, will be blessed.

LAND, DESCENDANTS, AND "CUTTING"

As the Abraham narrative continues, it can be divided into two sections, one dealing primarily with the promise of land (Gen 12:4–15:21), and the other with the promise of descendants (Gen 16:1–22:24). God is at work to restore Eden (land) and the creation mandate to be fruitful and multiply. Both promises, however, seem very much in jeopardy even though Abram obeys God's word. He and his wife finally have a child despite thinking the promise bordered on the absurd.[5] Moreover, Abraham never acquires land until the purchase of a grave for his wife, Sarah, near the end of their story.[6] But three texts stand out as important to the story: (1) God cuts a covenant with Abraham in Genesis 15, (2) a covenant sign is cut in Genesis 17, and (3) after the chief bearer of promise is almost cut, the covenant promise is confirmed by an explicit divine oath in Genesis 22. Each text has important kingdom ramifications, since the covenant, its sign, and the explicit divine oath, guarantee the promise that will bring about worldwide blessing. Also, when the sign is given, Abraham and Sarah are promised that they will beget a line of kings, and when the divine oath is sworn, one such descendant will conquer the gates of his enemies in bringing about worldwide blessing.

In Genesis 15 Abram has been in the land for a long time without any sign of the fulfillment of God's promises—no progeny and no land. God reassures him of progeny by stating that his descendants will be as numerous as the

---

[4]There are three categories of people in this blessing: the elect, the anti-elect, and the non-elect. The elect have the purpose of blessing the non-elect while the anti-elect seek to subvert this blessing. For the three categories see Joel Kaminsky, *Yet I Loved Jacob: Reclaiming the Biblical Concept of Election* (Nashville: Abingdon, 2007).

[5]As the writer of Genesis 17 is aware, the name Isaac means "laughter" and it seems like a joke both to Abraham and Sarah that they could have a child (Gen 17:17-19; 18:12-15).

[6]Gen 23.

stars in the sky. At this point the narrator comments that Abram's belief in the promise changes his moral status before God: God now considers him righteous (Gen 15:6). Then God reassures him of the promise of land by making a covenant with him. Abram dismembers animals to indicate the gravity of covenant violation. If the parties breach the covenant, they invoke on themselves the fate of the mutilated animals (cf. Jer 34:8-20).[7] Abram falls asleep and has a vision in which he perceives the history of his descendants for the next four hundred years: descent to Egypt, Egyptian oppression, exodus, and conquest of the Amorites in the land of Canaan (Gen 15:13-16). But in the vision, he sees a smoking, burning fire—a theophany—passing between the pieces of the animals (Gen 15:17). Yahweh himself guarantees the promise with this covenantal rite. As if to ensure the proper interpretation of the rite, the narrator adds: "In that day, Yahweh cut a covenant with Abram" to give to him the land (Gen 15:18). The kingdom of God will come through a promise guaranteed by a covenant.

After a significant time has passed, when Abram is approaching one hundred years old and Sarai her ninetieth birthday, they still do not have a child (Gen 17). Sarai's womb is dead, and Abram certainly does not seem to have the regenerative power to make a difference. There is no land to rule over nor any potential subjects. It is at this point that Abram hears an obligation to follow in the train of Enoch and Noah, that is, to walk blamelessly with God. He has been declared righteous but now he must embody that righteousness in his life. Then God gives him the sign of the covenant which will ensure him of numerous progeny—abundant life in the midst of death. The sign is circumcision, the removal of the foreskin from the male sexual organ. It is particularly fitting as a sign of the faith of Abram since the promise and the sign refer to the miracle of descendants. But it also suggests a type of death to a trust in human resources and potential. Abram and his future family must walk with God and trust in him. In other words, be devoted to God. Thus, this is an outward sign of an inward devotion. This

---

[7]See also the comparative evidence from the first (Neo-Assyrian) and second (Alalakh) millennium BC treaties. See further William S. Morrow, "Ancient Near Eastern Treaties/Loyalty Oaths and Biblical Law," in *The Oxford Handbook of Biblical Law*, ed. Pamela Barmash (Oxford: Oxford University Press, 2019), 319-32.

was its meaning in ancient Egypt, where it was often practiced on royalty and the priesthood.[8]

It is in this context that God promises Abram and Sarai not only numerous offspring but a royal line of kings (Gen 17:6, 16). It is not coincidental that the aged couple are renamed in this text: Abram is renamed Abraham, and Sarai becomes Sarah. The change in name reflects a change in destiny—Abraham's expanded name means an expanded progeny and Sarah's name reaffirms the royalty associated with her previous name. Their son is named Isaac (*yiṣḥāq*), a wordplay on Abraham's laughter (*wayyiṣḥāq*) when God assured him that the promise of a child would be fulfilled, despite all obstacles (Gen 17:17-19).

Shortly after this time, the child is conceived and nine months later Isaac is born (Gen 21:1-7). Life has defeated death. But no sooner is the child of promise born in the narrative than Abraham is called by God to sacrifice this long-awaited promise of life and hope for the world (Gen 22:1-19).[9] The audience is informed that this is a test of obedience but nevertheless it appears that death will triumph over life (Gen 22:1). This text is the climax of Abraham's journey of faith, and it resounds with its beginning when he was called to give up his past to follow the leading of the divine promise. Now, at the end of this journey, he is called to give up his future—the promise of God that his son would be the bearer of universal blessing.[10]

Nonetheless, the man of faith, in the greatest struggle of his life, his dark night of Gethsemane, believes absolutely in the word of God even when it flatly contradicts everything that he holds dear, including the divine promise! Near the end of the Abraham story we might be expecting Abraham to become king over Canaan, but here the blessing seems to have turned into

---

[8]John D. Meade, "Circumcision of the Heart in Leviticus and Deuteronomy: Divine Means for Resolving Curse and Bringing Blessing," *Southern Baptist Journal of Theology* 18 (2014): 59-85.

[9]Note the difference between narrative time and real time. While the events of Genesis 22 immediately follow that of Genesis 21, many years have passed since Isaac is the one who is doing the heavy lifting in Genesis 22. He is probably a teenager, perhaps around fifteen years old (Gen 22:6).

[10]Genesis 12:1-3 and Gen 22:1-2 remarkably parallel each other. The Hebrew phrase "go for yourself" (*lek-ləkā*) occurs only twice in the Bible in Gen 12:1; 22:2. Abraham's past and future are emphasized with three descriptors: past—your land, your birthplace, your father's house (Gen 12:1), and future—your son, your only one whom you love, Isaac (Gen 22:2).

a curse.[11] However, by virtue of this stupendous "obedience of faith," at the last possible moment God supplies Abraham with a ram in the place of his son, an anticipation of a future salvific act of God where the death of an animal will save the firstborn son in every Israelite home, and be the means by which the nation is redeemed from slavery and death (Ex 12). God swears to him for the first time with an oath that all the nations of the earth will be blessed through his descendants and that the latter will be like a conquering army, possessing the gates of their enemies and, in the prediction of the Messiah much later, even the very gates of hell itself (Mt 16:18).

It is striking that God has made these unconditional promises before (Gen 12:2; 13:16; 15:5; 17:6; 18:18), but not in such an emphatic manner.[12] But now Abraham's obedience becomes integrated as a fulfilled condition of the promise, now sworn with a divine oath: "Because you have done this . . ." (Gen 22:16). Abraham's deep faith in the promise of God produces his profound obedience, which in turn leads into God's emphatic reaffirmation of the promise.[13]

If this test shows Abraham's absolute commitment to God and God's absolute commitment to him, these commitments display expectations of kingdom life. The greatest command in the kingdom will be to place love for God above every other love, but God is committed to no less a love for the citizens of the kingdom. This is supremely shown in the provision of the lamb for the sacrifice. Someday God himself will experience the cutting of the covenant as his citizens will eat of his body and drink his blood to experience true life.

The next chapter, Genesis 23, focuses on Abraham procuring some land for his "kingdom"—a grave site for Sarah who has recently died. The text

---

[11]I owe this insight to Gary Anderson: "The election of Abraham does not end with his becoming king over the land of Canaan; its literary apogee is Abraham's call to free himself of what he holds most dear." Gary A. Anderson, *Christian Doctrine and the Old Testament: Theology in the Service of Biblical Exegesis* (Grand Rapids, MI: Baker Academic, 2017), 81.

[12]Note the infinitive absolutes in Gen 22:17.

[13]"It is not that the promise has become contingent on Abraham's obedience but that Abraham's obedience has been incorporated into the divine promise." R. W. L. Moberly, "Christ as the Key to Scripture: Genesis 22 Reconsidered," in *He Swore an Oath: Biblical Themes from Genesis 12–50*, ed. Richard S. Hess, Gordon J. Wenham, and P. E. Satterthwaite (Carlisle, UK: Paternoster Press, 1994), 161.

presents a meticulous description of the necessary proof required for Abraham's purchase. An outlandish sum of money changes hands. What explains this inordinate attention to such detail by the narrator? The text bears signs of being a legal document, complete with the amount of transaction and the many witnesses, and the specific description of the location (Gen 23:17-20). If Isaac is the first sign of many descendants for the nation, this graveyard is the first sign of the nation's territory. Admittedly these are inauspicious beginnings, but the kingdom of God is becoming a reality on the earth. Life is overcoming death.

DISCUSSION QUESTIONS

1. How does the naming of people in the Abraham cycle contribute to the storyline?

2. While Isaac's name indicates Abraham's view of the absurdity of the promise, what other points do you think are being emphasized by God's choice of this name?

3. Many people in the contemporary world think that Genesis 22 is a classic text in which the biblical God is depicted as a moral monster and Abraham is an extreme example of a child abuser. Yet in the biblical text Abraham is praised for his obedience to the divine will. How would you answer the contemporary objections?

Chapter Seven

THE PATRIARCHAL NARRATIVES AND THE KINGDOM OF GOD, PART 2

JACOB AND BLESSING OVER CURSE; JOSEPH AND GOOD OVER EVIL

THE NEXT TWO MAJOR SECTIONS, the Jacob cycle and the Joseph story, further develop the ideas of kingship and nationhood (Gen 25:19–35:29, 37:2–50:26). The larger world of the ancient Near East is in the background in the Jacob cycle while it emerges to the foreground in the Joseph story. In the Jacob narrative, the family that is the carrier of worldwide blessing begins to grow and the nation of Israel is born. In the Joseph story the family begins to be a blessing to the nations, and by the end one of the sons will rise to prominence to bless the world in the distant future.

THE JACOB CYCLE

Blessing over curse. Three texts are crucial for the Jacob cycle, programmatic ones in which key divine encounters occur. This account focuses on the transmission and procurement of *the blessing*, despite the possibility of curse. The first divine encounter occurs when Isaac's wife, Rebecca, is unable to conceive. Through prayer the barrier of infertility and death is overcome, and she becomes pregnant with twins (Gen 25:21). In the darkness of her womb, a struggle takes place between the siblings, and Rebecca seeks a divine explanation. She is told that these are not just individuals but nations, and the younger will have precedence (Gen 25:22-23). This develops the original promise to Abraham that he would be a great nation. Here, the least likely to rule—the younger—becomes the blessed one. When the children finally emerge from the womb, they are still fighting for dominance with the youngest clutching at the heel of his older, hairy brother. Thus, the older is named Esau because of his hair, while the younger is named Jacob, for grasping at the heel.

On earth as it is in heaven. The background to the second divine encounter occurs much later when their father is ready to transmit the blessing to his eldest son (Gen 27). Because of his blindness he is unable to detect the one whom he will bless, and his wife and Jacob deceive him into conferring the blessing on Jacob. Jacob then flees to Mesopotamia to escape the murderous wrath of his brother. While fleeing, the exhausted and bedraggled fugitive stops for a rest, and using a stone for a pillow, falls fast asleep (Gen 28).

In his deep sleep he has a dream where the stone has become the base of a ramp on which angels are ascending and descending, receiving their orders from heaven and descending to the earth to perform them. The Lord himself is at the top of the structure (Gen 28:10-22). Jacob may well have expected a curse for his previous behavior, but instead he is struck by God's amazing grace.

The vision is significant for kingdom theology, for the ramp represents the bridge between the kingdom of God and the earth, and the channel of the kingdom in which God's will is being done on the earth is located on the head of Jacob. This is confirmed by the divine voice that blesses Jacob and promises him the gift of the land on which he is sleeping and a vast progeny of descendants, as well as the promise of not only universal blessing through them but also protection and guidance on his way to Mesopotamia.

This is a promise that the kingdom of God—God's will being done on the earth as it is in heaven—is going to take place in the nation that Jacob will father and will be the means by which the entire world will be blessed. Heaven

and earth will someday be united! When Jacob awakens, he calls the place
Bethel—the house of God, the place of God's habitation. Jacob could hardly
anticipate then that his dream that night would someday become a reality
when a distant descendant would say to a fellow Israelite: "You will see heaven
open and the angels of God ascending and descending on the Son of Man"
(Jn 1:51). Someday the entire earth will be Bethel (Jn 4:21-24)!

Jacob becomes Israel. The background to the final encounter with God
comes after a twenty-year period where the deceiving Jacob has met his
deceptive match in a father-in-law named Laban. Laban's mendacity results
in Jacob marrying two sisters instead of the younger one he loves. In the
ensuing narrative there is a description of the growth of Jacob's family under
less-than-ideal circumstances (Gen 29–30). His polygamous marriage is the
sordid scene of rivalry and competition, and out of this domestic chaos emerge
twelve children, while Jacob has slaved for his father-in-law night and day.
When he finally escapes from his controlling relative, and flees for home in
Canaan, he is pursued by Laban who cannot afford to lose such an asset
(Gen 31). After divine intervention, Laban and Jacob make a nonaggression
pact and the beleaguered patriarch crosses the Jabbok River with his clan
into Canaan. When he hears the news that his offended brother, Esau, is
approaching with four hundred armed men, Jacob soon realizes that he has
been delivered from the proverbial frying pan into a blazing fire (Gen 32).
Ever the manipulator, Jacob sends out plenty of gifts to pacify his brother's
murderous anger, then divides up his family into groups so that at least some
can escape if Esau seeks to kill them. But the cowardly Jacob remains at the
rear. He is desperate. He has run out of human options. And in that precise
moment he is attacked by a man who wrestles with him all night.

This is a resounding echo of Jacob's birth in which he wrestled with his
brother in the darkness of the womb, grabbing his brother's heel as both
emerged, resulting in his name as a heel-grabber. But this opponent is no
Esau. And in the midst of the struggle, the assailant simply touches Jacob's
hip, paralyzing him with pain as his femur is wrenched out of its socket. Jacob
becomes aware for the first time that he has been wrestling with someone
far above his weight class. It is really no contest. But still Jacob hangs on
because the identity of his divine assailant has finally dawned on him. He

has been wrestling with Him his entire life. Seizing the moment, Jacob, the deceiver, ever the manipulator, the low-down heel-grabber, hangs on for dear life and realizes that what he needs most of all is the divine blessing. He cannot steal it—that has not really worked. Moreover, it would be impossible to deceive his divine assailant anyway, even in the darkness, as he did to his father. Nevertheless, in this life and death struggle, he will not release his opponent from his grip, continuing to demand the blessing, despite the searing pain.

Remarkably the one prerequisite that his supernatural assailant requires of Jacob is simply to declare his name: his identity. In the darkness of his father's mind, Jacob lied to steal the blessing by saying that his name was Esau. Now he must declare himself in the darkness to eyes that can see everything in the darkness for "darkness is not darkness with you" (Ps 139:12). No deception. No lying. Just the unvarnished truth. And if he tells this person his name, it must also mean a confession of his character—Jacob, the manipulator, the heel-grabber, the deceiver. What could he be thinking? Perhaps that he would be cursed forever, destroyed by this person who just a few moments before had crippled him with a slight touch. Yet he still manages to blurt out his name. And in that instant, he is blessed beyond measure, for he has been given a new birth in his struggle and he acquires a new name: "Your name is no longer Jacob, but Israel for you have struggled with humans and God and won!" (Gen 32:28).

Here Jacob is a new man, although crippled, and he names the place Penuel, for he has seen God face-to-face and survived. It is as if he has had a Garden of Eden experience. But it has been costly. He will never walk the same. He is broken but *blessed.*

This wrestling has been a metaphor for Jacob's entire life but now he is a new man because he finally admits his identity. Now he has been born again as Israel, which means the struggler with God, or the one with whom God has struggled. As Samuel Balentine writes, "The new name is meant to embody a new character, a change from one who seeks to control to one who is controlled."[1] He is the one whom God rules!

[1]Samuel E. Balentine, *Prayer in the Hebrew Bible: The Drama of Divine Human Dialogue*, Overtures to Biblical Theology 20 (Minneapolis: Fortress, 1993), 71.

Face-to-face. He has struggled and overcome. *Jacob* (*ya 'ăqōb*) struggled (*yē 'ābēq*) at the *Jabbok* (*yabbōq*) and when he is born again as *Israel* (*yiśrā 'ēl*), he changes the name of *Jabbok* to *Peniel* (face of God, *pənî 'ēl*). The one whom God rules sees his face. Surely this text not only echoes his birth narrative where he struggles in the womb with Esau and comes out as Jacob, but also the dream scene when he sees heaven touching earth on his head, and he changes the name of Luz to Bethel. Now he changes the name of Jabbok to Peniel. He has graduated from a meeting in the house of God to an actual experience of the living God. To be engaged in a struggle to get the blessing to bless the world, and to wrestle for it with God himself, and to be crippled, and to survive this encounter, he becomes a new Adam, a new royalty. Jacob is no longer the controller—God is! Thus, Israel bequeaths his name to the nation. Now as Israel, who has seen God face-to-face and survived, he moves to the head of the family procession to meet his dreaded enemy face-to-face; he now reaches out to greet him, to embrace him, and sees his face as the face of God (Gen 33:10).

Perhaps this is what it means to be Israel, to see in the wrinkled red-headed face of his enemy, the face of God. To experience God's face is to see God's face in his brother, and embrace him, unlike Cain who attacked the face of God in his brother. It is a long way in time before Jesus will take up the towel and wash the feet of his disciples being their royal servant. But it has come already here in Israel in his new attitude to his brother. He is no longer the competitor who steals from him but the servant who blesses him. Later Jacob receives another blessing from God reaffirming his new name, his progeny, the land of promise, and the prediction that he would be the father of a line of kings (Gen 35:1-15).

THE JOSEPH STORY

Good from evil. The next major story in the account of the patriarchs develops the royal dimension in several ways, and it is a story of great evil being turned to great good (Gen 37-50). There are two protagonists, first Joseph and then Judah, and royalty is associated with each. First, Joseph is singled out for prominence at the beginning of this story by his father, Jacob, as he is given a coat of many colors. This coat distinguishes Joseph from his brothers as it is associated with favoritism and royalty. The only other time a coat like this appears is much later and it describes a royal robe of a king's daughter (2 Sam 13:19). Did Jacob foreshadow this greatness in Joseph's life when he gave him such a coat? At any rate dreams are the engine driving this story, and they are all connected with royalty: two dreams of Joseph that presage royalty, two dreams of royal officials of the Pharaoh of Egypt, and two dreams of the Pharaoh himself.

Kingdom dreams. The first pair of dreams are those of Joseph, and he shares them with his jealous brothers, who are left unimpressed as the dreams predict his future dominance (Gen 37:5-7, 9-10). But these dreams about future rule carry the story in the same way that the promise to Abraham (Gen 12:1-3) and the oracle to Rebekah (Gen 25:22-23) did for the previous narratives. All are about blessings, rule, and authority. In all of them there are crises to undergo before the blessed one proves himself. Abraham passes the fiery trial at the beginning and ending of the story, as does Jacob throughout the story and particularly at the end when he is born again as Israel. Joseph seems to be destined to rule according to these dreams. Consequently, the expectation of a trial looms ahead before a victory, a cross before a crown. Jacob sends Joseph to check on his brothers, but when they see him coming from a distance, they decide to send his dreams to oblivion. They say, "Here comes this dreamer! . . . Let us kill him . . . and see what will become of his dreams!" (Gen 37:19-20). In fact the rest of the Joseph story becomes an outworking of their diabolical plan. The irony is thick.

No sooner had Joseph arrived than the brothers set into motion their sinister scheme. Instead of killing him, Judah hatches a plan to make a profit: they will sell him to merchants heading to Egypt, and then kill a goat, rip up his royal robe, splatter it with blood, and present it coldly to their father who will draw the desired conclusion that his favorite son has been killed by a wild animal (Gen 27:26-36). The deception will be perfect. The brothers sell Joseph to merchants, and their plan works flawlessly. Their father is deceived by his son's robe stained with goat's blood (just as he once deceived his own father with goatskin). Jacob's grief knows no bounds as his sons harden their hearts to his tears and grief. It seems as if Joseph's dreams of royalty and rule have come to nothing.

The account of Joseph's fate is interrupted in the narrative with an account from Judah's life, that same brother who orchestrated the fate of Joseph and the grief of his father to make a few shekels. Yet Judah will bring about reconciliation and forgiveness in the Joseph story by admitting his crime and that of his brothers. This is foreshadowed in the narrative of Genesis 38. And from his descendants will come one who has an identity tag as a ruler, to whom the entire world will pay homage (Gen 49:8-12).

But what has this to do with the kingdom of God?

If Genesis 37 relates to one special character, Joseph, having to do with rule, Genesis 38 focuses on Judah and a line of descent. It seems that here the problem or obstacle is not women who are barren but the sinful progeny of Judah. He marries a Canaanite woman and marries his son to a Canaanite woman, Tamar, an act that seems to contradict Abraham's prohibition of marriage to a Canaanite (Gen 24:3). But the problem here is not the Canaanites but the Israelites. In the ensuing story Judah comes to recognize his own sin against his Canaanite daughter-in-law, Tamar, and it is Tamar who is able to bear the child of promise through unconventional means despite the sins of Judah and her previous husbands, Judah's sons.

Without going into great detail, this story highlights the chutzpah of a Canaanite woman who provides a descendant for Judah against all odds—even against the odds created by Judah himself! It also shows the beginning of a personal transformation in Judah's life. The one who deceived his father with clothing that implied the death of Joseph, confesses his own sin when Tamar presents him with his personal staff and seal. These articles are evidence of his sin against Tamar. Someday one of his descendants will be able to wield a staff or scepter with compassion and grace.

Joseph and Judah. As the Joseph story progresses there is further development of the characters of Joseph and Judah. Joseph is enslaved and later imprisoned by another lie, but he is never abandoned by God. While in prison, he accurately interprets the dreams of two other prisoners and is released to interpret two dreams of the Pharaoh, resulting in his promotion to become the king's majordomo. Since the dreams predict an imminent time of prosperity followed by a worldwide famine, Joseph organizes a massive effort to store food during the prosperous period to distribute during the famine not only to Egypt but to the surrounding nations. One must not miss the underlying theme: Abraham's seed is blessing the world.

From this royal position Joseph meets his brothers, who traveled to Egypt to buy much needed grain. When Joseph sees his brothers, he not only remembers the dreams but devises a plan for their moral transformation:

> Although Joseph recognized his brothers, they did not recognize him. Then he remembered his dreams about them and said to them, "You are spies! You have come to see where our land is unprotected." (Gen 42:8-9 NIV)

He intends to put them into the same situation they were in when they sold him into slavery and deceived their father. As the story develops, the brothers become increasingly aware of their guilt as Joseph tests and transforms them. Finally, when the opportunity arises to abandon their younger brother Benjamin—Joseph's full brother—as a slave in Egypt and gain their own freedom, Judah rises to the occasion. In the third longest speech in Genesis, Judah substitutes himself for his brother because he knows that the failure to return Benjamin will kill his father with grief (Gen 44:18-34).[2]

Judah's impassioned speech compels Joseph to reveal his identity. Their terrified response is met by Joseph's reassurance of God's sovereign plan. God had a global rescue plan in mind when Joseph was sold into slavery: "Do not be aggrieved that you sold me into slavery because God sent me ahead for you for the preservation of life. . . . What's more God has made me ruler over all the land of Egypt" (Gen 45:5-8). This is really the climax of the Joseph story, but it is a story in which an Israelite rises from slavery and imprisonment to become a ruler in Egypt to save not only Egypt but the surrounding nations during a global famine while also using his power to bring about moral transformation in his own family. Moreover, it is about Judah, the linchpin of that transformation, growing in stature.

When Jacob and the rest of the family migrate to Egypt, it is noted that there are seventy Israelites, including Joseph's family who are already present in Egypt. This is a round number, but it is hardly coincidental as the seventy Israelites probably represent the seventy nations in the Table of Nations in Genesis 10. Here is the kingdom of God—a new humanity—being marked

---

[2]The longest speech is Jacob's in Gen 49:1-27, the second longest is Abraham's servant in Gen 24:34-49.

out from the kingdoms of the world. God's salvation project for someone from this large extended family to bless the world is well on its way.

This is dramatically illustrated when Pharaoh meets Jacob (Gen 47:7-10). Here the most powerful ruler in the world meets a decrepit old Jacob, a powerful study in contrast. But shockingly it is Jacob who blesses the Pharaoh. And this happens not once but twice. There could be no more dramatic irony, as all expectations are reversed. The key to universal blessing does not reside in the all-powerful Pharaoh but in this fragile old Israel, who walks with a noticeable limp. He is the one, ruled by God, who rules the world!

Before Jacob dies, he passes on the blessing to his sons, describing their future destinies "in the latter days." This phrase may generally mean "in days to come" or it can have a specific technical expression meaning the end of history (Gen 49:1-27, esp. Gen 49:1). The future orientation is clear.

JUDAH AS FUTURE KING

As the book of Genesis reaches its conclusion, one might expect this blessing to resound with the theme of dominion. Nonetheless there is something of a shock since it is Judah who is singled out for the blessing of dominion. Though Joseph ruled Egypt, Judah will rule the world.

> The scepter will not depart from Judah,
>   nor the ruler's staff from between his feet,
> until he to whom it belongs shall come
>   and the obedience of the nations shall be his. (Gen 49:10 NIV)

The text begins by emphasizing the meaning of Judah's name: his brothers praise him; he is a triumphant warrior who has defeated his enemies, with his hand on their neck (Gen 49:8). His lion-like qualities indicate formidable strength for dominion, expressed by his staff, which awaits a future descendant (Gen 49:9). This leads to universal dominion and a transformation of nature: vineyard branches will be so plentiful they will serve as hitching posts for donkeys, and wine will be more plentiful than water as it will be used for washing clothes (Gen 49:11).

Here the staff that Judah gave to Tamar as a down payment for sex now becomes a symbol of rule. Judah has undergone a transformation by acknowledging his own guilt and saving the family with his intercession for Benjamin. It is Judah who is going to defeat the primeval enemy of humanity. It is through Judah that universal blessing will happen; he will be the universal ruler who will restore the kingdom of God. Within the story of Joseph, it is his brothers who bow down to Joseph, but in the larger story of the Torah it will be the nations that will bow down to Judah.

Many scholars understand Genesis 49:10 to point to the Davidic monarchy and its hegemony under David. While this is surely the case, it does not exhaust its meaning. Within the structure of the Tanakh it points beyond David to the Davidic covenant and its universal ramifications. Psalm 72 and Psalm 89 describe the grandiose fortunes of this individual. He will be a blessing to the entire world, there will peace in his dominion from sea to sea:

> May he rule from sea to sea
>   and from the River to the ends of the earth.
> May the desert tribes bow before him
>   and his enemies lick the dust. . . .
> May all kings bow down to him
>   and all nations serve him. . . .
> Then all nations will be blessed through him,
>   and they will call him blessed. (Ps 72:8-9, 11, 17 NIV)

> I have found David my servant;
>   with my sacred oil I have anointed him. . . .
> I will crush his foes before him
>   and strike down his adversaries. . . .
> And I will appoint him to be my firstborn,
>   the most exalted of the kings of the earth.
> I will maintain my love to him forever,
>   and my covenant with him will never fail. (Ps 89:20, 23, 27-28 NIV)[3]

Both poems describe a Davidic king who will triumph over his enemies, have universal sway, and transform nature. There is even a direct echo of Genesis 12:3 regarding universal blessing. These are the characteristics of the king in Genesis 49:8-12. There are many more examples of these texts in the Prophets

---

[3]For a lucid description of this development of the messianic line in Genesis see T. Desmond Alexander, "Royal Expectations in Genesis to Kings," *Tyndale Bulletin* 49 (1998): 198-206.

that point to a Davidic descendant who will incarnate Davidic rule over the world, with Jerusalem at the center (e.g., Is 9:5-6; 11:1-10; Mic 4–5).

Genesis ends on a note of eschatological hope. The blessing of Jacob not only gives a preview of the history of the various tribes, but a preview of the end of history and the dominion of Judah. Genesis captures the entirety of human history from its "beginning" in Genesis 1 (*rē'šît*) to its end in Genesis 49 (*'aḥărît*). The ancient kingdom of God at the beginning of time will return at the end of time. Nothing will stop this movement, as the Joseph story clearly indicates: even great evil can be turned into a great good to bring about a great salvation (Gen 50:20).

DISCUSSION QUESTIONS

1. Jacob, Joseph, and Judah were all transformed, not through great blessings, but through great suffering, and in very different ways. The path to blessing went straight through suffering. How can these stories about the kingdom speak to therapeutic cultures that have no place for suffering?

2. How can the biblical characters in these stories with all their faults and problems help us to have a more realistic understanding of God's grace and his desire to work in our lives today?

3. Any ideas of why Isaac, the miracle child, is not given all that much narrative attention in the biblical text?

Chapter Eight

EXODUS-DEUTERONOMY, PART 1

EXODUS AND THE BEGINNING OF A NATION

THE REST OF THE TORAH is centered on the growth of the nation and the life of Moses, who is called as its leader. The text essentially begins and ends with the birth and death of Moses (Ex 2; Deut 34). Key movements focus on the kingdom of God irrupting into the world in the Israelite exodus from Egypt, the Sinai covenant, the building of the tabernacle, and God's enthronement among the people of Israel. Leviticus shows how this divine presence is maintained, and the book of Numbers focuses on the fraught-filled journey of this nascent nation into the Promised Land, while Deuteronomy renews the national covenant before entrance into the Promised Land—their new Eden.

A CLASH OF KINGDOMS

Over the course of a prolonged period, long after Joseph and his generation have died, the family of Israel rapidly increases in size, thus fulfilling the mandate given to humanity at creation and the promise to the patriarchs of numerous progeny. But a massive obstacle will stand between the flourishing and extension of the kingdom of God on the earth. Previous obstacles of family ties, infertility, domestication of the promise, and family strife had plagued the patriarchs. But now the opposition will dramatically escalate. A new dynasty arises in Egypt that is unaware of Joseph and his legacy in Egypt and sees the proliferation of the Israelites as a clear and present danger since they could easily ally themselves with Asiatic enemies and conquer the Egyptian empire (Ex 1:6-22). The Egyptians enforce punitive working conditions to keep the Hebrew population in check, but the harsher the conditions the more the population increases. Then attempts are made to destroy all newly born male babies through covert genocide and failing this, overt extermination. Every newborn male is taken from its parents and cast into the Nile River.

Within the larger context of the biblical story, this is a clash of kingdoms. Indeed, given the promise to the woman that there would be enmity between her seed and the seed of the Serpent, the enmity of the Serpent here takes the form of genocide. And the cobra that projected from the Egyptian Pharaoh's crown in the posture of attack could not help but emphasize the theological nature of this struggle.[1] Such an event becomes a type in the biblical story as many centuries later a future prince is saved as a baby from the slaughter of a ruthless queen of Judah (2 Kings 11:1-3), and the clash reaches a climax in the slaughter of the innocents of Bethlehem in the attempt to kill the infant Messiah and the future persecution of his disciples (Mt 2:16-18; Rev 12:16-17; cf. Rom 16:20).

Into the Egyptian context, a baby—an extraordinary symbol of weakness— is born who becomes the deliverer of his people. The story of Moses' birth is instructive about God's methods in establishing his kingdom (Ex 2:1-10). Concealed by his family in an ark made of bulrushes on the Nile River amid the papyrus reeds near the bank, he becomes a new Noah in this makeshift mini-boat, one who will save his nation.[2]

When the princess of Egypt approaches with her retinue of servants, the ark is discovered and brought to the daughter of the Pharaoh. A Hebrew

---

[1]The cobra was a protective guardian of the Egyptian ruler and was a symbol of his sovereignty.
[2]Keith Bodner, *The Ark on the Nile* (Oxford: Oxford University Press, 2016).

literary device is used to narrate the removal of the ark's top, giving the audience the perspective of the princess: "*Behold* the child is crying!" (Ex 2:6). The princess responds with compassion. One can say in retrospect that in the heartbreaking cry of the infant is heard the eventual collapse of the Egyptian kingdom. For this Moses, this new Noah, becomes a prince of Egypt who will lead his nation through deep waters to the other side, and drown the Egyptian army with the wave of his staff. And the goal of this exodus is nothing less than the reign of God, as Moses and Miriam sing, anticipating the future in the light of their freshly experienced salvation from the depths: "Yahweh reigns forever and ever" (Ex 15:18). This liberation becomes the catalyst for a covenant in which the people will become a kingdom of priests through whom the Lord will reign. As the divine King takes up residence in their midst, they will begin their journey to the land of promise.

BACKGROUND TO THE EXODUS

The child Moses grows up in the court of Pharaoh as the genocide continues not only in the slaughter of innocent children but in the experience of back-breaking slave labor. As an adult he is no longer able to endure the oppression of his people. He kills an Egyptian in his anger and soon finds himself a fugitive in the desert seeking to escape an Egyptian manhunt. There he languishes for forty years, marrying a Midianite girl and serving as a shepherd for his father-in-law, while his people continue to suffer, crying out for relief from their oppression.

The larger biblical narrative presses the questions: What has become of the kingdom of God? What has become of the covenant that God made with Abraham declaring that through his descendants, the pristine conditions of paradise would be restored, and that men and women would regain their status as the kings and queens of creation? In fact, God has been remarkably absent from this drastic turn for the Israelites as he has not even been mentioned once. But the narrator shows that the answers to these burning questions will soon be coming:

> During that long period, the king of Egypt died. The Israelites groaned in
> their slavery and cried out, and their cry for help because of their slavery
> went up to *God. God* heard their groaning and [*God*] remembered his covenant

with Abraham, with Isaac and with Jacob. So *God* looked on the Israelites and [*God*] was concerned about them. (Ex 2:23-25 NIV modified)

The fivefold designation of God in this passage shows his immense concern. Grammatically only one noun is necessary, but the repetition suggests a critical new period in redemptive history in which God will now take center stage announcing a momentous new development in the kingdom of God. Four hundred years earlier, he had appeared to Abraham and promised from the fire that his people would experience a time of testing in Egypt, after which he would lead them out to give them the land of promise. Now the time is fulfilled for him again to appear in fire to signal this new advance in the kingdom of God.

GOD'S NAME AND THE PASSOVER

Consequently, it is no accident that God appears in fire to announce to Moses his plan of salvation (Ex 3). From a burning bush in the desert, he announces to this octogenarian shepherd to prepare for a new role as shepherd, one of people not of sheep. He must lead his people out of Egypt. God gives his guarantee by revealing his own personal name to Moses, the covenant name of Yahweh. This name assures Moses and Israel of the divine presence, and thereby all the power of God to deliver them from the most formidable human power of that time. But in a preview of future events, God indicates that it will not be easy, as the Lord threatens to kill Pharoah's firstborn son (Ex 4:21-23).

The firstborn son represented the future rule of Egypt, while the firstborn son of God, Israel, represented the future rule of the world. No firstborn son, no rule; firstborn son, rule. Who is the real king and what does he do with his power? Pharaoh uses his power to exploit and destroy, to oppress and suppress. But God is going to display his powers through Moses for releasing his people from this oppression and exploitation. It is no coincidence then that the final act that brings about deliverance for the people of Israel is the slaying of firstborn sons throughout Egypt and the sparing of the Israelite children through the rite of Passover, in which the blood of a firstborn sacrificial animal was splattered on the doorposts of their homes (Ex 12:1-20, 29-41). Thus there was a death in every home in Egypt, but the Israelite homes had a substitute. Later at a covenant ceremony when Israelites become formally anointed as a royal priesthood, this rite will be partially repeated as the blood of sacrificial animals will be splattered over them, enabling them to have a vision of their divine King (Ex 24).

When this last plague, the death of the firstborn, occurs in Egypt Pharaoh orders the release of the Israelites and they hastily make their exodus to freedom. But soon after the Egyptians change their mind and pursue their former slaves, concerned that they have lost a great economic resource. In the greatest event in the Old Testament, the Israelites cry out, caught as they are between the devil and the deep Red Sea. As Moses raises his staff, the waters divide, and the people rush through on dry ground to the other side and to salvation. The pursuing Egyptian army perishes as the waters surge back on them in a fatal deluge (Ex 14). Moses, Miriam, and the Israelite women sing and dance on the other side, and the high point of their song is a celebration of the kingdom of God and its victory.

> By the power of your arm
>   they will be as still as a stone—
> until your people pass by, Lord,
>   until the people you bought pass by.
> You will bring them in and plant them
>   on the mountain of your inheritance—
> the place, Lord, you made for your dwelling,
>   the sanctuary, Lord, your hands established. (Ex 15:16-17 NIV)

This song proclaiming Yahweh's praise about his mighty feat in saving Israel at the Red Sea, quickly moves to the prophetic mode and describes future events in the land of promise. As the people moved through the Sea with walls of water on each side, they will move through the Promised Land with walls of enemies on each side, who have become completely immobilized as the Israelites pass through their midst.[3]

The goal of this salvation and liberation is nothing less than God living with his people on his holy mountain in his sanctuary under his reign. The

---

[3]As John Gray remarks, "In the psalm in Exodus 15:1-18 the opponents against whom Yahweh vindicates his Kingship are the Egyptians and other local enemies of Israel in her settlement of Palestine." John Gray, *The Biblical Doctrine of the Reign of God* (Edinburgh: T&T Clark, 1979), 8.

prime objective of the exodus is eventually to bring the world under the reign of God, so that "Yahweh reigns forever and ever" (Ex 15:18).

The language used in this exodus song recalls God's creative act in the beginning when his Spirit brooded over the waters before the organization of the cosmos under the supervision and stewardship of his human image bearers. In fact, some of the later prophets capitalized on exodus language to speak of God's new action in the future as a new creation, a reestablishment of the original order (e.g., Is 51:9-11; 52:7-10). God was setting up a new creation in the people of Israel, among whom he would reign, and that reign would one day extend to the ends of the earth.

COVENANT, CONSTITUTION, AND KINGDOM

Although the concept has been implicit in the biblical text, this is the first explicit reference to Yahweh's reign in the Bible.[4] This point becomes emphasized at Sinai where a covenant formalizes Israel as a nation under God's kingship. Yahweh has delivered them from slavery and brought them to himself—a picture of intimacy—and sets the terms for a covenantal relationship. The remainder of Exodus focuses on the covenant, its implications, its formalization, and the astonishing consequence—the building of a tabernacle, which indicates God's ruling presence among his people. The structure of Exodus 19–40 is as follows:

- Covenant ritual and formalization (Ex 19–24)

- Plans for the building of the tabernacle (Ex 25–31)

- Covenant violation: golden calf episode (Ex 32–34)

- Building the tabernacle (Ex 35–40)

In the first part, the offer of the covenant, there is the establishment of a new relationship. There are two statements each of which have an identical structure, compound sentences in which a ground is followed by a consequence:

> [Ground] Now if you obey me fully and keep my covenant, [Consequence] then out of all nations you will be my treasured possession.

---

[4]Jeffrey H. Tigay, "Exodus," in *The Jewish Study Bible*, ed. Adele Berlin and Marc Zvi Brettler (Oxford: Oxford University Press, 2004), 138.

> [Ground] Because the whole earth is mine, [Consequence] you will be for
> me a kingdom of priests and a holy nation. (Ex 19:5-6)

In each case the consequence leads to a unique status for the people of
Israel. The first indicates Israel's special value to God among all the nations.
A treasured possession means a personal treasure that a person has at his
or her disposal.[5] A king may be very rich by virtue of his position in society,
but his personal treasure belongs only to him. Similarly for God to be the
Creator of the world, he in a sense owns everything, but Israel by virtue
of its obedience from among all the nations of the earth, is his own special
treasure. It alone knows his revelation, and thus has a special value. But
that special value means a special purpose. Similarly, in the second case,
because God is the Creator of all the nations and kingdoms of the world,
Israel will become a kingdom of priests, and a holy nation. The phrase
"kingdom of priests" is best understood as a nation whose people are
priests, that is, people who have access to the divine.[6] Thus it is parallel
to "a holy nation," namely, a nation marked by holiness and therefore
the divine.

Although in the immediate context this nomenclature does not suggest a
particular mission to the nations, in the wider context of Abraham's call to
be a blessing to the nations, it has burning relevance. This is the first explicit
reference to Israel as a kingdom in the Bible. And what a kingdom it is! They
were to be a priestly kingdom, having a mediatorial role to the nations. Priests
within a society were a special class of individuals that were fully consecrated
to God and served as intermediaries, channeling people to God and vice versa.
Israel was to be an entire kingdom of priests in the context of the world,
special representatives of God, bringing God to the nations and the nations
to God. They were to be a holy nation, a nation consecrated to the divine, for
if the word *priest* immediately invokes the deity, the adjective *holy* does the
same. The word *holy* is the word that is uniquely characteristic of God's
"godness" in the Old Testament. And this text is pervasive with holiness: "The
whole of Exodus 19 is a living narrative in which everything is holy, and

---

[5]Cf. 1 Chron 29:3 and Eccles 2:8, where the king's personal treasure is different from the nation's.
[6]John A. Davies, *A Royal Priesthood: Literary and Intertextual Perspectives on an Image of Israel in Exodus 19.6* (London: Bloomsbury, 2004), 103.

Yahweh's promise that Israel will become a holy nation (וגוי קדוש; vs. 6) is thus given its appropriate setting."[7]

The fact of Israel becoming a kingdom of priests and a holy nation is given embodiment in the formalization of the covenant in these chapters. After the people's agreement, preparations are made for the encounter with the holy God on the burning mountain: the people prepare themselves by washing, abstaining from sex, and being careful not to approach the mountain. They are to be totally focused on encountering Yahweh, through ritual purity and respect for boundaries (Ex 19:7-25).

Preparation leads to the revelation of the Ten Words or "Ten Commandments," which function as the constitution for this unique kingdom, specifying what it means to be a holy nation (Ex 20:1-14). These words have hermeneutical priority over all other Israelite legislation, not only because they are placed first but because they are the very words of God. All other words will pass through the filter of Moses and other prophets. When obedience to this charter happens, the divine nature, divine holiness, will be reflected through human lives. They will indeed image God and be a kingdom of priests: a people living under the rule of God.

Since these commands are addressed in the second person singular, they are addressed to each individual Israelite and all social classes stand equally under the word of God. Jeremiah Unterman observes that everyone heard the divine King from Sinai, not just the elites.[8] Everyone was to obey these commands and image God. The enumeration of the Ten Words can be divided differently but their content is radical. In the traditional division they are prefaced with Yahweh's redemption of Israel from Egyptian slavery in which God's name is exegeted by his actions: "I am Yahweh your God, who brought you up out of the land of Egypt, out from slavery" (Ex 20:1). Radical grace precedes his demands.[9] The following demands focus on obligations directly to God, the divine Authority, and obligations to each

---

[7]James Muilenburg, "Holiness," in *The Interpreter's Dictionary of the Bible*, ed. George Arthur Buttrick (Nashville: Abingdon, 1962), 2:620.

[8]Jeremiah Unterman, *Justice for All: How the Jewish Bible Revolutionized Ethics* (Lincoln: University of Nebraska Press, 2017).

[9]Cf. Carmen Imes, *Bearing God's Name: Why Sinai Still Matters* (Downers Grove, IL: IVP Academic, 2019), 11-12.

other. They can thus be summarized as duties to God (1-4) and to God's image (5-10).

After the utterance of the Ten Words the people were terrified because of the thunderous voice, the smoke, and the fire, and they sought Moses' intercession to protect them from the divine presence. Moses then relays all the words of the covenant, to which the people agree: "Everything Yahweh said we will do!" (Ex 24:3). He then writes down the words of the covenant in a papyrus document.

This document, known as the Book of the Covenant, deals with debt slave laws, homicide, the repudiation of parental authority, kidnapping, damages due to negligence, theft, seduction, sorcery, bestiality, sacrifices to foreign gods, prohibitions and injunctions regarding matters of social justice, and concern for the poor. It is telling that the first law deals with debt slave laws and homicide, and this is best explained by the people's recent exodus from slavery and genocide in Egypt (Ex 21:1-11, 12-20). But the legislation is a matter of making the constitution—the Ten Words—concrete in the culture. Thus, for example, the policy "you shall not murder" (Ex 20:13 NIV), becomes "anyone who strikes a person with a fatal blow is to be put to death" (Ex 21:12 NIV). This is followed by qualifications that determine if the blow was intentional or not, the latter being less serious (Ex 21:13-14). The laws show that the kingdom is far from utopian, but they take the people where they are, intending to move them toward a just society.

It is important to understand that these laws reflect the cultural moment of Israel as well as representing patterns or legal precedents. They are not intended to be exhaustive legislation but simply examples of legislation that function as models. As such they can be revised in the light of cultural changes, and they also reflect cultural mores in ancient Israel. Thus there are laws dealing with agrarian life, like restricting dangerous animals, marking pits in the ground, returning clothing offered as collateral for a debt, and gleaning laws providing a social safety net for the indigent.

The very next day this book becomes central in a unique rite that formally binds the people to Yahweh in the covenant (Ex 24). But it is doing more than that; it is officially consecrating the people to be a kingdom of priests and a holy nation. Moses builds an altar representing Yahweh and erects twelve pillars representing the twelve tribes of Israel, probably encircling the altar.[10] Then burnt offerings and peace offerings are offered. Burnt or whole offerings would later be used for rites of atonement to remove sin from the individual. Peace or fellowship offerings would indicate the wholeness or communion that takes place between God and the worshiper. Thus, Moses takes one-half of the blood that is shed (for atonement and fellowship) and puts it in bowls and the other half he splashes against the altar. Then he reads the Book of the Covenant to the people, receives their hearty agreement, and then sprinkles the blood from the bowls on the people, sealing the covenant with these words: "This is the blood of the covenant that Yahweh has made with you in accordance with all these words" (Ex 24:8). The significance of the reading of the book and the agreement between these two manipulations of the blood is critical. As John Davies comments, "The positioning of the reading of the document between the two halves of the blood rite is apparently designed to indicate the significance of the document as a hermeneutic for the rite."[11]

The blood ritual accomplishes three tasks. It purifies the people for service as priests, it unites them with God as the blood is applied to both the altar representing God and the people, and it binds both parties in a life/death oath. The effect of this ritual is seen immediately: seventy elders representing the people, Aaron and his two sons, now can ascend the mountain with Moses and enjoy a fellowship meal with God. This is clearly the conclusion to the covenant as they experience a beatific vision: "They saw the God of Israel, and under his feet was like the pavement of sapphire, as bright as the heavens, and he did not stretch out his hand against the leaders, and they saw God and ate and drank" (Ex 24:10-11). This is one of the first times that people have actually seen God in the Bible since the fall, and it is a group representing the entire people of Israel! Here is a Garden of Eden experience magnified.

The meal is also a throne room experience, as the people's vision is understood as seeing his feet. God, the great King, is surely sitting on a throne, surrounded by his treasures. Here the idea of vision is further developed because the statement about seeing God is mentioned twice. The first

---

[10]Kline, *God, Heaven and Har Magedon*, 123.
[11]Davies, *Royal Priesthood*, 211.

statement is bolder yet qualified by the vision directed to the pavement beneath God's feet (Ex 24:10). The elders seem to be looking up at the base of the throne through a prism of brilliant light. The second statement in Exodus 24:11 features the verb *ḥāzâ* ("to see"), often used for a particular type of visionary experience that prophets would later have, a more mystical visionary revelation. Both the life and death potential of this encounter are emphasized by the fact that God did not stretch out his hand against them, and they ate and drank. In the presence of the transcendent King, fear and terror are absent, unlike in Exodus 19 and Exodus 20, but rather this is a time of rich fellowship and communion. This scene may echo Jacob's experience after his encounter with his supernatural, nocturnal visitor at the Jabbok: "I have seen God face to face and survived" (Gen 32:31). Yet this scene was so radical in its claims that the Septuagint translator had to tone it down considerably: "They saw the place where the God of Israel stood and the things under his feet were as the work of slabs of sapphire" (Ex 24:10).[12]

The covenant rite also had a binding and oath function. The blood united the two parties in addition to making Israel holy by removing impurities. Thus, the two parties could now enjoy fellowship and become fictive kin. This rite now fitted Israel for its role of being a priestly kingdom, a holy nation. But there was also probably a maledictory function with the blood symbolizing the death of a covenant breaker.[13]

Psalm 114 provides a later exegesis of this text: "When Israel went forth from Egypt, the house of Jacob from a people of foreign language, Judah became his sanctuary, and Israel his dominion" (Ps 114:1). Adele Berlin remarks that this text recalls Exodus 19:5-6 whereby entering the covenant, Israel became the place of God's rule, which would later be localized in the temple and in the land. It is nothing less than an event of "such cosmic

---

[12]Perhaps this is why they did not see a problem with the Israelites being in the direct presence of God, so they translated the subsequent verses as: "And of the chosen ones (the leaders) of Israel there was not one missing, and they appeared in the place of God [i.e., where God was] and did eat and drink."

[13]These blood rituals were often multidimensional. See Theodore J. Lewis, "Covenant and Blood Rituals: Understanding Exodus 24:3-8 in Its Ancient Near Eastern Context," in *Confronting the Past: Archaeological and Historical Essays on Ancient Israel in Honor of William G. Dever*, ed. Seymour Gitin, J. Edward Wright, and J. P. Dessel (Winona Lake, IN: Eisenbrauns, 2006), 341-50, esp. 348.

proportions that it turned the world upside down; indeed, it caused the world to be recreated."[14] Consequently, the remainder of Exodus is about the instructions for the building of the tabernacle and its construction for God's presence. In language that recalls the creation of the world in seven days in Genesis, the tabernacle is planned in seven stages, and its entire purpose has already been foreshadowed in the conclusion to the Song of the exodus:

> You will bring them in and plant them
> > on the mountain of your inheritance—
> the place, LORD, you made for your dwelling,
> > the sanctuary, LORD, your hands established.
> "The LORD reigns
> > for ever and ever." (Ex 15:17-18 NIV)

Thus, the purpose of the sanctuary is transparent:

> Then I will dwell among the Israelites and be their God. They will know that I am the LORD their God, who brought them out of Egypt so that I might dwell among them. I am the LORD their God. (Ex 29:45-46)

This building will now become the place of God's reign on earth. For the sanctuary is a microcosm of the creation, with the outer court representing the earth, the mountains, and the sea, the inner court heaven, and the innermost court the divine throne room where the ark of the covenant, representing the visible footstool of the invisible divine throne, is located.[15] Inside the ark would be the Ten Words, representing the covenant and the divine law. Israel becomes a kingdom within the kingdoms of the world—the kingdom of the Serpent—pointing the way to the future.

Israel is a kingdom with a mission as a further development of the covenant with Abraham by which his seed would bring about universal blessing. In Genesis, the promises to Abraham were that of election to blessing and election to worldwide mission. Similarly in Exodus, Israel experiences the

[14]Adele Berlin, "The Message of Psalm 114," in *Birkat Shalom: Studies in the Bible, Ancient Near Eastern Literature, and Post-biblical Judaism Presented to Shalom M. Paul on the Occasion of His Seventieth Birthday*, ed. Chaim Cohen et al. (Winona Lake, IN: Eisenbrauns, 2008), 347.
[15]See, e.g., Jon D. Levenson, "The Temple and the World," *The Journal of Religion* 64 (1984); Gregory K. Beale, *The Temple and the Church's Mission: A Biblical Theology of the Dwelling Place of God* (Leicester, UK: Apollos, 2004).

personal privilege of being Yahweh's own personal treasure, but now the nation has a universal mission defined by its new identity as a kingdom of priests and a holy nation.

FACE TIME

In a clear rebellion against Yahweh's kingship—the equivalent of treason in the political sphere, Israel worships a golden bull. The first two commands have been broken by the worship and construction of an idol. The bull was a prominent fertility symbol particularly in the land of Canaan, the destination of Israel. It represented power and fecundity. Here it was a representation of the divine as Aaron had said: "Here are your gods who brought you out of the land of Egypt" (Ex 32:4).

The construction and worship of the golden calf—Israel's original sin—nearly led to complete disaster as God threatened to destroy Israel and start again with Moses. And Moses underlined the severity of the breach by smashing the stone tablets that encapsulated the covenant after he saw the idolatry. Yet Moses successfully intercedes for Israel, sparing the nation. But Israel is now in jeopardy because of the danger of living with a holy God. When God decides to send his angel with the people into the Promised Land as a substitute for his presence, Moses sees this as a theological catastrophe. He argues that the divine presence is the hallmark of being the people of Israel: "If you do not go with us, how will we be distinguished, I and your people, from all the peoples of the earth?" (Ex 33:16). Moses highlights Israel's role among the nations, reminding God that they are his treasured possession, a kingdom of priests, and a holy nation: "Because all the earth is mine you will be for me a kingdom of priests and a holy nation" (Ex 19:5-6). Without the divine presence, without the divine King living among them, they have lost their reason for existence. As Christopher Wright remarks, *"And only by Israel being distinct from the nations was there any purpose in being Israel at all* or any hope for the nations themselves eventually."[16]

When God relents and promises to go with his people, Moses seeks to get a further revelation of the divine glory by asking for a face-to-face encounter. The word *face* is a leading idea of this section, and one might label this entire

---

[16]Christopher J. H. Wright, *The Mission of God: Unlocking the Bible's Grand Narrative* (Downers Grove, IL: InterVarsity Press, 2006), 335. Emphasis original.

section "face time." God's face is turned against Israel in the previous chapter and Moses' intercession saves Israel from disaster. God promises to send an angel before Israel's face, but he will not go with the Israelites lest he consume them in his wrath because of their sinful recalcitrance. A tent of meeting is erected on the outside of the camp and there Moses speaks to God as a person speaks "face to face" with a friend (Ex 33:7-11). This suggests that God's face (i.e., his presence) has been removed from the camp, creating a necessary distance between a holy God and a sinful people. Moses intercedes again for the people based on his own personal relationship with Yahweh, since Yahweh knows him by name (Ex 33:17). So Yahweh relinquishes his decision not to accompany the people and promises his presence, that is, his face.

Moses then presses on to get a further revelation of God and his ways. Since he has this personal relationship with God, he seeks a vision of the divine glory. Yahweh grants him a partial vision, saying he will pass all his goodness before him, pronouncing his name, while he sets Moses in a cave where he can see the trail of the glory—God's back—but not his face (Ex 33:18-23). No human being could survive seeing the full revelation of the glory expressed in the divine face.

The subsequent text does not so much focus on what Moses sees but what he hears, and it is essentially a further definition of the divine name that was revealed earlier in the burning bush (Ex 34:6-7). Here God pronounces his own name twice, just as he did in the burning bush, and in thirty concise words in the Hebrew there is a description of both merciful and judicial qualities, fifteen each. The text, however, is symmetrically presented in terms of God's character and his actions:

- Identity: Yahweh Yahweh
- Character: A merciful and gracious God
  Longsuffering and full of steadfast love and faithfulness
- Actions: Maintaining steadfast love for thousands
  Forgiving iniquity, rebellion, and sin
  But certainly not acquitting the guilty
  Visiting the sins of the fathers upon their children and grand-children to the third and fourth generation.

There have been many studies of this text, which is the most explicit definition of the divine name in the Old Testament. In his own words, Yahweh has provided a self-description, his own personal portrait.[17] When Moses sees that God's very nature is grace and mercy, and that these attributes can be relied on for thousands of generations, though there is by comparison an incomparably brief expiration date for his justice, he lands the theological plane and pleads for complete forgiveness for the people. Having reascended Mount Sinai, Moses meets God once more, and God grants forgiveness and restores the covenant completely, with a new set of stone tablets. This time when Moses descends the mountain, his face is shining with the radiance of God (Ex 34:29). In Moses' intercession for his people and in his dialogue with God, Moses has discovered something he never knew about the divine nature. He has entered the burning bush himself and his face has been set on fire. For this seems to be the meaning of the shining face of Moses. Rays of light emanate from his face. And he has seen only the back and not the face of God!

But what does all this have to do with the kingdom of God? It seems that Moses' intercession guarantees the building of the tabernacle, which has been called into question by Israel's sin. With that tabernacle built, the kingdom of God will be a reality in the life of Israel. God will rule his people from his invisible throne whose footstool is the ark of the covenant in the holy of holies—the innermost sanctum. And when the tabernacle is completed, not even the great Moses will be able to enter, the presence of God will be so palpable (Ex 40:35). All of which suggests that the divine presence that was on the mountain in all its transcendence now has condescended to the tabernacle, living among the people. The kingdom of God has become a reality on the earth in a small corner of the Sinai Peninsula. Someday it will spread out to the entire earth.

DISCUSSION QUESTIONS

1. What is the difference between Moses' first descent from Mount Sinai (Ex 32) and his second descent (Ex 34)? What did he learn?

2. What does the law of God tell you about the rule of God?

---

[17]R. W. L. Moberly, "How May We Speak of God? A Reconsideration of the Nature of Biblical Theology," *Tyndale Bulletin* 53 (2002): 177-202; Mark J. Boda, *The Heartbeat of Old Testament Theology: Three Creedal Expressions* (Grand Rapids, MI: Baker, 2017).

Chapter Nine

EXODUS–DEUTERONOMY, PART 2

LEVITICUS–DEUTERONOMY AND THE ESTABLISHMENT OF A NATION

THE NEXT BOOK OF THE TORAH, Leviticus, details how a holy King can coexist with his sinful subjects. Sacrifice is the instrument by which sin can be removed from the people so they may live with their divine Ruler. Leviticus thus emphasizes this particular ritual repeatedly and it culminates in an annual rite of atonement that purges the community from even unintentional sins that have accumulated throughout the year. With a holy God, a kingdom with sinful human subjects cannot exist without atonement. Sacrifice provides an antidote for human sin so that the people can coexist with a holy God. For without atonement there are two options: no people or no King. The people would not be able to endure God's presence, as one later text indicates:

> Sinners tremble in Zion, panic seizes the defiled, "Who can endure a consuming fire? Who can endure an eternal flame?" Only the one who walks in

righteousness, who speaks truthfully, who rejects oppressive greed, who keeps his hands free from taking hold of a bribe, who refuses to listen to plots of murder and shut their eyes from contemplating evil. (Is 33:14-15)[1]

Experiencing God's presence and acceptance means that the people "will see the King in his beauty . . . and it is the Lord who is our King who will save us" (Is 33:17, 22). This is not an exaggeration because the King's residence is dedicated in Leviticus. Fire from heaven descends and consumes the offerings on the altar, and the people praise God and fall prostrate on their faces (Lev 9:23-24). But the very next chapter describes what happens when priests bring unacceptable offerings to the Lord. The same divine fire that consumed the offerings the day before, leading to ecstatic worship, consumes the priests for their sin (Lev 10:1-3). Being in God's presence can result in ecstasy or misery, collapsing in adoration or death. Hence the importance of atonement and obedience.

ATONEMENT

Atonement in the Old Testament essentially means the removal of sin so that the divine-human relationship can continue. The key element in the atonement rite is the manipulation of blood. The classic articulation is found in Leviticus 17:11: "For the life of a creature is in the blood, and I have given it to you to make atonement for yourselves on the altar; it is the blood that makes atonement for one's life" (NIV). Clearly animal blood is used for human beings as an exchange for life, as a type of substitution, and it functions also as a ritual detergent for any impurities. It also functions to bring about communion between alienated parties, and in the case of the sinner, reconciliation with God.[2] The first half of Leviticus emphasizes the importance of rituals for atonement, climaxing with one entire day every year consecrated for an atonement rite in which the sins of the people are confessed over the head

---

[1]For further theological reflection on the need for atonement, see L. Michael Morales, *Who Shall Ascend into the Mountain of the Lord? A Biblical Theology of the Book of Leviticus* (Downers Grove, IL: InterVarsity Press, 2015).

[2]Theodore J. Lewis, "Covenant and Blood Rituals: Understanding Exodus 24:3-8 in Its Ancient Near Eastern Context," in *Confronting the Past: Archaeological and Historical Essays on Ancient Israel in Honor of William G. Dever*, ed. Seymour Gitin, J. Edward Wright, and J. P. Dessel (Winona Lake, IN: Eisenbrauns, 2006), 341-50.

of a goat, which is then led into the wilderness. This scapegoat graphically removes the sins from the Israelite tribal encampment (Lev 16). But the last half of Leviticus—the so-called Holiness Code (Lev 17–26)—focuses on the importance of Israelites living "atoned for" lives, which leads to considering the crucial concept of holiness. Since the Israelites are to be a kingdom of priests, and a holy nation, they are to reflect the essential nature of their King.

HOLINESS

One chapter detailing the holiness necessary to mark the Israelite nation is Leviticus 19. An initial injunction for the Israelites to be holy commences the chapter and it reads literally: "Holy be, for holy am I, Yahweh your God" (Lev 19:2). As one commentator remarks: "This is the caption; what follows is the elaboration."[3] The elaboration is a series of commands that expound the details of this injunction, and they are divided from each by the divine identity formula: "I am Yahweh your God" or "I am Yahweh." This concluding formula occurs fourteen times in the text.

In this chapter holiness does not distinguish between the spiritual and the physical, the sacred and the secular. In the first section, the secular (honoring parents) is juxtaposed with the sacred (keeping Sabbaths) (Lev 19:3). This juxtaposition is maintained throughout so that the third section highlights cultic sacrifices to God (Lev 19:5-8) with material help for the poor (Lev 19:9-10). But the main point in this lengthy chapter is that holiness must pervade all of life. All of life is devoted to Yahweh, especially in showing concern for those less fortunate. Significantly there is no essential difference between loving one's neighbor as oneself and loving a foreigner in the same way (Lev 19:18, 34). What is the motive for this type of life? Nothing less than the imitation of God. As Donald Gowan observes,

> The Holiness Code (Leviticus 19-26) offers a rationale for all of law, "You shall be holy, for I the LORD your God am holy" (Lev. 19:2, etc.), insisting that the people of God must reflect the character of God himself.[4]

---

[3]Baruch Schwarz, "Leviticus," in *The Jewish Study Bible*, ed. Adele Berlin and Marc Zvi Brettler (Oxford: Oxford University Press, 2004), 253.
[4]Donald E Gowan, *Theology in Exodus: Biblical Theology in the Form of a Commentary* (Louisville, KY: Westminster John Knox, 1994), 80.

By living this way Israel will make visible the invisible holy God in the world. No doubt this is one of the reasons why the Israelites were forbidden to make images of Yahweh to be used in the sanctuary.

Consequently, as God's kingdom of priests, as his holy nation, Israel was to image their God to the rest of the world. Living holy lives, they would reflect the character of God himself and bear visible witness to God's presence.

The relevance of the impact of the blood oath that has bound the people to Yahweh is clearly shown by the end of the book. The people will experience many blessings and a flourishing life if they embody Leviticus 19. But if they fail, the result will be death in the form of a plenitude of curses, leading finally to exile from their prized land of promise. Nevertheless, this will not mean the end of the promise to the patriarchs. With repentance in exile, Yahweh will remember them, and their uncircumcised hearts will be humbled. Then Yahweh will return them to the land and not break covenant with them (Lev 26).

NUMBERS AND THE DIVINE KING

The book of Numbers advances the narrative as the people make their departure from Sinai to the Promised Land. They are organized in tribes around the newly built tabernacle in the wilderness, showing the centrality of the divine throne (Num 2). When they are on the move, the priests carry the ark of the covenant, the footstool of the invisible throne, out in front of the camp as the people follow the ark and the cloud/fire to the next destination (Num 9:15-23). The stationary arrangement of the tribes at rest around the throne, and the linear arrangement of the tribes traveling behind the ark show the centrality of the rule of God. An important text summarizes this rest and movement at the behest of God:

> On the day the tabernacle, the tent of the covenant law, was set up, the cloud covered it. From evening till morning the cloud above the tabernacle looked like fire. That is how it continued to be; the cloud covered it, and at night it looked like fire. Whenever the cloud lifted from above the tent, the Israelites set out; wherever the cloud settled, the Israelites encamped. *At the LORD's command* the Israelites set out, and *at his command* they encamped. (Num 9:15-18 NIV, emphasis mine)

Israel is under the rule of God; its every move in the desert results from obedience to the divine command.

Another summary statement of the Israelites' departure from Mount Sinai reflects the importance of the divine rule and presence for the Israelites and the opposition to this rule:

> The Cloud of Yahweh was over them by day when they travelled from the camp. When the ark departed, Moses said, "Rise up Yahweh and let your enemies be scattered. May those who hate you flee from before you!" When it rested, he would say, "Return Yahweh to the thousands of Israel! (Num 10:34-35)

This is clearly a kingdom moving into enemy territory. God's presence is necessary for victory. And that presence is formalized in a priestly blessing to the people when Aaron confers an overflowing benediction on the people:

> May Yahweh bless you and keep you!
> May Yahweh shine his face upon you and grace you!
> May Yahweh lift up his face upon you and give to you shalom! (Num 6:24-26)

Israel is to be so filled with blessing that it will eventually cascade to the entire world (Gen 12:3; Ps 67).

ISRAEL'S ORIGINAL SIN REPEATED

There are many crises in the book of Numbers but the critical one is the people's rebellious refusal to conquer the land of promise (Num 13–14), a clear violation of their divine ruler's command, and an indication of the truth of the dictum: "We have seen the enemy and he is us." This rebellion has a similar significance to that of the golden calf episode where Israel escaped annihilation because of the intercession of Moses (Ex 32). The people lack faith in the power of their divine King, who is seeking to fulfill his promises to Abraham, not only to give to his people the land but to judge the Amorites for their sins.

Twelve men are chosen representing each tribe of Israel to reconnoiter Canaan before the planned conquest (Num 13:1-25). Forty days later they return with a majority report lauding the land's benefits but decrying any attempt to conquer it because of its massive fortresses and gigantic population (Num

13:26-29, 31-22). A minority report by two individuals, Caleb and Joshua, believes in the power of God to bring about success (Num 13:30). Needless to say,
the majority report proves more persuasive and creates despair, turning the
people against their leadership, even threatening to kill Moses and Aaron (Num
14:1-10). It is only because of Moses' intercession again that the people are
spared. They are forgiven but there is a consequence for their unbelief: the
adult generation is condemned to wander in the wilderness for forty years
until it dies, one year for each of the days spent investigating the land
(Num 14:10-24). Their unbelief amounts to a type of prostitution. Dennis Cole
explains that "the term used to describe this infidelity is *zĕnûtêkem*, which is
normally used in the context of sexual immorality and (metaphorically) for
idolatry."[5] Thus, faithlessness is found where there has been a change of the
human heart's affection (Num 14:33). But in an offhand remark in which Yahweh
uses two oaths to formalize the punishment of this generation, the divine intent
for the world is revealed: "As surely as I live, and *as surely as the glory of Yahweh
will fill the whole earth*, not one of those who saw my glory and the signs I
performed in Egypt . . . will ever see the land promised on oath to their ancestors"
(Num 14:21-22). The glory that will someday fill the whole earth is paralleled
to the revelation of Yahweh's glory in the defeat of the Egyptians to save the
Israelites and to show his kingship. Notwithstanding the rebellion of his people,
Yahweh's kingdom will eventually triumph not just over Egypt but over the
entire world. This future certainty guarantees their present punishment.

Nevertheless, judgments do continue in the desert wanderings and after
one example of blatant disobedience and divine judgment (Num 15:32-36),
a remedy is provided to help the Israelites remember their King and his
commands. No longer is oral teaching and memory regarded as enough to
follow the divine rule; they are called to make tangible signs of that rule so
that they will not follow their natural instincts and impulses (Num 15:37-41).

The context clarifies the importance of this law. No longer is it enough to
have the oral teaching of the commands by priest and leaders from texts, to
keep the people aware of the divine rule; external symbols are now necessary.
Thus, fringes or tassels on the garments are reminders of the importance of

---

[5]R. Dennis Cole, *Numbers*, The New American Commentary 3B (Nashville: Broadman & Holman,
2000), 237.

regulating life by the divine rule instead of one's own wandering heart. Whenever the people are tempted to follow their eyes rather than the word of God, they need to fix them on the tassels and hear the call to obedience. In fact, some commentators think that the blue color of one of the chords was meant to remind the Israelites of the sky and therefore the divine ruler and their own identity as a royal priesthood. Later Jewish interpreters suggest that these tassels are the equivalent of jewelry, which God sees as something beautiful on his people.[6] But the problem remains. The human heart needs to be transformed, and this need will be an ongoing problem in Israel's history.

ABRAHAMIC BLESSING REAFFIRMED

The remainder of Numbers provides some details of the Israelites' struggles in the desert, but as the older generation dies out and as the new generation heads toward the Promised Land, an enormous threat looms over their mission as the kingdom of God to which the people are oblivious. Balak, king of Moab, believes that the only way to stop the nascent nation is to curse them. He hires a renowned prophet as a "hit man" for this purpose. Baalam, son of Beor, from distant Mesopotamia, is renowned for the fact that "whoever he blesses is blessed and whoever he curses is cursed" (Num 22:6), a clear challenge to Yahweh's promise to Abraham (Gen 12:3). But ironically, in three attempts, instead of cursing the Israelites he blessed them. Each blessing forcefully echoes the Abrahamic blessings and the blessing on Judah. Thus, the blessings of Balaam advance the kingdom of God. It is worth briefly considering parts of each.

The first "curse" (Num 23:7-10) deliberately echoes the first blessing to Abraham and shows the impossibility of counteracting that blessing. God called the patriarch and said explicitly, "I will bless those who bless you and curse those who curse you" (Gen 12:3).[7] Moreover Israel is a distinct *nation* with an innumerable population (Gen 13:16; Ex 19:5; 33:16).

---

[6]Yehudah Cohn, *Tangled Up in Text: Tefillin and the Ancient World* (Atlanta: Society of Biblical Literature, 2008), 159. Cf. Jacob Milgrom, "Of Hems and Tassels," *Biblical Archaeology Review* 9 (1983): 61-65.
[7]"The wording here recalls the Lord's word to Abram (Gen. 12:3) and must surely be deliberate." Alec Motyer, *Roots: Let the Old Testament Speak* (Ross-Shire, UK: Christian Focus, 2009), 66.

In the second prophecy (Num 23:18-24) there is the echo of immutable blessing pronounced on Abraham coupled with the immutable character of God to guarantee it. Whereas the first prophecy focused on the distinctive character of Israel among the nations and their impressive numbers, this prophecy describes their acceptance by God and their strength, echoing both the futility of any curse, the exodus from Egypt under the kingship of God, and the blessing of Judah who was compared to a lion who would rule the nations.

The third prophecy (Num 24:3-9) begins by drawing attention to the luxurious bounty of the people of Israel. Instead of a rag tag bunch of nomads, God views them as beautiful and glorious, like mighty cedars beside flowing waters. Then there is a shift to the greatness of their kingdom, as their King will be more exalted than Gog, a mythical-eschatological figure of great power (Num 24:7).[8] The strength of this kingdom is described as stronger than an ox, shattering nations before it, and again the image of a lion is used, this time directly citing Genesis 49:9 about Judah's triumph. Then there is a direct citation of Genesis 12:2 reaffirming the promise to Abraham. Abraham's blessing is thus strongly linked with the rulership of Judah, and the success of God's king and kingdom!

The last of these passages (Num 24:15-19) rings the changes on the king who will emerge from Israel in the distant future—the last days (Num 24:14)—and thus this passage is directly linked to Jacob's prophecy about Judah's rule over the nations in the last days (Gen 49:1) that will bring about this universal blessing through a violent act. Again, words are selected from Genesis to describe this king. The word *kôkābîm* ("stars") was used in Genesis to describe the multitude of descendants that were promised to Abraham (Gen 15:5). Here a *kôkāb* ("star") will arise from Jacob (Num 24:17). This parallels the reference to a *šēbet* ("scepter") rising from Israel (Num 24:17). The word *šēbet* is chosen again from the passage about a ruler emerging from Judah to rule the nations: "A scepter will not be turned aside from Judah" (Gen 49:10). The Septuagint understood the scepter as messianic: "A *man* will arise from Israel."

---

[8]Reading with the Septuagint and not the Hebrew.

The rest of the passage describes the smiting of Israel's enemies—Moab and others—on their heads and Israel's triumph and dominion. While the text is difficult in places, it describes the conquest of all enemies to fulfill the promise of universal blessing. Balaam pronounces three more oracles (Num 24:20, 21-22, 23-24) to complete the predictions of Israelite conquest to a tally of seven, thus indicating the comprehensive, final destruction of all enemies who would thwart Israel's mission to be a blessing to the nations.

The kingdom of God will not be destroyed but will eventually triumph over every nation or person that opposes the mission of Israel to be a universal blessing. This anticipates the Old Testament fulfillment of that petition in the Lord's prayer: "Let your kingdom come, your will be done on earth as it is in heaven!" (Mt 6:10). But that time is still a long way off in the distant future.

But perhaps the most formidable enemies that Israel faces are not external but rather internal. No sooner does this series of prophecies predicting the advance of God's kingdom into the world appear than another major setback occurs (Num 25). On the very verge of entering the Promised Land to become a great nation and state, another "golden calf" episode occurs. This time Israelite men are led astray by Moabite women to engage in ritual sex in the religious rites of the local Baal deity (Baal Peor). A plague ensues and then a priest makes atonement through the execution of two leaders in the idolatry. But the incident right on the verge of the land of promise points to serious problems within Israel itself that may jeopardize the covenant.

DEUTERONOMY AND THE GREAT COMMANDMENT

When the new generation finally reaches the outskirts of the Promised Land, Moses gives them a last sermon, essentially the book of Deuteronomy. Moses renews the covenant and reviews their journey from Egypt through the wilderness while looking ahead to their future. This covenant renewal is a constitution for the new nation-state in the land. Moses reminds them of their identity. The nation is to be a kingdom ruled by the divine law, and every Israelite household is to reflect that law by internalizing it in such a way that it captivates the mind and enthralls the heart. Thus, there is a reflection on the failures following the Sinai covenant, and the Shema is introduced, which focuses on the nature of the real demand of Sinai and the importance of getting the Torah written on stone and papyrus into the deepest recesses of the human heart (Deut 6:6-9).

Every Israelite is reminded that they must have wholehearted allegiance to the one God. It is not enough for the words of the King to be inscribed on tablets of stone. Their purpose as external symbols on their hands and between their eyes, as inscriptions on the door frames of their houses and on their city gates, is to inculcate the divine rule in their thinking and action, their domestic and civic life.

A FUTURE SERVANT-KING

When the time comes for Israel to choose a king, the kind of king they are to choose must reflect the rule of God; he must not be like the kings of other nations. He himself must be an Israelite who embodies the Shema, providing for every member of the nation a role model. His qualifications and "job description"[9] make him to be almost an anti-king in terms of the ancient Near Eastern conception of a ruler. He is a king who is clearly a servant of his people and under the authority of a higher King (Deut 17:14-20).

As many commentators point out, Deuteronomy 17:14-20 is unique in the ancient world: "There is no parallel in ANE legal texts to the law of the king: a king's power limited by a written text. . . . Whereas in ANE societies the king was supreme, Yahweh is the 'fountainhead' of law and Torah is an expression of his will."[10]

Three negatives mark his identity (Deut 17:16-17): he is not to amass military power (horses); nor to rely on political diplomacy (wives from other cultures); nor to acquire economic affluence (money). These negative commandments are offset by three positive ones (Deut 17:18-19): he is to write out a copy of the Torah, keep it with him for consultation, and read it every day. The purpose of these activities is also threefold (Deut 17:20): to learn to fear Yahweh by obeying his commands, to become humble, and to enjoy a

---

[9]Robin Branch, "The Messianic Dimensions of Kingship in Deuteronomy 17:14-20 as Fulfilled by Jesus in Matthew," *Verbum et Ecclesia* 25 (2004): 378-401.

[10]Peter T. Vogt, *Deuteronomic Theology and the Significance of Torah: A Reappraisal* (Winona Lake, IN: Eisenbrauns, 2006), 219.

long and successful reign for himself and his descendants. The king is the
ideal citizen, and with a Torah mind he simply represents Yahweh's will. In
theological terms, he is Yahweh's vicegerent. Thus this "extraordinary re-
striction of royal authority" in which the king does not promulgate his own
law but is subject to divine law and is required to know it essentially by heart
is astonishing.[11] With a king like this on the throne, Israel may be a monarchy
in name but in spirit it is still a theocracy. There need be no distinction between a true theocracy and a monarchy. "The king doesn't make people bow
before him. Instead as an ideal Israelite, he introduces people to the real king
of Israel."[12]

It would seem to be the case that while there is provision for a king in the
earlier books of the Torah, the focus on this new constitution recognizes that
the wish for a king will come from the people, who want a king like all the
nations around about them. The legislation recognizes this eventual desire
but safeguards such a king from being like that of the other nations. In the
same way, the people are not to have prophets like the other nations but are
to have a prophet like Moses, who eschews the complex apparatus of occult
rituals but will simply speak the words of God (Deut 18:9-22).

THE GRAMMAR OF THE LAW

Repeatedly this new national constitution forbids the rampant idolatry characteristic of the indigenous population of the land. There is a zero-toleration
policy. Even the native people must be expelled from the land (Deut 7).
Kingdom come means idolatry gone. When the covenant was made with
Abraham, there was the provision that there would be a delay in the fulfillment
of the promise of the land because there was to be a postponement of judgment
for the peoples of Canaan (Gen 15:13-17). Divine judgment only occurs when
the sins reach a tipping point, a principle found in other passages of Scripture
(e.g., Amos 1:3, 6, 9, 11, 13; 2:1, 4, 6). The coming of the kingdom means that
Israel must be agents of divine judgment, purging the land of its sinful population, preparing it for the presence of the holiness of God. This concept will

---

[11]Bernard Levinson, "Deuteronomy," in *The Jewish Study Bible*, ed. Adele Berlin and Marc Zvi Brettler (Oxford: Oxford University Press, 2004), 405.
[12]Branch, "The Messianic Dimensions of Kingship in Deuteronomy 17," 384.

be discussed further when considering the texts dealing with the conquest and settlement in the land of promise.

Deuteronomy emphasizes the importance and relevance of the Ten Commandments in its structure and for the legislation that forms the heart of the book (Deut 12–26). These laws are thus creative applications of the fundamental values embodied in the Decalogue, similar in degree to the Covenant Code in the original Sinai covenant. The application of the first two commandments entails the abolition of all foreign cult centers to pagan gods in the land (Deut 12). There can be no competitors for the divine rule. One of the first concerns for the application of the Sabbath law is relief from debt slavery during the sabbatical year (Deut 15). The command to honor parents expresses concern for the right attitude to authority in general (Deut 16:18-18:22). The sixth command applies to perjury, manslaughter, warfare, as well as murder (Deut 19-21). The prohibition of adultery deals with a variety of sexual offenses (Deut 22). Moses is thus interpreting the Decalogue, opening it up instead of shutting down its relevance through a woodenly literal understanding. If the Decalogue is the *grammar* of the law, the statutes and decrees of Deuteronomy 12–26 are the expression of the *language* of the law, how to apply the grammatical rules in everyday speech and life. Jesus gives another application of the grammar in the Sermon on the Mount (Mt 5–7). Thus Deuteronomy 12–26 is far from exhaustive but is a paradigm of how to interpret the Decalogue. The literal application of the ten commands is the interpretive ground floor while their potential application is the sky.[13] This requires wisdom, which is what the law is all about (Deut 4:6-8).

Moses renews the Sinai covenant in a way that reconfigures the project in the light of the forty years in the wilderness.[14] One can infer some significance in some of the changes which modify the Ten Words. No longer are the people to remember the Sabbath, they are to keep it (Deut 5:12; cf. Ex 20:8),

---

[13]"Laws generally set a floor for behaviour within society, they do not prescribe an ethical ceiling." Gordon J. Wenham, *Story as Torah: Reading Old Testament Narrative Ethically* (Grand Rapids, MI: Baker Academic, 2003), 80.

[14]Scott Hahn, *Kinship by Covenant: A Canonical Approach to God's Saving Promises* (New Haven, CT: Yale University Press, 2019), 62-83. Without agreeing with all of Hahn's points, I think he is generally correct with his understanding of Deuteronomy as a reconfiguration of the Sinai covenant.

which may suggest that Israel has been lax in its observance of the Sabbath day. Also, the pattern of God's creation week in Genesis 1:1-2:3 is no longer the basis for Israel's work week of six days of labor and one day of rest, but rather God's redemption of Israel from Egyptian oppression (Deut 5:12-15; cf. Ex 20:8-11). The people are reminded how God had mercy on them and relieved their backbreaking labor. Thus, they must remember not to be a slave to their work, and to give everyone under their charge—including their animals–relief. It is interesting that the more inclusive word *all* is added to ensure a more comprehensive interpretation of animals designated for relief from labor: "Your oxen, your donkey and *all* your livestock" (Deut 5:14). Why would this addition be necessary in a legal text if there was not some problem? Interestingly a new motive is also added: "in order that your servant and maidservant may rest like you" (Deut 5:14). One is to imagine that one's servants require relief just like oneself! Similarly, the prohibition of coveting someone's spouse has a separate entry at the first of the list of prohibitions. Moreover, she is not considered under the rubric of a neighbor's house, which suggests that the forty years of wandering in the wilderness has made the importance of female rights more prominent, as well as the danger of adultery.

Moreover, the commandments are linked in a way that binds them together into two segments, the love of God (commands 1-5) and the love of neighbor (commands 6-10).[15] This slight change clarifies the overall understanding of the covenant obligations.

DEALING WITH AN INTERNAL ENEMY

All of these factors suggest that Israel has an enemy within as well as without. The addition of other commands suggests fundamental problems in the nation. The multiplication of laws in any community is a symptom of a problem with human nature. More and more circumstances and situations must come under scrutiny and be regulated because of the need to deal with skewed desires and increased lawlessness. Thus, there is now a divorce law that is

---

[15]Notice the presence of the conjunction *waw* that begins commands seven through ten, thereby connecting commands six through ten in Deuteronomy. The *waw* is absent for these commands in Exodus. Jason DeRouchie first alerted me to this change and its significance (personal communication).

necessitated to protect the woman in marriage from being a mere commodity to be recycled (Deut 24:1-5). Other commands note inheritance problems that might arise in a polygamous family (Deut 21:15-17) and restrictions on sexual exploitation during military campaigns (Deut 21:10-14).

That the heart—the center of the will, intellect, and emotions—is absolutely crucial is shown when Israel is instructed to reaffirm the covenant when they enter the land at Shechem with half the tribes standing on Mount Gerizim, the mountain of blessing, and half on Mount Ebal, the mount of curse. Then twelve curses are pronounced by the tribe of Levi on individuals, mainly for "secret" sins dealing with idolatry, social relations, sexuality, and murder. This remarkable list shows that the Torah is aiming at nothing less than the transformation of the heart since none of these sins can be regulated by the courts (Deut 27:9-26).[16] Only the divine King who knows all hearts can enforce these curses.

Probably nowhere more pertinent is this point emphasized than in the rewards and punishments that are listed for obedience and disobedience near the final section of the book. The curses (Deut 28:15-68) vastly outnumber the blessings (Deut 28:1-14). The people are viewed as needing far more negative incentives to be loyal to the covenant than positive ones—the proverbial stick rather than the carrot. When this characteristic is combined with Moses' own prediction that Israel will apostatize sometime in the distant future (Deut 4:25-26; 30:1-2), it is clear that the citizens of the kingdom need something that only God can finally give: a new heart. Moses makes this exact point at a critical part of the discourse: Israel needs to circumcise its heart to be able to keep the Shema and be loyal to the covenant and their Divine Suzerain (Deut 10:14-22, cf. Deut 30:1-6).

In a ritual enactment of the covenant on the plains of Moab, understood as an addendum to the Sinai covenant, all the people gather to hear a history lesson about how God had brought them to this place (Deut 29:1-8). A formal

---

[16]Citing Albrecht Alt, Martin Noth remarks: "Here we are dealing with transgressions which would normally take place in secret, and would therefore seldom figure in the realm of human jurisdiction; consequently, transgressors, who would scarcely be reached by human law, were to be punished by a curse." Martin Noth, *The Laws of the Pentateuch and Other Essays* (London: Oliver and Boyd, 1966), 118.

imprecation follows to ensure loyalty (Deut 29:9-28), concluded by a reassurance of restoration in the future should the covenant be broken
(Deut 30:1-10). The formal imprecation is particularly graphic in its attempt
to negatively reinforce the covenant with extremely strict penalties. If anyone
secretly says *in their heart* that they will disobey the covenant, they will be
dealt with mercilessly like the peoples of Sodom and Gomorrah (Deut 29:19-21).

HOPE FOR THE FUTURE

Remarkably, should the covenant be broken and Israel ends up in exile, there
is hope for the future, just as at the end of Leviticus. If repentance truly takes
place in exile, that is, an authentic return to God, then God will surely return
Israel to the land, and there he will circumcise their hearts so that they will
fulfill the Shema (Deut 30:6)! This is the only solution for Israel to conquer
the enemy within. They must subject themselves fully to the rule of God and
thereby mediate blessings to the world. Thus, they will need a circumcised
heart; the internal circumcision must match the external circumcision, just
as it had with their first forefather, Abraham. This shows that the people of
the kingdom must have the faith of Abraham.

So here at the end of the Torah, with Moses saying his farewell to the
people and formalizing a covenant renewal with the people, there is an
awareness that all may not be right in the kingdom as Israel, God's kingdom,
takes its place among the nations. If this priestly kingdom, this holy nation,
lives up to its calling, there will be a dramatic impact on the nations. As Israel
manifests the visible image of God to the nations, as it embodies his divine
rule in their lives, the nations will say in response:

> "Surely this great nation is a wise and understanding people." What other
> nation is so great as to have their gods near them the way the LORD our God
> is near us whenever we pray to him? And what other nation is so great as to
> have such righteous decrees and laws as this body of laws I am setting before
> you today? (Deut 4:6-8 NIV)

As Moses bids his people farewell and as Joshua takes new leadership of
the nation, there is suspense about the prospects of this kingdom mission.
A dark cloud also looms on the horizon for this kingdom, as shown by the

preponderance of curses and their apparent inevitability.[17] What will the future portend for Israel? And what about the promise of blessing to all the nations?

DISCUSSION QUESTIONS

1. What can we learn from the fact that Israel's worst enemy was internal?

2. How is the circumcision of the heart related to the Shema? What relevance is this for the Kingdom?

---

[17]Note in particular Deut 30:1-10 and the expression "as it is now" in Deut 29:28, which was probably added by a later editor who knew all too well about the judgment of exile. Note also how much the curses (Deut 28:15-68) outnumber the blessings (Deut 28:1-14). Cf. also Deut 4:25-28 and Deut 31:24-29, which anticipate the exile.

Chapter Ten

THE FORMER PROPHETS

KINGDOM GROWTH AND DECLINE

THE NEXT SECTION IN THE HEBREW BIBLE (Joshua–2 Kings) moves quickly from the end of the Torah to the middle of the Hebrew Bible.[1] The story follows Israel from their preparations to enter the land of promise to their initial success in the land. But then the story follows an almost continuous decline of the nation until it has been destroyed and its people deported, first to Assyria and then to Babylon. All the promises of God appear to be intact at the beginning of Joshua, but by the end of 2 Kings they are in

---

[1]In the rest of the book, I am generally following the tripartite order for Israel's Scriptures found in early Jewish documents. After the Torah (Pentateuch) follow: the Prophets (Former Prophets: Joshua, Judges, Samuel, and Kings; Latter Prophets: Jeremiah, Ezekiel, Isaiah, and the Twelve) and the Writings (Ruth, Psalms, Job, Proverbs, Ecclesiastes, Song of Songs, Lamentations, Daniel, Esther, Ezra–Nehemiah, Chronicles. This is an order found in an early source from the Talmud [Baba Bathra 14b]). The three groups of writings are often referred to with the acronym Tanak (Torah [Law], Nevi'im [Prophets], Ketuvim [Writings]). This tripartite designation was probably the earliest version of the Christian church's Bible and gave rise to different sequences of the church's Old Testament. The middle of this Bible occurs at the ending of the Former Prophets. From another point of view, there is an overall narrative structure of the Tanak (Genesis to Kings is interrupted by the Latter Prophets and the first half of the Writings [Ruth–Lamentations], and then Daniel continues the narrative to the end of the Tanak in Chronicles).

radical doubt. Moreover, the idea of God's kingdom being a powerful force at the end of 2 Kings seems nothing but a cruel joke. The very earthly kingdom of Babylon is in charge (2 Kgs 25:37-40).

JOSHUA AND THE DIVINE WARRIOR

After the golden calf debacle, the rebellion in the wilderness, and forty years of wandering aimlessly in the wilderness, Deuteronomy considerably escalated and intensified previous commands to expel the Canaanites from the land. There can be no "truck" with the inhabitants of the land, no intermarriage and assimilation; there must be a complete obliteration of idolatry (Deut 7, 12, 20). For the most part they are to be placed under a total ban. This ancient practice dedicated a conquered people and their wealth to destruction.[2] They were to be wholly set apart to God for destruction. Any precious metals that were taken were put through a fire to be purified (Num 31:21-24). There was no personal advantage for anyone, as all was dedicated to the Lord. This was clearly an act of divine judgment as God received what was his due as a last resort. The lives of the enemy, which came from God, were being used to destroy his image and corrupt his world and so were offered back to him in a religious act of judgment.

Therefore, the land was to become purified, and to become holy (Ps 78:54; Zech 2:12). The religious significance of warfare comes to the fore when Joshua is reconnoitering the land before attacking the first city of Jericho. He spies a soldier with a drawn sword nearby and approaches him with the question, "Are you with us or against us?" (Josh 5:13). The answer is striking: "Neither, but I am the Captain of the Lord of Hosts. . . . Take off your shoes for you are standing on holy ground" (Josh 15:14-15). This repetition of a theme before a critical moment in Israel's life is striking. A similar theophany before the exodus at the burning bush at Sinai calling Moses to new leadership (Ex 3:5) reoccurs now in Canaan. Joshua is a new Moses commissioned by a God who transcends nationalistic boundaries. He is holy. His words solemnly affirm

---

[2]There have been considerable attempts to "tone down" this rhetoric but it has been largely unsuccessful. For example, see Douglas S. Earl, *The Joshua Delusion: Rethinking Genocide in the Bible* (Eugene, OR: Wipf and Stock, 2011). For the major study, see Philip Stern, *The Biblical Herem: A Window on Israel's Religious Experience* (Atlanta: Scholars Press, 1991).

that the conquest is not just a political and military conflict but a matter of holy justice.

EXODUS, PASSOVER, AND JERICHO

Moreover, this conquest will be patterned after the exodus in other ways. When the people cross the Jordan River into the Promised Land, they cross over on dry ground just as the previous generation traversed the Red Sea when departing Egypt (Josh 3–4). Similarly, there is a Passover that coincides with this crossing, just as a Passover preceded the exodus (Josh 5:1-12). As the Passover portended the judgment of Egypt, it now foreshadows the judgment of Canaan.

All of this provides an important theological framework for the imminent conquest. Obedience to the divine rule is critical, and the conquest of the city of Jericho is a paradigmatic case of the divine rule. While a battle and an Israelite victory certainly takes place, one would hardly discern this from the description of the victory in Joshua 6. Instead, the focus is on divine monergism not on human participation.[3] The battle is the Lord's. The procession around the city with the footstool of the divine throne in the lead and the collapse of the walls at the sound of the Israelite trumpets on the seventh day is a highly liturgical act. The quick conquest of the city with hardly a word about the battle suggests a highly theologized account emphasizing the divine royal Warrior and his judgment. Israel obeys the divine King and conquers the city easily.

Two important stories show the significance of obedience and disobedience to the divine rule. A Canaanite woman, Rahab, saves herself and her family from the judgment by trusting in Yahweh and helping Israelites (Josh 2). On the other hand, an Israelite, Achan, brings destruction down on himself and his family by disobeying Yahweh's orders (Josh 7). Before his sin is discovered and dealt with it also causes the deaths of thirty-five Israelites in a defeat at the city of Ai.

RENEWING THE COVENANT

After Israel defeats Ai, the people gather at Shechem in accordance with the Deuteronomic constitution and there reaffirm their commitment to the

---

[3]For a focus on human participation, see Josh 24:11.

covenant (Josh 8:30-35). It was here that Abraham had first entered the land, and where Jacob returned from "exile" in Mesopotamia (Gen 12:6; 33:18). It will be near here over a millennium later when Jesus introduces a Samaritan woman to a new covenant (Jn 4). But in the present text, Joshua builds an altar on Mount Ebal, on which sacrifices are offered, and then he writes on the stones of the altar a copy of the Torah. This was probably a few verses summarizing the Torah, perhaps the Shema. Then in obedience to Moses' command in Deuteronomy 27, and very much like the covenant ritual in Exodus 24, with the people gathered facing the ark of the covenant, the foot-stool of Yahweh's invisible throne, Joshua solemnly reads the pronouncements of their King from his Torah, in particular the blessing and the curse, to remind Israel of its allegiance to its Lord.

The remainder of Joshua recounts the division of the land among the various tribes, after the initial conquests (Josh 13-22). The book concludes with two speeches by Joshua, which sound ominous. In the first speech, Joshua solemnly warns Israel that it will be destroyed if it makes accommodations with the remaining Canaanites in the land. This will lead to idolatry and thus disloyalty (Josh 23). In the second speech, Joshua exhorts the tribes to elim-inate any idols that they may have among them and to worship Yahweh alone. In a covenant renewal ceremony, even when the people solemnly vow to follow Yahweh alone, Joshua—in a moment of prescience—denies that it is possible because God is so holy, and sin is endemic (Josh 24:19-20). The in-evitability of human failure to obey Yahweh raises its ugly head once again. Nevertheless, the covenant is renewed and thus the kingdom has come into the world as Israel takes its place among the nations—a nation under the rule of God. The kingdom now has a domain, the land of Canaan, and a job to do—to be a holy nation, a kingdom of priests, and be a means of universal blessing. What remains to be seen is how successful this vocation will be.

JUDGES AND NATIONAL DECLINE

The book of Judges continues the theme of the coming of the kingdom, as it depicts life in the land after the initial conquest. The framework of the book indicates that instead of moving forward the kingdom goes around in circles and even spirals downward from the divine intention. It begins well but after the death of Joshua and the entire generation that knew the work of Yahweh, there is the beginning of apostasy, reflected in political and moral chaos (Judg 2:6-10). The people fail to complete the conquest as there are significant pockets of Canaanite enclaves and towns that serve to contaminate the faith of the Israelites with the local Canaanite fertility cults. Baal, the Canaanite god of the storm, becomes a principal competitor for Israelite devotion.

As mentioned before, the narrator of this period in Israelite history provides a framework through which to understand the events that take place (Judg 2:1–3:6). When the Israelites sin and fall away from Yahweh, he sends a foreign power to discipline them, and then the people repent and cry out to Yahweh, who then sends a deliverer, a judge, to save them. They continue to serve God until the judge dies, and then the cycle repeats. Unfortunately, deliverance by the judges is never enough, and it is not as if the people simply repeat this cycle through the generations. Every time the Israelites sin again, it is worse than the time before, and by the end of the book the land is in moral and political shambles. It is not as if the Israelites have just been "Canaanized," rather they prove much worse than their Canaanite neighbors and end up in a bloody civil war (Judg 17–21).[4]

THE NEED FOR A KING

An important theme of Judges is the inadequacy of a divinely appointed judge to save Israel permanently. The office of a judge is charismatic not dynastic. When the judge dies, leadership ends. What is needed is clearly a king, and a king implies continuing leadership through the establishment of a dynasty. By the end of the book this is a constant lament: "There was no king in Israel" (Judg 17:6; 18:1; 19:1; 21:25).

About midway through the book, the people wish to anoint the judge, Gideon, to become king because of his military success: "Rule over us, you, your son and your grandson as well, for you have saved us from the Midianites" (Judg 8:22). Their choice is based on his military prowess not God's perspective found in Deuteronomy 17. Gideon realizes this and responds, "I will not rule over you, nor my son, but God will rule over you" (Judg 8:23). In other words,

---

[4]This is the major theme according to Daniel Block, *Judges, Ruth*, New American Commentary 6 (Nashville: Broadman & Holman, 1999).

he rejects their choice, because he sees in their request for monarchy a rejection of theocracy.

Yet despite Gideon's "humble refusal" the context indicates that he stylizes himself after ancient kings, by collecting gold and by having a large harem, as evidenced by his seventy sons! He names one of his sons by a Canaanite concubine, Abimelech, which means, "My father is king!" (Judg 8:30-31). And this from the man who rejected kingship! Clearly his actions belied his words. This sets the scene for Abimelech, who is not a full Israelite, to seize kingship for himself. With the help of local Canaanites in Shechem, he massacres seventy of his brothers, eliminating any competition (Judg 9:1-6). Gideon hypocritically rejected kingship, but his son has no such qualms. He embraces kingship with a vengeance.[5] Significantly this claim to kingship is contested by one of the half brothers who survived the massacre, Jotham. After Abimelech has been appointed king in a ceremony in Shechem, from the top of Mount Gerizim Jotham bellows out a parable about kingship (Judges 9:7-15).

This parable has largely been seen as an antimonarchical tract, which seems like a natural reading of the text. No one wants the job of king except a despised bramble bush. Many commentators conclude that this text reveals the absolute idiocy of kingship in the ancient world. Nonetheless, given the fact that almost all the surrounding nations had kings, and that kingship is even envisioned for Israel in its early traditions, what is more likely described in this parable is a particular type of kingship against which even the book of Deuteronomy protests: a tyrant. In the parable all the trees want a king, but the point of the parable is not that kingship is the problem—in fact, it is desired, but the trees "must beware of the thornbush and look carefully for a suitable tree."[6] And Abimelech is not the suitable tree but rather a useless thornbush who burns up his subjects and is in fact burned up by them (Judg 9:20; cf. Judg 9:46-57).

---

[5]It may be that there is ambiguity here with Gideon intending this name as a reference to divine kingship and not a self-reference. Y. Amit argues for the former, but in my judgment the latter is more likely. Y. Amit, "Judges," in *The Jewish Study Bible*, ed. Adele Berlin and Marc Zvi Brettler (Oxford: Oxford University Press, 2004), 530.

[6]Amit, "Judges," 531.

Abimelech, one-half Israelite, self-appointed, ruthless assassin of any possible competitor, takes no directions from anyone, never mind the Torah. His reign is an ironic parody of Deuteronomy 17:14-20. And in contrast to the judges, he was certainly not endowed with the Spirit, but rather an evil spirit (Judg 9:23), which will later mark a rejected Israelite king (1 Sam 16:14). After his "brief and bloody reign," which "marks the failure of the first attempt at monarchy" in Israel,[7] the succession of judges resumes, and the downward spiral continues.

Among the judges following Abimelech's failed reign are Jepthah and Samson. Jepthah has been so influenced by the indigenous culture of Canaan that he sacrifices his daughter to Yahweh after a military victory (Judg 11:34-40). Samson, who is raised up by Yahweh as a type of Hercules figure to help the Israelites fight against Philistine oppression, is a fitting model to climax the parade of judges within the book (Judg 13-16).

Table 10.1. Parallels between Samson and Israel

SAMSON	ISRAEL
Nazarite—set apart for God	Holy nation—set apart for God
Unique physical power	Unique spiritual strength
Physically promiscuous	Spiritually promiscuous
Lost physical identity	Lost spiritual identity
Lost physical strength	Lost spiritual strength
Lost physical vision	Lost spiritual vision

The final description of Samson's physical blindness at the end of his story provides an apt analogy for the spiritual blindness of his own people. This does not happen until he discloses the secret of his great strength to a Philistine femme fatale, who finally extricates it from his exasperated mind—Nazarites must never shave their head in fulfillment of a spiritual vow. It was the mark of their dedication to God and thus when Samson's hair was shorn, he lost his supernatural strength. When his hair begins to grow again, he can accomplish a great victory over the Philistines, greater than anything he had done before (Judg 16:21-31). There may be the suggestion that any hope for

---

[7]Amit, "Judges," 530.

Israel will be found in recovering its spiritual identity as the people of Yahweh, under his rule.

As if to put an exclamation point on this view, there is a total collapse of the Israelite nation in the last five chapters of the book that mirror the social and spiritual fragmentation of the first few chapters (Judg 17–21). Israel has become worse than its Canaanite neighbors! This much is clear as the ringing refrain throughout these chapters indicates, "There was no king in Israel. Everyone did what was right in their own eyes" (Judg 17:6; 21:25; cf. Judg 18:1; 19:1). In fact, these references indicate four episodes that highlight Israelite idolatry: a gang rape, a civil war, the virtual annihilation of a tribe, and a mass kidnapping of Israelite women to ensure the tribe's survival.

These episodes show the depths to which the kingdom of God has sunk. Israel has become like Sodom and Gomorrah.[8] The solution must be a true king, not one like Abimelech. Moreover, a sporadic judge equipped by the Spirit of God will not do. What is needed is a royal house to ensure that chaos will be held at bay. Where is a king who will re-establish the kingdom of God in the world?

SAMUEL AND THE END OF THE JUDGES

As the book of Samuel begins, the sequence of events regress from bad to worse. The general context is a nation in which even the priesthood has become corrupt. The high priest is an elderly man, whose physical obesity, spiritual vacuity, and moral laxity have enabled his sons to use their priestly occupation to exploit the people to satisfy their insatiable appetite for food and sex. Moreover, politically the nation is on the brink of being conquered by the Philistines, part of a migration of sea peoples, settled on the Mediterranean coast of the southern Levant.

Into this dire social and political context there is the introduction of a domestic scene between the two wives of a man named Elqanah while the family is at a religious festival (1 Sam 1:1-20). One, Hannah, is barren and the other, Penninah, is the mother of many children. Penninah cannot resist rubbing in the shame of Hannah's infertility at these annual festivals. Finally,

---

[8]The behavior of the populace in the Israelite city of Gibeah and Sodom are described in similar language in Judg 19 and Gen 19.

on one such occasion, matters reach a boiling point and Hannah cannot endure the torment any longer. She rushes to the sanctuary and pours out her soul to Yahweh, asking for a child to end her humiliation, and promising to return him to the sanctuary and commit him to a lifelong Nazarite vow (1 Sam 1:9-11). She addresses God as "Yahweh of Hosts," a name particularly suited to Yahweh seated on the throne above the ark of the covenant. This is the first appearance of this name in the Bible, and it is associated with "the ark of the covenant of Yahweh of Hosts who sits on the throne above the Cherubim" (1 Sam 4:4). The high priest has such keen spiritual perception that he mistakes Hannah's sincerity for intoxication. This will not be the last time such religious dullness mistakes genuine spirituality for inebriation (Acts 2:13-21). After being corrected by the grief-stricken woman, he then assures her of the efficacy of her prayer.

Women often play a pivotal role in major advances of the storyline of the kingdom of God. The promise comes to Eve of a future descendant who will conquer the Serpent and restore the lost conditions of paradise (Gen 3:15). Before the birth of Isaac, God announces to Sarah the coming event despite her disbelief (Gen 18:1-14). The primary actors in the birth of Jacob's children, and the ones who give them names, are his wives (Gen 29–30). Tamar takes the initiative to bear a son for the interrupted line of Judah (Gen 38). Hebrew midwives, in addition to Jochebed and Miriam, feature prominently in the salvation of Israel from oppression in Egypt (Ex 1:16-21; 2:1-10). Miriam and her entourage praise Yahweh at the Red Sea. Deborah and Jael generate a great victory over the Canaanites in the time of the Judges (Ex 15:20; Judg 5). Now it is time for other women to step into the fray during this critical period of the time of the Judges, when Israel has sunk to such an abysmal level that even its priesthood is corrupt. And Hannah is going to do this by bearing a child, Samuel, who will become a kingmaker for the nation.

AN UPSIDE-DOWN READING OF HISTORY

After Hannah gives birth to Samuel and weans him, she takes him to the sanctuary to fulfill her promise. As she delivers him over to the sanctuary personnel, she sings a thanksgiving song about the kingdom of God

(1 Sam 2:1-10). It resonates with earlier poems about the kingdom from old Jacob on his deathbed, Miriam and Moses at the Red Sea, Baalam on the plains of Moab, Moses giving a parting blessing to the people at the border of Canaan, and Deborah at Mount Tabor. Hannah resumes the kingdom cadence with a song that charts the future of the kingdom and can be called the Old Testament Magnificat.

While Hannah's poem is a personal thanksgiving song, it is also much more. Hannah takes her own experience in which she, as a downcast, infertile, and miserable woman, has been raised from her humiliation by Yahweh's unique intervention. She connects the theological dots moving from the personal to the historical to the universal. She begins by praising Yahweh's unique power in raising her horn from the ash heap and ends by praising Yahweh's power to lift a king's horn. The ram's horn is a symbol of power. When rams are fighting their horns are lowered as they attack one another and the one whose horn is raised at the end of the battle is regarded as the victor. Hannah has seen herself locked in a battle with her culture and her rival wife. With the miraculous birth of her son, Yahweh has given her victory. That is why Hannah says one should not speak arrogantly or proudly boast. What the Hebrew text literally says, is that one should not say "Tall! Tall!" (gəbōhâ gəbōhâ, 1 Sam 2:3). This word will become a dominant theme in the following narrative as anyone who is tall will become small, and anyone who is small will become tall. In Yahweh's kingdom the proud will be abased and the humble raised.

Hannah then segues in praise of Yahweh's unique holiness, and his method of working in history: the powerful are defeated and the weak triumph, the satiated starve and the starving are satisfied, the fertile become barren and the barren fertile (1 Sam 2:4-5). The reversal of the normal order of things in the world is not the result of chance but it is the result of Yahweh the Great Reverser: he kills and resurrects, he impoverishes and enriches, he humbles and exalts, and he raises up the poor and needy to make them royalty (1 Sam 2:6-8).

Connecting the dots from Yahweh's methods, Hannah concludes that human strength does not guarantee victory. One does not fight Penninah's thunder with one's own but with Yahweh's. As a result, Hannah concludes that this great Creator will establish a universal reign in the future, and the way he will do this is to anoint a king and raise his horn (1 Sam 2:9-10)! The birth of one child, in a little home in the hill country of Ephraim, has cataclysmic ramifications—the prediction of a universal kingdom. This is truly an upside-down reading of history![9]

HOW ARE THE MIGHTY FALLEN!

After Hannah's song the mighty begin to fall, and the small become tall. The little boy Samuel is juxtaposed to the adult and powerful Elide household (1 Sam 2:11-21). But God circumvents the normal channels of communication and speaks through the little boy to pronounce judgment on the corrupt priests (1 Sam 3). Not long after, the priests carry the ark of the covenant—the footstool of the divine throne—to help ensure a military victory against the Philistines. But in one fell swoop, the Israelites are defeated, the priests killed, and the ark captured. Upon hearing the news of defeat old Eli falls off his "throne" and breaks his neck (1 Sam 4). The mighty are being pulled down from their thrones. For many in Israel this would have been a theological crisis of the first magnitude.[10] Their King has been captured. But it is no less a crisis for the Philistines. When they set up the ark in their pantheon, their chief god, Dagon, collapses before it, disarmed and decapitated (1 Sam 5:1-5). Yahweh's kingship will not be domesticated, whether in Israel or in Philistia. The Philistines realize they must return the ark to Israel because it wreaks havoc everywhere it goes in their land (1 Sam 5:6-12). They want to avoid it like the plague because it causes a plague everywhere it goes! There may be no human king in Israel, but their divine King is teaching his people a valuable lesson, the same valuable lesson that Joshua learned when he met the Captain of Yahweh's hosts on the outskirts of Jericho. Yahweh is holy, and those who would live in his presence must take off their shoes for they are standing on holy ground. It seems that Yahweh has let the ark be

---

[9]Thomas R. Schreiner, *The King in His Beauty: A Biblical Theology of the Old and New Testaments* (Grand Rapids, MI: Baker, 2013), 137.

[10]Patrick D. Miller and J. J. M. Roberts, *The Hand of the Lord: A Reassessment of the "Ark Narrative" of 1 Samuel* (Baltimore: Johns Hopkins University Press, 1977).

captured in order to punish Israel and its chief priestly house, and to show that Yahweh alone could overcome the Philistines and compel them to return the ark to Israel.[11]

When the Philistines finally send the ark back to Israel, it reaches Beth-shemesh. The Israelites rejoice, and remove it from the cart, split the wood of the cart, and sacrifice the cows pulling the cart as a burnt offering. But some of the people try to look inside the ark and are struck down (1 Sam 6). The remaining townspeople cry out, "Who can stand in attendance before Yahweh, this Holy God? To whom shall he go up from us?" (1 Sam 6:20). One of the important lessons of Hannah's song is learned the hard way by Israel: "There is no one holy like Yahweh!"

Throughout the rest of Samuel, the themes of the song of Hannah resound like a drumbeat. When Samuel grows old the people want a king, but they really are not interested in a king like the one described in Deuteronomy 17. They want a king who will be a military warrior to fight their battles (1 Sam 8). This means the rejection of the king of Deuteronomy 17, God's vicegerent, which also implies the automatic rejection of divine kingship. The king they want will always be "on the take," rather than a giver: he will take sons for soldiers, daughters for servants, seed, fields vineyards, and household servants.[12]

ISRAEL'S FIRST KINGS: THE TALL AND THE SMALL

The people get their king in Saul the son of Kish. A head taller than everyone else, Saul distinguishes himself as a military hero. At first he relies on God's Spirit, but more and more he depends on his own strength and prowess (1 Sam 9–12). Saul's conspicuous height is clearly an ominous sign. It does not take long before he has been rejected by Yahweh for disobeying the divine commands (1 Sam 13–15). As a result, Samuel says, "because you rejected the word of the Lord, God has rejected you from being king." There can only be one king in Israel, and that is Yahweh, and Saul learns that lesson in his rejection. Therefore, even though Saul remains

---

[11]G. Henton-Davies, "Ark of the Covenant," in *The Interpreter's Dictionary of the Bible*, ed. George Arthur Buttrick (Nashville: Abingdon, 1962), 1:224.

[12]Note the repetition of *lāqaḥ* ("take") in 1 Sam 8:11, 13, 14, 16.

king officially, God seeks out his own servant-king, one who will be small but whom Yahweh will make tall. The theocracy will be preserved with such a king.

Samuel travels to Bethlehem in response to Yahweh's call to anoint clandestinely this new king (1 Sam 16). He is told to seek out a man named Jesse and anoint one of his sons. When the sons are paraded before him, even the discerning old prophet must be reminded of Yahweh's upside-down values:

> When they arrived, Samuel saw Eliab and thought, "Surely the LORD's anointed stands here before the LORD."
>
> But the LORD said to Samuel, "Do not consider his appearance or his height, for I have rejected him. The LORD does not look at the things people look at. People look at the outward appearance, but the LORD looks at the heart." (1 Sam 16:6-7 NIV)

The word for "height" in 1 Samuel 16:7 is two words in Hebrew (*gəbōah qômātô*), literally the "tallness of his stature." It evokes those arrogant words that one should never personally claim for oneself: "Tall! Tall!" (1 Sam 2:3).

Last, when the youthful David appears, he is God's choice, even though his own father did not consider him royal material. As the youngest (lit. smallest), David was disregarded and left looking after the sheep. But he is Yahweh's choice, and that is what matters.

Throughout the subsequent storyline the narrator focuses on David's rise, even though Saul is king. The young lad even maintains the ruler's sanity by using his musical skill to exorcise an evil spirit troubling the king (1 Sam 16:17-23). In the very next chapter David, the small one, topples an ancient version of The Terminator, Goliath, the tall one, who has challenged and terrified every Israelite warrior (1 Sam 17). Again, David's speech in the face of Goliath's bombast is a riff on Hannah's song and becomes a type of the ongoing battle between the seed of the woman and the Serpent, in which the Serpent's head is crushed:

> You come to me with a sword, a spear and a javelin, but I come to you in the name of Yahweh of Hosts, the God of the Armies of Israel, whom you have despised . . . and I will smite you . . . so that all this assembly will know that not with the sword nor spear does Yahweh save, for to Yahweh belongs the outcome of war. (1 Sam 17:45-47)

Later, when David becomes a fugitive because of the king's jealousy, he is constantly being saved from difficult situations (1 Sam 19–26). When the tall Saul and his sons die in a battle at Gilboa against the Philistines in a resounding Israelite defeat, Saul's corpse—like Dagon's and like Goliath's—is beheaded and his body hung on the walls of the town of Beth-Shan (1 Sam 31). Upon hearing the news, David laments their death by composing a song that reverberates with the main theme of Hannah's poem: "How are the mighty fallen!" (2 Sam 1:18-27, esp. 2 Sam 1:19, 25, 27). Military equipment and prowess perish. It is interesting that David composed this song with the title "[The Song of the] Bow," and it was to be taught to the people of Judah (2 Sam 1:18). Perhaps it was to engrain in them the lesson of the song of Hannah: "The bows of the mighty are broken!" (1 Sam 2:4). The final line of "The Song of the Bow" belies the power of the bow, and therefore trust in human strength: "How are the mighty fallen, and the weapons of war perish!" (2 Sam 1:27).

THE RETURN OF THE KING (THE ARK)

After David becomes king over the nation, two significant events emerge as important in the biblical narrative about the kingdom of God. In the first, David returns the ark to the new capital of the kingdom, Jerusalem (2 Sam 6). The tabernacle is there but no ark, and the ark represents the real Ruler of the nation. But the first attempt is a disaster, caused by the failure to follow divine protocol. When the oxen pulling the cart carrying the ark stumble, a man named Uzzah, who is not a priest, reaches out his hand to steady the ark and is instantly struck down (2 Sam 6:6). David is reminded that he cannot domesticate the holy for his own purposes. Donald Murray argues that in this first attempt, David is acting like a king in the cultural context of the ancient Near East. He is in charge and religion serves the establishment. The priests are like the chaplains at modern secular universities, brought out from the shelf for significant events, dusted off, and asked to say a prayer to bless the occasion. But the real biblical idea of kingship is that of a *nāgîd* (leader), someone who is a steward of the divine government, who rules in the place of God and under God.[13]

---

[13]Donald F. Murray, *Divine Prerogative and Royal Pretention: Pragmatics, Poetics and Polemics in Narrative Sources About David (2 Samuel 5:17–7:29)*, JSOT Supplement Series 264 (Sheffield, UK: Sheffield Academic Press, 1998), 299.

However, in David's next attempt to return the ark, he follows the required protocols and dances with abandon before the ark in its procession into Jerusalem (2 Sam 6:12-23). The king's heart is on full display. Even when his wife, Michal, later scorns his total disregard for cultural propriety in humiliating himself before the lower classes, he responds by chastising her pride: he will even make himself lower in his own eyes, because Yahweh has chosen him to be a *nāgîd* in the place of her tall father (2 Sam 6:21). David is not concerned for his own reputation but God's and the common people in whose eyes he is honored. David now is singing and dancing the same tune as Hannah.

THE HOUSE THAT GOD BUILT

The second significant event happens soon afterward. When the kingdom is established, David's vision is turned to the great gap between the human *nāgîd* and the divine King, and the incongruity between his own permanent palace and the ark's temporary shrine (2 Sam 7). He decides to build a more enduring "house"—a temple—for the real king of Israel. But the prophet Nathan comes to him with a divine word rejecting his desire yet promising him that Yahweh would build him an enduring house, a royal line, one that would last forever. The play on the word *bayit* ("house") is marked. In fact, this word is the leading motif of the text as it occurs fifteen times in the Hebrew (2 Sam 7:1, 2, 5, 6, 7, 11, 13, 16, 18, 19, 25, 26, 27, 29 [twice])! David wanted to build a physical structure for Yahweh, but Yahweh will build him a dynasty! David and his line will be Yahweh's adopted sons, and David's son Solomon will be chosen to build the temple for Yahweh. If the dynastic kings fail to follow Yahweh, Yahweh will certainly punish them, but he will never remove his *ḥesed* (as he did for Saul).

David's response is profound gratitude. In one of the most powerful speeches in the narrative of the entire Bible, he praises God for his grace in establishing this dynasty, the means by which God's unique covenant with Israel will take further shape (2 Sam 7:23-24). His sense of gratitude is immense as he refers to himself ten times as God's servant. He concludes on the note of blessing, which was so emphatic in the Abrahamic covenant: "from your blessing the house of your servant is blessed forever" (2 Sam 7:29). David sees that this covenant will be a further means by which Israel will bless the world. He calls the covenant a Torah for humanity, or a decree for the human race, which could mean a lesson or instruction for humans to observe, that this covenant is for their benefit. Or more likely in the context of the entire biblical narrative, as Walter Kaiser argues, a charter for humanity, and thus the fulfillment of the Abrahamic covenant through David's dynasty.[14]

The event described here is the establishment of the Davidic covenant, where God makes a covenant with one person and his descendants, for an enduring dynasty over the nation of Israel. This is true even though the word *bərît* ("covenant") does not appear in the text. The idea of promise and oath are clearly here, and David's response surely understands the importance of this commitment of Yahweh. In addition, in other passages the term *bərît* is used to interpret this text (Ps 89:4-6, 35, 40; 132:11-12).

But it is also important to note the word *mamlākâ*, "kingship" or "kingdom," is virtually a synonym for this dynasty: "I will establish his kingship" (2 Sam 7:12), "I will establish the throne of his kingdom forever" (2 Sam 7:13), "Your house and your kingdom will last forever" (2 Sam 7:16). This is a dynasty ruling over a kingdom that will be enduring. The dots between David's covenant and Hannah's song can be linked now as she looked forward to God's abasement of the strong and powerful in favor of the weak, culminating with a human king who would reign to the ends of the earth. This line can be traced back to the Pentateuch's description of a king who would emerge from Israel, crushing hostile powers, and one to whom the nations would submit, and a dynasty of kings coming from the line of Abraham and Sarah.

Nonetheless, it becomes evident in the subsequent narrative that David's own personal house is in trouble, as he certainly does not act like the *nāgîd* of Yahweh but a typical ancient Near Eastern king (2 Sam 11–20; 1 Kings 1–2). He falls prey to adultery and murder in the sordid tale of his illicit liaison with Bathsheba (2 Sam 11–12). But when confronted by the prophet Nathan and given a severe punishment, he nevertheless admits his sin and intercedes for the newborn child, the result of his union with Bathsheba. His humility and repentance clear him for acceptance with Yahweh, but they do not

---

[14]Walter C. Kaiser, *Toward an Old Testament Theology* (Grand Rapids, MI: Zondervan, 1991), 152-55.

suspend the judgment, which falls like a sledgehammer. The newborn child dies (2 Sam 12:15-19); his own son, Amnon, rapes Tamar, his half sister and David's daughter (2 Sam 13:1-22); Amnon in turn his murdered by Absalom, his own half brother and Tamar's full brother (2 Sam 13:23-33); Absalom then leads a revolt that ends in humiliation for his father, David, and his own death (2 Sam 15-19), until finally another son born to David and Bathsheba succeeds David as king amid palace intrigue (2 Sam 12:24-25).

SOLOMON, SHALOM, AND CHAOS

Famous for his wisdom as the result of a divine gift (1 Kings 3), Solomon used it as a boon for his people and as a beacon for the nations. He organized his kingdom to ensure its success, extending its domain up to the Euphrates, down to the Egyptian border, and the kingdom was extremely prosperous. The kingdom was noted not only for its prosperity but also for the accompanying peace, described with imagery that would later be used to describe the new world of the Messiah's reign:

> He had peace [*shalom*] on all his borders roundabout. All the days of Solomon, Judah and Israel, from Dan to Beersheba, dwelt in safety, everyone under his own vine and his own fig tree. (1 Kings 4:24-25 [Heb. 5:4-5]; cf. Mic 4:4)

"Solomon's" (*Shelomo*) kingship was aptly marked by shalom. But his wisdom was regarded as surpassing the wisdom of the wisest in the outside world. Household names at the time, whose names were synonymous with wisdom, are rhymed off by the narrator to show Solomon's superior grasp of knowledge and wisdom: the narrator moves from countries and territories noted for their wisdom (probably Mesopotamia and Egypt, the great civilizations of the time) to individuals (Ethan the Ezrahite; Heman, Chalcol, and Darda, the sons of Mahol). His proverbial sayings (three thousand) and songs (one thousand and five) resulted from his study of creation covering both flora and fauna (1 Kings 4:32-33 [Heb. 5:12-13]). His knowledge of the natural world was virtually encyclopedic.[15] Through his wisdom, Solomon was mastering creation as the first king, Adam, did when he named the animals in Genesis.

---

[15]Z. Zevit, "First Kings," in *The Jewish Study Bible*, ed. Adele Berlin and Marc Zvi Brettler (Oxford: Oxford University Press, 2004), 682.

And this wisdom was not for personal intellectual growth, but it was to be disseminated to the wider world: "From all nations, people came to listen to Solomon's wisdom, sent by all the kings of the world who had heard of his wisdom" (1 Kings 4:34 [Heb. 5:14]).

TEMPLE AND KINGDOM

The real high point in the Solomonic narrative is the building and dedication of the temple (1 Kings 6–8). This is the permanent structure where heaven meets earth, and Yahweh reigns from Jerusalem, through his vicegerent, Solomon. While it takes Solomon almost twice as long to build his own palace, the real interest of the narrator is the temple. The narrator devotes much more literary output to the temple (seventy-five verses, 1 Kings 6:1-38; 7:13-51) than other buildings (twelve verses, 1 Kings 7:1-12). And then he spends another sixty-six verses on the dedication of the temple (1 Kings 8)! The temple with its structure is a model of the world, under the authority of the divine ruler in heaven, who in a sense takes up residence in his house. The innermost court reflects the divine throne, the main sanctuary reflects heaven, and the outer court with the bronze sea and altar, corresponds to the earth, with its seas and mountains. The temple connects heaven with earth and underscores the importance of the priests who officiate in the temple, as they serve as channels or mediums between heaven and earth. The dimensions of the temple, some 45 feet high, 150 feet long, and 75 feet wide, along with its complex and sophisticated design and architecture, would convey the divine magnificence in symbolic form to every visitor.

The temple's significance can be easily seen in a vision of the prophet Isaiah, who experienced an epiphany as he was visiting the temple courtyard (Is 6). He was able to see into the temple, where there was an altar of incense in front of the inner sanctum, where the ark of the covenant rested, the visible footstool of the invisible divine throne. On this particular day, the invisible became visible and he saw a towering throne on which Yahweh was seated. The train of his royal robe filled the entire temple, and angel-like creatures thundered, "Holy, Holy, Holy, the entire earth is filled with his glory" (Is 6:3). As the train filled the temple—"God is too magnificent for the temple to contain"[16]—in a similar way the entire earth would someday be filled with the glory of Yahweh. The temple is the prime location from which the divine rule extends over all the earth.

When Solomon dedicates the temple, he regards it as the place par excellence where all the nations of the earth can meet their divine ruler. His temple dedication prayer, the longest prayer in the narrative of the Hebrew Bible, is not so much a prayer to God as instructions to people for their prayers when they approach the temple![17] Solomon has seven petitions in his prayer, the number being representative of all possible requests. One petition urges God to grant the request of the non-Israelite in order that all the peoples of the earth may worship (1 Kings 8:41-43).

What is this about if not the reality of the kingdom of God extending into the wider world? "That all the peoples of the earth may know your name and fear you!" (1 Kings 8:43). This is very similar to the message of Psalm 67, which envisions the goal of the overflowing Aaronic blessing to Israel in Numbers 6:24-26 as the means through which the entire world will be blessed, and that the entire world will become the kingdom of God.

> May God be gracious to us and bless us
>   and make his face shine on us—
> *so that your ways may be known on earth,*
>   *your salvation among all nations.*
>
> May the peoples praise you, God;
>   may all the peoples praise you. . .
>
> May God bless us still,
>   *so that all the ends of the earth will fear him.* (Ps 67:1-3, 7 NIV,
>   emphasis mine)

THE DEMISE OF THE KINGDOM

While there may have been high hopes for the present Israel to fulfill this promise, the nation quickly failed in this vocation. While there were significant

---

[16]P. House, "Isaiah's Call and Its Context in Isaiah 1–6," *Criswell Theological Journal* 6 (1993): 207-22, esp. 217.

[17]Samuel E. Balentine, *Prayer in the Hebrew Bible: The Drama of Divine Human Dialogue*, Overtures to Biblical Theology 20 (Minneapolis: Fortress, 1993), 80-81.

achievements in Solomon's reign, he soon became one of Israel's worst kings. He began to violate systematically the Deuteronomic ideals. His harem became legendary in size, which eventually led to religious pluralism (1 Kings 11:1-8). Second, to ensure the rapid deployment of his military power, he fortified many strategic cities and multiplied chariots (1 Kings 4:26; 9:15-19; 10:26). Finally, his wealth multiplied to an enormous extent because of his trade and mining ventures (1 Kings 10:23-29). As for following Deuteronomy's positive commandments to write out a copy of the Torah and to read it every day, one can assume from his behavior that such practices were nonexistent.

As his government bureaucracy increased in size, so did the tax burdens on his own citizens, which were aggravated by the implementation of alienating policies (1 Kings 4:7; 9:15, 20-21; 12:1-4; cf. 1 Sam 8:15-17). If there was a small window open where the kingdom of God could be seen as a potential reality for the world, that was shut quickly. When Solomon died, the kingdom collapsed. The northern tribes broke away and formed a northern state (1 Kings 12:1-20). Yet God preserved the southern tribe of Judah's kingdom, to maintain his covenant with David, and preserve the hope of a ruler who would someday exercise dominion over the entire world.

Both nations, however, were fatally afflicted with a death wish. Idolatry was the major culprit, which led to covenant violation and social injustice. The northern kingdom met its end in 722 BC, when the Assyrians invaded and exiled most of the population while repopulating the country with exiles from other nations that they had conquered. The southern kingdom met the same fate over a century later in 586 BC at the hands of the Babylonians who destroyed their cities and temple. Their Davidic king, Jehoiachin, along with most of their population, was carried off to exile (1 Kings 12–2 Kings 25).

THE MIDPOINT OF THE BIBLE: DEATH AND RESURRECTION

At this point at the end of the Former Prophets, the halfway point in the Hebrew canon, the narrative about the kingdom of God begun in Genesis has reached a dead end. What has become of the promise of a descendant of the woman, restoring the lost glory of humanity and conquering the Serpent? What has become of the promise of universal blessing through Abraham's

seed? What has become of the Davidic covenant? Many promises were intact
at the beginning of the Former Prophets. Now they are all in radical doubt.
In fact, other voices from the Latter Prophets will depict this situation with
graphic language. Isaiah describes the nation as a devastated, uninhabited
ruin (Is 6:11-13); Micah like a plowed field (Mic 3:12); Jeremiah like precreation
chaos (Jer 4:23-26); Ezekiel like a valley full of dismembered skeletons
(Ezek 37:1-14). The temple, which was the major symbol of the kingdom, the
residence of the divine throne, lies in ruins. The ark of the covenant has
disappeared. The kingdom of God that would fill the earth seems nothing
more than a pipe dream. And yet . . . there are four verses at the very end of
the Former Prophets that indicate there may be a silver lining in the dark
storm clouds:

> In the thirty-seventh year of the exile of Jehoiachin king of Judah, in the year
> Awel-Marduk became king of Babylon, he released Jehoiachin king of Judah
> from prison. He did this on the twenty-seventh day of the twelfth month.
> He spoke kindly to him and gave him a seat of honor higher than those of
> the other kings who were with him in Babylon. So Jehoiachin put aside his
> prison clothes and for the rest of his life ate regularly at the king's table. Day
> by day the king gave Jehoiachin a regular allowance as long as he lived.
> (2 Kings 25:27-30)

Many scholars understand this passage to be little more than a pessimistic
or realistic understanding of the narrator.[18] This last reference is all the his-
torian has at his disposal to complete his history. It is a sad conclusion. Israel
is gone, Judah is in exile, and the Davidic king is a prisoner who has just been
released from prison and granted some privileges by the Babylonian king,
who has the real power. This means that any talk of the kingdom of God being
established in the world is an exercise in pure fantasy.

To be sure, this is one way to the read the evidence, but if one is attuned
to some of the clues in the biblical narrative of an upside-down reading of
history, one should take pause. Israel was caught between the all-powerful

---

[18]For a comprehensive discussion of the text, see Stephen G. Dempster, "The End of History and
the Last Man," in *The Seed of Promise: The Sufferings and Glory of the Messiah; Essays in Honor of
T. Desmond Alexander*, ed. P. R. Willamson and R. F. Cefalu, GlossaHouse Festschrift Series 3
(Wilmore, KY: GlossaHouse, 2020), 113-41.

Egyptian army and the deep Red Sea, and the Sea opened providing an exodus from certain death (Ex 14-15). On the cusp of the Promised Land, and unaware of the deadly danger of a shaman's curses, the curses are turned into blessings (Num 22-24). From the domestic squabble in an Israelite household, emerges a desperate woman's prayer for a child, and this child becomes the sign of a new world in which God would set the world "right side up" through a king who would reign to the ends of the earth (1 Sam 2:1-10).

In addition to these strategic clues, other texts suggested universal blessing through Abraham's progeny (Gen 12:1-3), as well as God's future circumcision of the heart of exiles to enable them to fulfill the Shema if they turned back to him (Lev 26:40-45; Deut 30:1-10). Also, there was the template designed for human kingship (Deut 17:14-20) and the covenant made with David that he would always have a ruler on the throne, and the universal significance of that covenant (2 Sam 7).

When combined with the messages of the next half of the Hebrew canon, these seemingly isolated dots in the trajectory of Scripture lead to a very different conclusion regarding the last four verses of 2 Kings. Rather than pessimism, perhaps biblical realism takes seriously the word of Yahweh to a barren Sarah at eighty-nine years of age: "Is anything too hard for Yahweh?" (Gen 18:14). It is such a word that defines reality for Sarah and Abraham and makes possible what other views of reality define as impossible.[19] Yes, there is the reality of the dead end of exile, and the kingdom of God appears to be a dismal failure, but from such dead ends God can make an exit. One is reminded of the first prime minister of Israel, David Ben Gurion, who once said, "In Israel in order to be a realist, you have to believe in miracles."

DISCUSSION QUESTIONS

1. What lessons can the contemporary church learn from the ups and downs of Israel in the Former Prophets?

2. Why do theocracy and monarchy not have to be contradictory in Israel?

3. How do you think a democracy might work in a theocracy?

---

[19]Walter Brueggemann, "Impossibility and Epistemology in the Faith Tradition of Abraham and Sarah (Gen 18:1-15)," *Zeitschrift für die alttestamentliche Wissenschaft* 94 (1982): 615-34.

Chapter Eleven

THE LATTER PROPHETS

THE ONCE AND FUTURE KINGDOM

THE LATTER PROPHETS (Isaiah, Jeremiah, Ezekiel, The Twelve) kept telling the people to return to the covenant, to keep faith with Yahweh, but their words fell often on deaf ears. At the same time, they did not leave the people without hope. Precisely because of the covenant, they were to be judged. But also precisely because of the covenant, there was hope. Accordingly, Jeremiah prophesied of a time when the ark of the covenant would become obsolete because the entirety of Jerusalem would be the throne of Yahweh, and all the nations would come and worship there, paying homage to the King, and not walking according to their sinful hearts (Jer 3:14-18). Ezekiel would say that although the exiles were like a massive killing field of dry bones, God would raise them up from the grave to be a mighty army, breathing life into them as he once did to Adam, and bringing them home (Ezek 37:1-14). Isaiah would prophesy that though the tree of Judah and Jesse had been cut down by judgment, a holy seed would survive in the stump of Judah; a shoot would sprout up from the stump of Jesse, and this Davidic king would bring healing to the nations and rule the world with Yahweh's Spirit (Is 6:13; 11:1-10).

The Twelve would make similar statements.[1] Although it seemed like the exile constituted a divorce, God would betroth Israel again in righteousness, ḥesed, and justice (Hos 2:14-23). The fallen tabernacle of David's kingdom would be rebuilt and be a beacon to the nations (Amos 9:11-12). The destroyed temple would be resurrected and bring about healing to the nations as they stream up to the magnetic hill of Jerusalem (Mic 4:1-5; cf. Is 2:1-5). And a new Davidic king would possess a worldwide kingdom (Hos 3:5; Mic 5:4 [Heb. 5:3]). Thus, these prophets, while excoriating Israel and Judah for their sins, offered hope beyond the judgment and spoke of a new future for not only Israel but the world. God's covenant with Abraham was not in jeopardy (Mic 7:18-20). It only appeared to be so. Despite Israel's failure to keep the Sinai covenant, God would fulfill the Abrahamic oath and address the central problem of that covenant—the failure of the people to obey the Torah and submit to their king. He would freely forgive their sins and write the Torah on their hearts, or give them a new heart, one of flesh for one of stone (Jer 31:31-34).[2] This would also be the way he would deal with the nations as well. This would all happen when God returns to Zion as King and brings his exiled people with him, making Jerusalem the center of the world and the place where he would rule the cosmos.

THE LATTER DAYS AND THE DAY OF YAHWEH

And yet in these prophets there was a day that loomed ahead ominously. The "latter days" was a time of salvation and *judgment*. This time was predicted in the Pentateuch as the time when God's kingdom would irrupt into history with a lion-like Ruler, whose reign would transform nature, demand obedience from the nations, and crush the enemies of God (Gen 49:8-12; Num 24:15-19). It was a time when Israel would be delivered from exile because of their repentance and return to God (Lev 26:40-45; Deut 4:29-31; 30:1-10). This theme is resumed in the Prophets in spectacular technicolor and refers

---

[1]The Twelve are the Jewish way of referring to most of the Minor Prophets and include Hosea, Joel, Amos, Obadiah, Jonah, Micah, Nahum, Habakkuk, Zephaniah, Haggai, Zechariah, and Malachi. Together they comprise one volume.

[2]The new covenant is a "new" covenant in relation to the Sinai covenant, but it fulfills the Abrahamic covenant.

to a complex period when God would bring about a decisive intervention in history by finally establishing his kingdom in the earth in a definitive way: the temple would occupy center stage in a new Jerusalem. The temple would be established on the highest mountain to which the nations would stream. There would be a time of withering judgment and a conclusive battle with the forces of darkness. But from this crucible would be a new world with a new Davidic king.

Such a time could be also described as the Day of Yahweh, a day when Yahweh would decisively act in history. In the past such days could refer to times when Yahweh saved Israel from its foes.[3] But in the prophets the day becomes a final day of judgment and salvation (Is 2:6–4:5; Obad 1:15, Zech 14:1). As preparation for that day, the people were called to ready themselves. Throughout the Book of the Twelve, this day is a leading idea, beginning in Joel, continued in Amos, and Obadiah, and virtually becoming the entire theme of Zephaniah, where it is classically known as *Dies Irae* (Day of Wrath):

> The great day of the LORD is near—
>   near and coming quickly. . . .
> That day will be a day of wrath—
>   a day of distress and anguish,
>   a day of trouble and ruin,
>   a day of darkness and gloom,
>   a day of clouds and blackness—
>   a day of trumpet and battle cry
> against the fortified cities
>   and against the corner towers.
> "I will bring such distress on all people
>   that they will grope about like those who are blind,
>   because they have sinned against the LORD. . . ."
>
> In the fire of his jealousy
>   the whole earth will be consumed,
> for he will make a sudden end
>   of all who live on the earth. (Zeph 1:14-18 NIV)

---

[3]This is the assumption behind its probable first occurrence in Amos 5:18-20. See also Is 13:6, 9; Joel 2:1.

By the time of Malachi, the theme builds to a climax as the last word of the prophetic collection:

> "*Surely the day is coming; it will burn like a furnace.* All the arrogant and every evildoer will be stubble, and *the day that is coming* will set them on fire," says the LORD Almighty. "Not a root or a branch will be left to them. But for you who revere my name, the sun of righteousness will rise with healing in its rays. And you will go out and frolic like well-fed calves. Then you will trample on the wicked; they will be ashes under the soles of your feet on the day when I act," says the LORD Almighty.
>
> "Remember the law of my servant Moses, the decrees and laws I gave him at Horeb for all Israel.
>
> "See, I will send the prophet Elijah to you *before that great and dreadful day of the LORD comes.* He will turn the hearts of the parents to their children, and the hearts of the children to their parents; or else I will come and strike the land with total destruction." (Mal 4:1-6 [Heb. 3:19-24] NIV, emphasis mine)

This great eschatological day is the decisive act of judgment by which the kingdom will be realized completely in human history. Sinners will be destroyed and the righteous vindicated. But before the turning point Elijah will appear to bring about the necessary preparations.

THE DIVINE KING

One of the striking facts about the Latter Prophets is God's kingship and reign over the nations. Compared to the idols, Jeremiah says, "But the LORD is the true God, he is the living God, the eternal King. When he is angry the earth trembles; the nations cannot endure wrath" (Jer 10:10). At his call to be a prophet, Jeremiah is commanded to have a ministry of destruction and reconstruction, not just to Israel but to the nations (Jer 1:9-10). God's sovereign word works through the prophet to accomplish his deeds among the nations. For example, both Moab and Babylon are judged by the word of the Lord who is "the King, whose name is the LORD of Hosts" (Jer 48:15; 51:57). In Babylonian exile, Ezekiel experiences a bizarre vision of the ark of the covenant transported on a vehicle with intersecting wheels, whose rims are covered with eyes, and powered by wing-like creatures. But above the ark is the appearance of a throne and on the throne is the appearance of a man, shining with a rainbow-like radiance. The vision is too much for Ezekiel as he collapses as a dead man, only to be "resurrected" by the Lord (Ezek 1). But the point is that the divine King has left Jerusalem because of its sin.

Isaiah's vision at his call is no less striking, causing him to come apart at the seams (Is 6). When the Davidic king dies, Isaiah has a vision in the temple of the real king of Israel, high and exalted, enthroned above the angelic creatures, with the train of his royal robe filling the temple. He is not one god among many but the only God, since it is his glory that alone fills the whole earth. His holiness is so intense that it reveals to Isaiah the disgusting filth of his own sin and that of his people. In each case, in these prophets the divine kingship over Israel and the world is not in question, but because of Israel's sin, the nation will be judged. This nation that was to be a light to the nations as a kingdom of priests and a holy nation must be transformed to be God's blessing to the world. And this will only happen through the crucible of judgment.

Jeremiah sees as the solution the divine King bringing about a new covenant in which forgiveness takes place and giving the people a heart on which the Torah is engraved so that they will all know Yahweh from the least to the greatest (Jer 31:31-34). The Shema will be not be just on their lips but as a reality in their lives as their hearts will finally be circumcised (Deut 30:5-6). Similarly, this covenant will coincide with a Davidic king and a Levitical priest, both of whom will rule and offer sacrifices, and have progeny as numerous as the stars in the sky and sand on the seashore (Jer 33:14-22).

For Ezekiel, the divine King will return his people from exile, cleanse them from all their impurities, and give them a new heart—a heart of flesh instead of a heart of stone, and put his Spirit in them to enable them to keep the Torah (Ezek 36:24-32). He will make a new covenant of peace with them (Ezek 34:25; 37:26). They will be placed in the land and the temple will be the center of life as a stream of water, like Eden's, will flow from it and grow to such an extent that it will bring healing wherever it goes, even including the Dead Sea (Ezek 47). Then the city will be called Yahweh Shammah because Yahweh's presence will be there (Ezek 48:35).

ISAIAH'S VISION OF THE SERVANT-KING

For Isaiah the divine King looms large in his prophetic visions. He has placed
Israel as a vineyard in the world to grow and produce the fruits of justice and
righteousness by which the world would be blessed (Is 5:1-7). But the project
has failed because of Israel's sin. In the first part of the book, Israel's king was
to lead the nation to become the means by which the world would be filled
with the knowledge and glory of God, but instead the nation became filled
with wealth, war machines, idols, and injustice (Is 2:6-8; 5:8-25).[4] The Davidic
dynasty was a sorry sight under Ahaz, and even the promising Hezekiah
failed (Is 7:1-17; 39:1-8). Thus, God promised a Davidic king who would come
and bring about a reign of such justice and righteousness that even nature
would be transformed and the world would be filled with the divine glory
(Is 2:1-5; 5:1-7; 9:5-6; 11:1-15). In the second part of the book, Israel has failed
miserably at being God's servant to the nations and has ended up in exile.
Thus, a servant is needed who will liberate Israel from not only physical exile
but spiritual exile. In royal language that links him both to Yahweh the King
and the Davidic king (Is 42:1-6), a servant takes upon himself the priestly
work of suffering for the sins of Israel and many nations (Is 52:13–53:12). The
result of his punishment leads to healing peace and a new covenant of shalom
with Israel. The servant's followers become servants who are taught by Yahweh
himself. In this everlasting covenant each person will have the same status
as David: a son and daughter of Yahweh (Is 54–55). The upshot of these actions will be that the new Jerusalem will illuminate the entire world with
God's glorious light (Is 60).[5] Sun and moon are unnecessary in this new world,
for Yahweh will be the everlasting light and God will fill the world with his
glory. This is the result of the action of God's royal servant (Is 42:1-7; 49:1-7;
50:4-9; 52:13-53:12).

HOPE DELAYED MAKES THE HEART SICK

The prophets expect that the return from exile will be the beginning of the
last days and lead to the establishment of the Kingdom of God in the world

---

[4]For the following discussion I am largely indebted to T. Desmond Alexander, *The Servant King:
The Bible's Portrait of the Messiah* (Vancouver, BC: Regent College Publishing, 2003).
[5]This chapter is really a much more elaborate description of Is 2:1-5.

in one fell swoop. The final three prophets of the Twelve (Haggai, Zechariah, and Malachi) are written after the return from exile when the great hopes for a new world order seem deflated. Questions linger: Where is the promise of the glory when there is little prosperity and hope (Hag 1)? Is not the Davidic covenant over as God has cast off the royal descendant as one throws away a signet ring? The modest rebuilt temple is a shadow of its former self—a day of small things (Zech 4). Many are even saying that it is futile to serve God (Mal 3:14-15). Nonetheless, these prophets seek to encourage the returnees to hope in the prophetic visions of the future. Haggai looks forward to a time when a Davidic monarch will be back on God's hand as his signet ring, and when a rebuilt temple, modest though it might presently appear, will be the sign of God shaking up the heaven and the earth in a new world order (Hag 2). Zechariah predicts a final day when God's kingship will be realized over the entire earth and the Shema will be universalized:

> On that day there will be neither sunlight nor cold, frosty darkness. It will be a unique day—a day known only to the LORD—with no distinction between day and night. When evening comes, there will be light. . . .
>
> The LORD will be king over the whole earth. On that day there will be one LORD, and his name the only name. (Zech 14:7, 9)

For Malachi, in a period of doubt and cynicism about prophetic hopes, he simply encourages the people to wait patiently because this Great Day of Yahweh is still coming, but before that day the great prophet Elijah will return to bring about reconciliation (Mal 4:4-6 [Heb. 3:22-24]).

The prophetic vision resurrects the nation with hope in the coming kingdom of God. In all its kaleidoscopic variety of the terror of divine judgment and the ecstasy of salvation in a new world transformed into a paradisal return to the beginning, the prophetic vision of the future is stunning. There is no overall description of any ordered sequence or plan for these events. Yet there are a number of certainties. Yahweh will come one day to put his world to rights. His appointed king will establish universal justice. It will be a time of withering judgment and unimaginable salvation. Be prepared!

DISCUSSION QUESTIONS

1. The prophets often had to deal with a hardhearted people who were unresponsive to their message. We know their discouragement from some of their writings. How can they help us in the face of similar problems as we pray and work for the coming of the kingdom?

2. While the prophetic visions were ruthlessly realistic about the endemic sinfulness of human nature, what made them optimistic about the future?

Chapter Twelve

THE WRITINGS, PART 1

THE PSALMS AND WISDOM LITERATURE—KINGDOM PRAYER, KINGDOM LIFE, KINGDOM HOPE

THE WRITINGS OFFER A SHIFT in the development of the vision of the Kingdom, emphasizing themes similar to the Prophets while introducing others. The little book of Ruth preceding the Psalms provides a fitting introduction to the Psalter and the Writings with a story about David's origins, the one with whom God made an everlasting covenant culminating in universal rule. In fact, the relationship of the Israelite king to the Gentiles becomes an important theme in the Writings as well as the book of Ruth, where it mentions Bethlehem, David's birthplace. Moreover, as mentioned before, desperate and often broken women like Naomi and Ruth emerge as pillars of the Kingdom in critical moments of redemptive history.[1]

---

[1] One only has to think of Sarah, Rebekah, Rachel, Leah, Shiprah, Puah, Jochebed, Miriam, Deborah, and Hannah, not to mention Elizabeth and Mary.

THE PSALMS

The Psalter—David's book—shows how David will be the key to God's salvation. The seams of the Psalter particularly emphasize this point. At the beginning it is stated that God will establish his universal reign through a Davidic descendant. To the Davidic king, the divine oracle pronounces: "Today I have begotten you. Ask of me and I will give to you as your inheritance the ends of the earth" (Ps 2:7-8). It must be remembered that this final form of the Psalter was produced when there was no Davidic king on the throne. At another crucial seam in the Psalter, the Davidic king will not only be the means by which justice will be done for the poor and the needy, but the one whose coming will transform nature and be the instrument through which all the nations will be blessed, a clear echo of the Abrahamic promise (Ps 72).[2] At the next seam, the Psalter reckons with the huge gap between the fact of exile (Ps 89:38-51) and the promise of the Davidic covenant (Ps 89:1-37). The situation, in fact, is one glaring contradiction between theology and reality. Yet the next (fourth) division of the Psalter intones the future kingship of God wherein all creation becomes a choir singing God's praises. A typical psalm in this division celebrates God's reign:

> Say among the nations, "The LORD reigns."
>> The world is firmly established, it cannot be moved;
>> he will judge the peoples with equity.
>
> Let the heavens rejoice, let the earth be glad;
>> let the sea resound, and all that is in it.
> Let the fields be jubilant, and everything in them;
>> let all the trees of the forest sing for joy.
> Let all creation rejoice before the LORD, for he comes,
>> he comes to judge the earth.
> He will judge the world in righteousness
>> and the peoples in his faithfulness. (Ps 96:10-13)

The world cannot wait for God's providential kingship to become an eschatological reality! At the end of the Psalter this eschatology almost becomes tangible. Immediately before a concluding fireworks of praise (Ps 146–150),

---

[2]Ps 72:17 functions as a climax for the entire psalm.

an acrostic psalm features the Davidic choir master leading Israel in praise of the great King and his coming Kingdom (Ps 145). No less than five times does this short psalm use words for kingship or dominion (Ps 145:1, 11, 12, 13 [twice]). The fireworks of praise to follow is a riff on this kingship, as the next psalm gives an understanding of what Yahweh's upside-down kingship looks like (Ps 146:5-9) and concludes with "Yahweh shall reign forever" (Ps 146:10). The imagery of praise in every line of the final psalm concludes with every living, breathing human being praising God and anticipates the fulfillment of Yahweh's glory flooding the entire earth (Ps 150:1-6).

THE FEAR OF YAHWEH: PROVERBS AND SONGS

The Wisdom literature—Proverbs, Song of Songs, Ecclesiastes, and Job, which are grouped together—provides a description of life in the kingdom of God under God's lordship, and in particular, how to live a flourishing life under the general framework of God's creation intentions, and how he is restoring them in Israel. Solomon is the one associated with wisdom preeminently in the Bible, and his humble prayer for the gift of wisdom—a hearing heart—at his accession indicates the importance of a relationship with God for understanding human life and the world that God made (1 Kings 3:5-9, esp. 1 Kings 3:9). His broad understanding, his many discourses about nature and life (1 Kings 4:29-34), the use of his reason to solve problems (1 Kings 3:16-22), his building projects (1 Kings 5), and his prosperity all indicate the result of a life based on the fear of Yahweh (1 Kings 10:14-29).[3] This important phrase "the fear of Yahweh," is the basis of his wisdom, for it points to a relationship with Yahweh—the God of the covenant—in trust and obedience. In the Bible, the fear of Yahweh is *the* prerequisite for wisdom.

Throughout the book of Proverbs where the structure of God's creation is emphasized, this relationship is an absolute priority and matter of the heart (Prov 1:7; 9:10). To be connected to the Creator in this relationship places one in a special relationship to the facts of creation. This framework of faith, that

---

[3]Solomon's wealth and especially the multiplication of his military arsenal and his wives eventually led to his trust in himself and other deities rather than in Yahweh, a clear violation of the Torah (Deut 17:14-20), all of which demonstrates that wisdom once gained can also be lost.

the creation is good, leads one to study insects and draw lessons for the lazy (Prov 6:6-11); to look at the field of a sluggard and take note (Prov 24:30-34); to make observations about rainless clouds and human boasting (Prov 25:15); to observe similar patterns in various phenomena that can help understanding (Prov 30:11-31); and to show that there are consequences for choices (Prov 1:8-19; 7:1-27).

A different epistemology is at work here: reason. Reason differs from the revelation of the Torah and the Prophets. Reason starts with the presuppositions of the Torah, especially the fear of Yahweh and the created order, and seeks to explore the world in this light. The world of experience is crucial. Thus, when Solomon confronts his first major problem as a king, namely, the contested claims of motherhood by two women over a child, he uses his reason to solve the problem, not revelation (1 Kings 3:16-22). The only revelation is the natural one—the maternal cry of the real mother, and his decision to return the child to her is just as certain as if he heard God himself pronounce the verdict.

The use of reason is often used to motivate a heart change in an individual. For example, where the Torah forbids adultery (Ex 20:14), and the Prophets condemn it (2 Sam 12:1-7), the Wisdom literature seeks to educate its audience about its perils (Prov 7).

Wisdom also opens one's eyes to experience the restoration of Paradise. It is not a matter of gaining life after death but experiencing life *before* death:

Length of days *is* in her right hand,
In her left hand are riches and honor.
Her ways are ways of pleasantness,
And all her paths *are* peace.
She *is* a tree of life to them that lay hold upon her:
And happy *is every one* that retaineth her. (Prov 3:16-18 KJV modified)

This tree of life is an important metaphor in Proverbs 11:30, 13:12, and 15:4, and many proverbs function "symbolically (and provisionally) as the tree of life which was lost in Genesis 3:22-24."[4]

---

[4]Bruce K. Waltke, *The Book of Proverbs, Chapters 1–15*, New International Commentary of the Old Testament (Grand Rapids, MI: Eerdmans, 2004), 260.

Rich imagery of flora and fauna pervades the Song of Songs, providing both the setting and description of erotic love between a man and a woman on equal terms. Far from idealizing just any marriage, this song's rich Garden imagery evokes the depiction of the first couple in Eden, where the first lovers became one flesh and were naked and not ashamed: "The Song confronts us with love as it was in the beginning and it lets us hear again the divine marriage benediction first addressed to the lover and his beloved in man's home primeval."[5] And it is not just a nostalgic reflection on this time, but it is also "the redemption of a love story gone awry," as the couple in all their nakedness are decidedly not ashamed any longer.[6] If the couple cannot get back to Eden, their King has brought it to them in this Song.

THE FEAR OF YAHWEH: JOB AND ECCLESIASTES

If Proverbs and Songs reflect in some ways on the restoration of the blessing of the first kingdom life, Job and Ecclesiastes are reminders of the curse and the fall.[7] These Wisdom books do not shirk the difficult questions. In both, the structure and order of creation is hidden or distorted to the protagonists. Instead of the presence of flourishing prosperity and life there is the reality of suffering and the stench of death and disorder. God seems conspicuously absent or extremely unjust, but both books conclude that the Sovereign One is in control, and one must have faith in him come what may. In both books the fear of Yahweh/God appears strategically to show the importance of this faith stance (Job 28:28; Eccles 12:13).

In Job, as a prelude to the conclusion of the book, a poem about wisdom emphasizes that despite extraordinary ability humans cannot discover the ultimate secrets of the universe, implying the presence of evil in the world and the suffering of the righteous (Job 28). Consequently, the great Creator offers humans a secondary wisdom—to fear the Lord and to turn from

---

[5]Meredith Kline, "The Song of Songs," *Christianity Today*, April 27, 1959, 39.
[6]Phyllis Trible, *God and the Rhetoric of Sexuality* (Philadelphia: Fortress Press, 1978), 144.
[7]I am indebted to John Goldingay's seminal article for this perspective, "The 'Salvation History' Perspective and the 'Wisdom' Perspective Within the Context of Biblical Theology," *Evangelical Quarterly* 51 (1979): 194-207.

evil. The ending of the book reaffirms this view by presenting a panorama of creation showing God's absolute sovereignty over all things, including death and evil, and the human incapacity to understand this (Job 38:1–42:6). Surely an implication of the beatific vision, which Job experiences at the end of the book, is that someday all will be well and that this Sovereign God can be trusted.

In Ecclesiastes, a human king has searched for meaning through many means and has concluded that "under the sun," the oppression, disorder, and injustice do not seem to add up. "Everything is meaningless and a chasing of the wind" (Eccles 1:14). The smell of death is everywhere. The king concludes with a poignant picture of an old house in decline, a sobering metaphor for death (Eccles 12:1-8). Just the same, he prefaces this image with an appeal to youth to remember their Creator before the onset of old age and death (Eccles 12:1). An editor, a frame narrator, who has provided the thematic introduction and conclusion to the book (Eccles 1:1-11; 12:8-14), affirms the king's teaching by summarizing the theological purpose of this meditation on life: "Fear God, and keep his commandments; for this is the whole duty of man. For God will bring every deed into judgment, with every secret thing, whether good or evil" (Eccles 12:13-14). Despite the problems, God is in control. Meaninglessness is not the last word.

LAMENTATIONS: JUDGMENT AND HOPE

Another book in the Writings, which is separate from the Wisdom literature but is the last book of poetry in this section, also deals with the reality of curse, death, and sin. The book of Lamentations mourns over the destruction of Judah and Jerusalem because of the sin of the people. Throughout its five chapters, which use an acrostic to indicate the fullness of God's judgment, human sin is viewed as the principal cause.[8] Repeatedly this is stressed, and the hopes for the kingdom of God have come crashing down with the destruction of the temple, the throne of God. Yet the book concludes with the recognition of the providential kingship of God, which implies hope for the future—God's eschatological kingdom on earth:

---

[8]Lam 1–4 is in acrostic form, with Lam 3 an extended one. Lam 5 does not use the acrostic form, thereby indicating that the grief can no longer be contained.

You, LORD, reign forever;
   your throne endures from generation to generation.
Why do you always forget us?
   Why do you forsake us so long?
Restore us to yourself, LORD, that we may return;
   renew our days as of old
unless you have utterly rejected us
   and are angry with us beyond measure. (Lam 5:19-22)[9]

In many ways the ending of this poem recalls the Deuteronomic promise of repentance in exile and restoration (Deut 30:1-10). The anticipated restoration wishes that God's heavenly reign would become a reality on the earth once again.

DISCUSSION QUESTIONS

1. In order to appreciate the difference between wisdom and prophecy, compare and contrast the prophet's choice of David for kingship (1 Sam 16:4-13) with Solomon's adjudication of a problem (1 Kings 3:16-28). Which is the better method?

2. Which of the books in this section do you most resonate with? Why?

---

[9]The last two clauses are negative, mentioning God's continued judgment as a possibility, but only in a rhetorical way to emphasize that he will not forget mercy; cf. Lam 3:19-24, 31-33; cf. the function of the rhetorical questions in Ps 77:7-9; 88:10-12.

Chapter Thirteen

THE WRITINGS, PART 2

DANIEL-CHRONICLES—WAITING FOR THE KINGDOM

AT THIS POINT WE NEED TO CONSIDER AGAIN the structure of the Hebrew Bible. The narrative, which was suspended before the Latter Prophets, now resumes after a type of poetic commentary. When we left the narrative, the nation was in exile, with Jehoiachin being released, but the commentary of the Latter Prophets and the poetic books of the Writings make it clear that judgment is not God's last word. God is going to restore Israel's fortunes and re-establish his kingdom in the world. His glory will one day fill the whole earth, as the waters cover the sea, just as the train of the robe of the divine King filled the temple in Isaiah's vision.

DANIEL AND THE KINGDOM

When the storyline resumes in Daniel, there is a resumption of the situation of exile mentioned in the last few verses of 2 Kings. Although Jehoiachin is not mentioned, the kingdom is. However, it seems that the real kingdoms worth mentioning are those of Babylon and Persia. The people of Judah are in an exilic prison, and they are subject to the will of their captors. It may seem surprising, then, that this book has probably more information about the kingdom of God than many others.

First, from one point of view this book is a tract for the times about how to live amid intense persecution in a foreign culture that is seeking to assimilate everything and everyone it encounters. As exiles, Daniel and his friends are put to the test, and they are models of how to live by the laws of their divine King rather than the laws of the hostile culture of Babylon. Second, Daniel interprets the dream of Nebuchadnezzar king of Babylon (Dan 2:27-45) similar to the way Joseph interprets the dream of the Pharaoh in Egypt (Gen 41:1-46). As the latter dream provided a template for the future salvation of the world during a coming famine, this dream of the Babylonian king near the end of Israelite history provides a template for the course of history leading to the ultimate salvation of the world.

Daniel's use of the highly charged prophetic term *latter days* confirms this understanding (Dan 2:28). Nebuchadnezzar's dream of a gigantic statue made of four different materials presages an outline of a succession of the kingdoms of the world finally destroyed by a rock that grows into a mighty mountain encompassing the entire world. The head of the statue is gold, its chest and arms silver, with a bronze midsection, and legs and feet comprised of iron mixed with clay. As Daniel interprets the vision, the head is Babylon, the chest and arms are Persia, the midsection is Greece, and the legs and feet are probably Rome. But the most important consideration is that the stone, which destroys all these kingdoms and fills the entire earth, is the kingdom of God.

Daniel is convinced that the Hebrew God is the ruler of the world and that even though his effective reign is not acknowledged yet, he nevertheless reigns. This truth is underscored in Daniel 4 when Nebuchadnezzar has another vision of a gigantic tree whose height represents the overweening pride of the king. Nebuchadnezzar imagines that he is the king who rules the world. But the tree is cut down to size until only a stump remains for a period of seven years. As Daniel interprets the dream, the seven years represent a time when the king will be humbled and reduced to a raving beast, until he is enlightened after the ordeal. He now has a completely new perspective about kingship and kingdoms:

> At the end of that time, I, Nebuchadnezzar, raised my eyes toward heaven, and my sanity was restored. Then I praised the Most High; I honored and glorified him who lives forever.
>
> His dominion is an eternal dominion;
> > his kingdom endures from generation to generation.
> All the peoples of the earth
> > are regarded as nothing.
> He does as he pleases
> > with the powers of heaven
> > and the peoples of the earth.
> No one can hold back his hand
> > or say to him: "What have you done?" (Dan 4:34-35)

God is the real ruler of the world. As John Gray has remarked about Daniel's understanding of God's rule, "God's sovereignty throughout is unassailable for instance in his disposal of kingship to Nebuchadnezzar (Dan 2:37) and others (Dan 5:21), particularly Israel (Dan 7:14, 21) and as expressed throughout in hymns of praise."[1] This shows that while God is sovereign over the earth and occasionally intervenes to show his effective rule, not all recognize and submit to it yet. God is king and he will become king! Eschatological rule will someday become a reality.

THE SON OF MAN RULES THE "BEASTS"

Two further crucial revelations in the book indicate how and when this rule will be realized and recognized in the world. First, in Daniel 7, Daniel himself has a vision of four successive beasts emerging from a chaotic sea, each successor seeming more vicious and macabre than its predecessor, until the final one appears: a monster with ten horns. These beasts represent kingdoms, like the materials of the colossal statue in Daniel 2. The final beast conquers the earth and makes war on the people of God. Furthermore, his mouth is filled with blasphemies. However, his kingdom will come to an end.

---

[1]John Gray, *The Biblical Doctrine of the Reign of God* (Edinburgh: T&T Clark, 1979), 236.

The destruction of the final beast's kingdom is presaged by the installation of God's throne and the coming of the Son of Man, on the clouds of heaven, to whom the kingdom will be given, and the eternal kingdom of God established on earth (Dan 7:1-14). This Son of Man stands in stark contrast to the beasts ascending from the watery chaos. Like Adam in Genesis, he is commanded to subdue the creation and to have dominion over the beasts. And he can do this because, although he is clearly human, he represents God on the earth as a royal figure.

It does not take much interpretive skill to note the similarity of this succession of four kingdoms and their destruction with the succession of four kingdoms and their destruction in Daniel 2. In each scene, the kingdom of God triumphs and God reigns over the earth. This much is clear. But the identity of the Son of Man seems a mystery since, in the interpretation of the vision in Daniel 7, the kingdom is given over to the saints of the Most High rather than the Son of Man. The most probable conclusion is that while the Son of Man is an individual figure, he also represents the saints of the Most High who are being persecuted. It is interesting that "after the kingdom is given over to the saints of the Most High, *his* kingdom will be an everlasting kingdom, and all dominions shall serve and obey *him*" (Dan 7:27). Whether this refers to the Most High or to the people viewed as a collective entity represented by the Son of Man remains ambiguous. Most likely there is a fluidity between an individual who represents the nation and the nation itself.[2]

THE ULTIMATE JUBILEE

The second revelation provides more detail about the coming of this universal kingdom. Daniel 9 provides a revised timeframe for this future development. Daniel reflects on the passage in Jeremiah where Israel's exile in Babylon is predicted to be seventy years (Jer 25:8-14; Dan 9:1-2), after which it will be

---

[2]This is shown clearly in the books of Kings and Chronicles, when the lives of the kings are followed and their piety or lack thereof determines whether the nation waxes or wanes. Note also in some of the Psalms (e.g., Ps 20–21) that the fate of the nation is tied directly to the leader. And in Psalm 80 the psalm oscillates between the nation and a son of man. The pleas to revive the nation go together with the request to restore a leader.

liberated and God's program for the kingdom will be reinstated after the land achieves its sabbatical rest. Daniel is told that the seventy years needs to be revised to seventy weeks of years (490 years), which signifies a superlative ideal period, after which there will be an ultimate Sabbath Jubilee. When this limit is reached—in the far distant future for Daniel—there will be six results, three that eliminate evil and three that produce positive additions: (1) restraining transgression, (2) making an end of sin, (3) covering iniquity, (4) bringing in everlasting righteousness, (5) sealing up the vision and prophecy, and (6) anointing the holy of holies (Dan 9:24). These results further describe the consequences of the final presence of the kingdom of God. The first three results use the three words—*pešaʿ* ("transgression"), *ḥaṭṭāʾt* ("sin"), *ʿāwōn* ("iniquity")—that refer to the conditions eliminated from Israel on the Day of Atonement, which would happen on the tenth day of the seventh month, and in particular, on the tenth day of the seventh month after seven sabbatical cycles of years, in the fiftieth year of Jubilee (Lev 16:21; 25:8-55).[3] Sin is finally and fully dealt with in this ultimate Jubilee. Corresponding to the removal of sin, is the gift of everlasting righteousness, which brings to completion all the prophetic hopes of the Scriptures and culminates in the dedication of sacred space. The entire earth will be holy when God's righteousness will be established. God's rule will finally be realized on earth at the end of the ages.

ESTHER AND KINGDOM "ABSENCE"

After this description of the future prospect of the kingdom of God, the next book, Esther, reveals the present gap between the kingdom as a present reality and its glorious future.[4] Jewish exiles living in Persia during its hegemony are on the verge of extermination. The burning question concerns the absence of any divine King, as the name of God is not even breathed in this book. But by using the literary device of irony, the writer indicates that although God is not mentioned by name, and although his kingdom seems very absent, he is actively present and is working through the historical

---

[3]Jubilee was the ultimate Sabbath, a time when all debts were canceled, all sins were forgiven, and land was restored to its original owners.

[4]Cf. the canonical order I am following here where Esther follows Daniel (Baba Bathra 14b).

process.[5] There is such a range of remarkable coincidences throughout the narrative that one would have to conclude that although God is visibly absent, he is palpably present.[6] The divine absence is so conspicuous that it implies a mysterious presence.[7]

God's absence can also be traced when Mordecai tells Esther that she must risk her life by seeking an audience with the king in order to save her people. He warns her that if she refuses to act, salvation will surely come from "some other place," which is probably a circumlocution for God (Esther 4:14). God has not given up on his people through whom he will manifest his kingdom to the world. The upshot is that Esther does save her people with her courage and ingenuity, and thus the people of the kingdom are preserved.

EZRA–NEHEMIAH AND KINGDOM DISAPPOINTMENT

The last book chronologically of the Old Testament is Ezra–Nehemiah and it details the return of the exiles from Babylon and the reforms that occurred in the new Persian province of Judah. It describes the return and its subsequent history from Cyrus's decree down to the time of Artaxerxes II. As it ends the Old Testament it seems full of hope. It is about building and rebuilding, about the kingdom of God. Restoration is happening. In line with earlier prophecies, many were probably expecting that the glory of the Lord would soon be revealed, and all flesh would see it together (Is 40:5).

The larger structure of both books of Ezra–Nehemiah emphasizes building in a centrifugal manner: the building of the temple, the building of the people, and the building of the city walls. God's rule and presence objectified in the temple works its way into the lives of the people and the entire city. All that is necessary now is for God to show up and bless his people so that Jerusalem would become the center of blessing for the entire world. The kingdom of

---

[5]The literary term that describes the processes is *peripety*: sudden reversals brought about in the nick of time that produce the opposite of their intention.

[6]For example, on a crucial night the king has insomnia and reads a chronicle where he discovers that his life was saved by Mordecai, for whom Haman has constructed gallows (Esther 5:14–6:2). Also, Haman prepares a script for his own glorification but it is used for his enemy, Mordecai (Esther 6:6-10). Haman eventually hangs on the gallows made for Mordecai (Esther 5:14; 7:8-10).

[7]Cf. Chloe T. Sun, *Conspicuous in His Absence: Studies in the Song of Songs and Esther* (Downers Grove, IL: IVP Academic, 2021).

God would be like that little stone that would grow into a great mountain and fill the entire earth, and all the kingdoms would be given to the authority of the Son of Man representing the saints of the Most High.

But one does not have to read very far into the text of these books to see disappointment. When the people see the current building of the foundation of the temple and compare it to what they knew of the previous temple, many of them grow disheartened and give up (Ezra 3:12-13). Then when Ezra returns, he finds that many of the people have become assimilated through intermarriage with the surrounding pagan population and they are not following the Torah (Ezra 9:1-15). Reform takes place, but the last chapter of Ezra simply notes those guilty of such intermarriage and assimilation (Ezra 10:18-44).

Later, Nehemiah returns from the capital city of the Persian empire to burned down walls and burned-out lives in Jerusalem. He rebuilds the city's walls despite much opposition, and he institutes reforms in the land, and dedicates the walls to the Lord (Neh 1–12). After accomplishing much he returns to the Persian capital. When he returns to Jerusalem sometime later, he finds a people who no longer keep the Torah, whose children can no longer speak Hebrew as a result of cultural and religious assimilation through intermarriage. He is exasperated (Neh 13:1-29). The kingdom of God does seem a distant reality. What about the prophetic word? What about the hope? These hopes seem like beautiful ships dashed against the rocky shore of reality. That reality is what has revealed its ugly form at key junctures repeatedly in the narrative: the intractability of the human heart. After the people build the city walls, Ched Spellman astutely observes:

> The towering walls have been rebuilt; but the most lethal enemy of the people resides within them. Ezra-Nehemiah's final warning to its readers is clear: *Remember who the real enemy is.* As one of Tolkien's characters in *The New Shadow* notes, "a man may have a garden with strong walls . . . and yet find no peace or content there. There are some enemies that such walls will not keep out."[8]

---

[8]Ched E. Spellman, "Nehemiah's New Shadow: Reading and Rereading the Ezra-Nehemiah Narrative," *Southeastern Theological Review* 9 (2018): 22, emphasis original.

CHRONICLES: A CONCLUDING SUMMARY AND HOPE

The final book that closes the Hebrew Scriptures is Chronicles, though it is chronologically prior to Ezra–Nehemiah.[9] It ends where Ezra–Nehemiah begins (2 Chron 36:22-23; Ezra 1:1-3). Ezra–Nehemiah postdates the exile, and Chronicles mainly records events down to the exile. Its last recorded words are those that begin Ezra–Nehemiah.

The position of Chronicles after Ezra-Nehemiah is probably not accidental for it functions as a concluding summary of the entire Old Testament, as Jerome once remarked, a recapitulation of the entire biblical narrative.[10] Thus it begins with Adam, the first human being in the first book of the Bible, and ends with the words that begin the last book chronologically in the Hebrew Bible (2 Chron 36:22-23; Ezra 1:1-2). It commences with nine chapters of genealogies and when it ends, King David arrives, and his life becomes the focus. It is as if all history is a preface to David, with whom God made an everlasting covenant, ensuring the perpetuity and glory of a Davidic kingdom. The story follows David's life and then the reign of Solomon and the subsequent Davidic kings. None of the Israelite kings of the north are really considered in this history. Consequently, this book is about the house of David: the Davidic dynasty and the house that David wanted to build but was left for his son Solomon to construct. At the end of this book, when it seems that the whole dream of the kingdom of God on earth is over, since there is no more temple, king, and land, the Chronicler introduces Jeremiah's prediction of seventy years of exile and Cyrus's decree:

> The land enjoyed its sabbath rests; all the time of its desolation it rested, until the seventy years were completed in fulfillment of the word of the LORD spoken by Jeremiah.

> In the first year of Cyrus king of Persia, in order to fulfill the word of the LORD spoken by Jeremiah, the LORD moved the heart of Cyrus king of Persia to make a proclamation throughout his realm and also to put it in writing:

[9]This is according to the sequence found in Baba Bathra 14b of the Talmud, which may be one of the earliest sequences.

[10]Jerome, *Prologus Galaetus*, often translated as "Helmeted Prologue of Kings," is Jerome's preface to *Liber Regum*, his Latin translation of 1–2 Samuel and 1–2 Kings.

> "This is what Cyrus king of Persia says:
>
> "'The LORD, the God of heaven, has given me all the kingdoms of the earth and he has appointed me to build a temple for him at Jerusalem in Judah. Any of his people among you may go up, and may the LORD their God be with them.'" (2 Chron 36:21-23)

The book ends on the note of exile, even though from its perspective there are many exiles who have returned (1 Chron 3:17-24, cf. 1 Chron 9). Accordingly, it draws attention to the fulfillment of Jeremiah's prediction of seventy years of exile (2 Chron 36:21), which itself draws on the Torah's curse for disobedience (Lev 26:34-35). One cannot help but think of the future fulfillment of all those prophetic promises regarding Jerusalem, the Davidic scion, and the temple. Cyrus, to whom all earthly authority has been given as God's appointed agent, concludes the Bible with a command for exiles to return to build the divine temple where God's throne will be set up once again. One cannot help but remember Daniel's reinterpretation of the seventy years as being the ultimate Jubilee—the time limit when the kingdom of God will finally come to the earth in all its fullness. The eschatological clock to the ultimate year of Jubilee has begun to tick, and thus, from the perspective of the Hebrew Bible, this would encourage hope for the return of the kingdom.

DISCUSSION QUESTIONS

1. How could the book of Esther help you understand your role in a secular culture?

2. What difference does the placement of Chronicles at the end of the Hebrew Scriptures make?

Chapter Fourteen

THE CENTER OF THE BIBLICAL STORYLINE, PART 1

THE GOSPEL OF MATTHEW

AFTER THE END OF ISRAEL'S SCRIPTURES, it is evident that the glory prophesied by the prophets and the cataclysmic judgment and salvation did not occur. Ezra and Nehemiah indicate the frustration and the heartbreak of unrealized eschatology. Later, during the Maccabean period, there was a time of intense persecution, when tracts for the times like the book of Daniel became electric with relevance. Under Antiochus Epiphanes, a Greek ruler, there was a concerted attempt to assimilate the Jews to Greek culture. Copies of Holy Scriptures were burned, the temple was desecrated, the gymnasia became more important than the synagogues and spiritual disciplines, and many Jews were killed (1–2 Macc). The rebellion of the Maccabees and the rise of devoted people of faith, the Hasidim, led to an all-out war against this effort, which achieved a measure of success with a rededicated temple and the Jews under the Maccabees gaining some measure of independence. But all of this ended in 63 BC. The Roman general Pompei conquered Judea and established a state under Roman rule and under which many Jews were oppressed and embittered. The Jews were in exile even though they were in their homeland.

From the writings of early Judaism there seem to be several concerns. Some may have given up hope but for many the prophetic hope of a Davidic scion who would bring about a universal peace was very much politically and theologically alive, particularly hope that a conqueror would liberate the Jews from oppression. The current dire situation of the Jews emphasized this political salvation. The Psalms of Solomon, a Jewish document written in the second and first centuries BC, reveal some of the current eschatological beliefs. For example, consider the seventeenth psalm with its focus on kingship and kingdom:

> See, Lord, and raise up for them their *king*, the son of David, *to rule over* Israel, your servant, in the time which you chose, O God. Undergird him with the strength to destroy the unrighteous rulers . . . to crash the ar-rogance of sinners like a potter's jar; to smash all their substance with an iron rod; to destroy the lawless nations with the word of his mouth. . . . *He will judge* peoples and nations in the wisdom of his righteousness. And he will have gentile nations serving him under his yoke and he will glorify the Lord in [a place] visible [from] the whole earth. . . . And he will be *a righteous king* over them, taught by God. There will be no unrighteousness among them in his days, for all [will be] holy, and *their king* [*will be*] *the Lord Messiah*. For he will not trust in horse and rider and bow, nor will he multiply his gold and silver for war. Nor will he narrow for many na-tions the hopes to a day of war. *The Lord himself is his king*, the hope of the strong. . . . This is the beauty of *the king of Israel* which God knew, to raise him over the house of Israel to discipline it. (Pss. Sol. 17:22-46, Brenton translation)[1]

Such a psalm is rife with quotations from the Hebrew Bible, a virtual catena of such statements. The psalmist cites Psalm 2 with the coming king's de-struction of the rebellious nations like a potter's jar, and the smiting of the lawless with an iron rod (Ps 2:9). Similarly, his rejection of trusting in horse and rider and bow, and his lack of interest in multiplying gold and silver draws on the law of the king in Deuteronomy 17:16-17. Other texts from this

---

[1]Emphasis added.

period also point to the eschatological temperature rising among different Jewish groups (e.g., 2 Esdr 13; 1 En. 46; 4Q248 II).

THE BEGINNING OF THE NEW TESTAMENT PERIOD

By the time the New Testament period arrives, and Jesus is born, a melting pot of views is full to the brim and the eschatological temperature has reached a boiling point. Or to use another metaphor, the political and religious situation in Judea is extremely volatile—Judea is like a powder keg ready to explode. The explosive intensity can be seen throughout the Gospels in the supercharged atmosphere. Not only is the little Roman province of Judea chafing under Roman rule, but Jesus almost has to walk on eggshells to avoid aligning himself with particular religious and political views (e.g., Mk 12:13-17).

This probably explains the reluctance of Jesus to declare his messianic identity in the Gospels. He fundamentally disagreed with the purely political understanding of the Messiah by his contemporaries and did not want to be prematurely drawn into a confrontation with the authorities before his ministry was finished.[2]

Of course, there are examples of these proverbial land mines exploding in the New Testament. A paramount example is John the Baptist's ministry. Using Old Testament prophecies, John preached the coming of God's kingdom, which attracted a large following in the desert, inflaming eschatological fervor (Mt 3:1-12). But his criticism of the ruler in Galilee at the time, Herod Antipas, over his adultery with his brother Philip's wife, Herodias, and Herod's consequent divorce of his own wife to marry his paramour, led to his imprisonment and eventual execution (Mt 14:1-12).

In another example, Jesus refers to Pilate's slaughter of worshipers on the temple mount (Lk 13:1-2). No extrabiblical knowledge of this exact historical incident exists, but other examples around this time attest to rulers gratuitously murdering Jews to demonstrate their authority and to quench the fires of potential rebellion. Josephus writes of Archelaus slaughtering three thousand Jews in Jerusalem at the time of the Passover because of their

---

[2]This is a better explanation than Wilhelm Wrede's theory of the messianic secret, that this reluctance on the part of Jesus is due to the early church's explanation for his failure to declare his identity. See Wrede, *The Messianic Secret in the Gospels*, trans. J. C. G. Greig (Cambridge, UK: Clarke, 1970).

protests of injustice over the deaths of previous Jewish leaders (Josephus, *Ant.* 17.9.3). Later, a Galilean named Judas took political action in influencing people not to register for the Roman census because it constituted religious treason. This action resulted in a bloody backlash by the Roman authorities (Josephus, *Ant.* 18.1; Acts 5:37).

Thus by the time of the New Testament period of first century Palestine, eschatological fervor abounds in anticipation of the coming kingdom of God. I want briefly to consider the structure of the New Testament canon to see if there is any way to gain some insight on a more developed and mature understanding of the kingdom of God "after the dust had settled" and when the early church was born.

NEW TESTAMENT STRUCTURE

In the initial structure of the New Testament,[3] there are four Gospels followed by the Acts of the Apostles. The four Gospels focus on the life of Jesus of Nazareth and are so closely related to each other that Acts is separated from the Gospel of Luke, even though it forms its sequel as volume two of its history. John, the fourth Gospel, displaces Acts and forms the conclusion to the Gospels with its unique style and emphasis. The Gospels present the story of Jesus of Nazareth—the Messiah—from four different perspectives, and Acts presents a history of the messianic community—the church—the "body" of Jesus of Nazareth. Both the collection of Pauline letters and the Catholic corpus of letters follow the Gospels and Acts. They present teaching for the various communities in how to live the life of the kingdom in this present age as they await the kingdom's consummation at the end of history. The book of Revelation concludes the New Testament and signals this consummation, bringing about a complete unity between heaven and earth.

The very structure of the New Testament points to the centrality of Jesus of Nazareth—his birth, life, death, and resurrection. He is the kingship of God returning to Zion, ushering in the promised kingdom of the Old

---

[3]For the complex development of this overall structure, which only emerges later, see E. Gallagher and John Meade, *The Biblical Canon Lists from Early Christianity* (Oxford: Oxford University Press, 2017), 30-56.

Testament hope. The account of his life, death, and resurrection is repeated four different times to show its importance in the overall structure of the Christian Bible. Jesus has become the central focus.

To be sure there are significant differences between the Gospels, and particularly between the Synoptics (Matthew, Mark, Luke) and John, but the fourfold narrative repetition of the life of Christ is unparalleled in the Scriptures. The only significant comparison in the Old Testament are the two histories of the kingdom in Samuel–Kings and Chronicles. Christ is thus the goal of the Old Testament. And if the Old Testament hope was all about the king coming to Jerusalem, the return of the King to Zion to establish his kingdom, then somehow these four Gospels relate to this fact.

MATTHEW

The kingdom of God is the main theme throughout the Synoptic Gospels, which form the foundation of the New Testament. In fact, the phrase *kingdom of God*, and similar expressions, occurs over one hundred times in these documents.[4] As Matthew is written for a Jewish audience it clearly parallels the Old Testament as it begins, "This is the book of the genesis of Jesus Christ, the son of David, the son of Abraham" (Mt 1:1). Here begins a new Genesis, a new beginning. It is not only a new Genesis, but also a new Torah. Jesus' speeches are structured in five discourses, paralleling the foundational document in Judaism, the Torah (Mt 7:28; 11:1; 13:53; 19:1; 26:1).[5] Matthew presents Jesus as a new Moses with a new Torah, which he also announces from a mountain (Mt 5–7). In other places in the book, Jesus appears on a mountain where he reveals his nature, whether it is the Mount of Transfiguration (Mt 17), the Mount of Olives (Mt 26:30), or the mountain of Galilee from which he commands the Great Commission (Mt 28:16-20).

---

[4]Matthew frequently uses the term "kingdom of heaven," which probably represents a Jewish respect for avoiding the divine title, and it also may well represent the idea of heaven's rule finally coming to earth. For the use of *heaven* as a circumlocution for deity, see Craig Evans, *Matthew* (Cambridge: Cambridge University Press, 2012), 90-91.

[5]The five main sections are each closed with similar phraseology and are enveloped by a prologue and an epilogue.

THE PERFECT SEGUE

But Matthew is the Gospel par excellence presenting Jesus as the fulfiller of the Old Testament prophecies, the long-awaited messianic Son of David, the king of Israel and the nations. As such it perfectly segues into the New Testament. Like Genesis and Chronicles, the first and last books of the Hebrew Bible, respectively, Matthew begins with a genealogy. And like Genesis, it closes with a prophecy of a ruler of the nations from Judah's line (Gen 49:8-12), thus culminating in the goal of the genealogical structure of the book. The Matthean genealogy rapidly focuses on this royal line after introducing Abraham (Mt 1:3-17).

The book of Chronicles spotlights the Davidic line in its genealogy since it only begins its narrative story with the arrival of David.[6] Likewise, Matthew's genealogy is structured according to David: from Abraham to David, from David to the exile, from the exile to the birth of the Messiah (Mt 1:2-6, 7-11, 12-16). At its beginning, Matthew follows the genealogy of Abraham, who was promised a descendant through whom the whole world would be blessed, to show the universal blessing that would come with the birth of Christ. But Christ is not only the son of Abraham, he is also the Son of David. God's covenant with David anticipated a descendant who would rule the world and thus be the agent of universal blessing. If anyone would miss this connection with Abraham and David, all they would have to do is look to Psalm 72 where the climax presents the Davidic king as the one in whom all the nations of the world would find a blessing (Ps 72:17).

Matthew's forty-two-member genealogy zeros in on the goal of the Hebrew Scriptures, the goal of Israel: the kingship of Jesus. Kingship and the number fourteen (forty-two being a multiple) are key characteristics of this genealogical line that highlight the kingship of David. There are fourteen generations from Abraham to David, fourteen from David to the exile, and fourteen from the exile to the birth of Jesus the Messiah. The Hebrew letters of David's name add up to the number fourteen. Jesus is the new David, the new King of the kingdom of God. As the culmination of

---

[6]Walter Brueggemann, *David's Truth in Israel's Imagination and Memory* (Philadelphia: Fortress, 1985), 100.

Matthew's genealogy, he is viewed as the Christ, the anointed one of God, the Messiah (Mt 1:16-17).

Jesus is the goal of the Israel's Scriptures. If it is true that the structure of the last book of those Scriptures presents David as the one for whom all history has been waiting,[7] then it is doubly true of Matthew's introduction to his Gospel.

But Matthew probably has another point to make with his genealogy that reflects on Daniel's seventy weeks, which when completed would usher in the ultimate Jubilee, God's perfect kingdom. As N. T. Wright observes, this moment had come with Jesus. Not only could Israel's entire history be summed up in three groups of fourteen generations, but also in six sevens. When Jesus arrives, the seventh seven, "the jubilee in person," has come.[8]

FULFILLMENT OF PROPHECY

As if to underline that this moment has arrived, the subsequent narrative first describes Jesus' miraculous birth, which is far more phenomenal than the birth of the first child of promise, Isaac, and the many miraculous births in the Old Testament (Mt 1:18-20). Here there is a *virgin* birth, and the child's name is to be called Joshua, for like the previous one he will be a Savior, but he will deal with the real problem in human history, not just the salvation from political enemies, but from spiritual ones, from one's own sins (Mt 1:21). Thus, the problem of the intractably evil human heart will be finally solved. Then comes a string of prophecies that this Messiah fulfills: his birth means that God is with his people again, not for a moment, but forever (Mt 1:22; 28:20).

The Magi following a star from the East leading to the birthplace of Jesus in Bethlehem are the fulfillment of Balaam's prophecy—a star would rise and smash the head of God's enemies (Mt 2:1-2). His birth in the Davidic hometown of Bethlehem fulfills an ancient prophecy of Micah about a universal ruler (Mt 2:5-6; cf. Mic 5:2-4 [Heb. 5:1-3]). Herod's massacre of infants there and the devastating grief of their Jewish mothers is not an arbitrary act

[7]Brueggemann, *David's Truth*, 100.
[8]N. T. Wright, *How God Became King: The Forgotten Story of the Gospels* (New York: HarperOne, 2012), 71.

but together manifests the wrath of the Serpent against the woman's seed. It also relives the grief of Rachel's death in the throes of childbirth, and the personification of her mourning for her distant grandchildren as they experience the suffering of exile (Mt 2:16; cf. Gen 3:15; 35:16-20; Jer 31:15). The flight of the holy family to Egypt to escape Herod's wrath shows the young boy identifying with his people by going down to Egypt and experiencing his own exodus (Mt 2:15; cf. Hos 11:1). Even the fact that the family settles in Nazareth fulfills prophetic texts (Mt 2:23; cf. Is 11:1 [most probably]). The point is clear. This child is no ordinary Israelite: he is Israel and the Son of David par excellence. By their actions both the Magi and King Herod see very clearly: this birth is about kingship and kingdom, and it means there can be no neutrality: either worship or murder.

BAPTISM AND TEMPTATION

John the Baptist, the last of the line of the prophets, moves on to this new stage of history as the herald of this new king and his kingdom. His message is a withering warning for people to prepare for the arrival of this new world order: "Repent for the kingdom of heaven has drawn near" (Mt 3:1). This is no time for hesitation or equivocation. Immediate action is required.

This is underlined when John meets Jesus and baptizes him (Mt 3:13-17). John recognizes him as the Coming One, the King, the One for whom he is preparing the way. Thus, when Jesus is baptized, identifying with sinners, three signs occur that mark this new era of the beginning of the eschatological reign of God: (1) the splitting of the heavens, (2) the sealing of the Spirit, and (3) the divine voice giving its imprimatur on his person.[9] The divine voice speaks nothing new but simply rehearses Israel's Scriptures. Citing Psalm 2:7, the heavenly voice identifies Jesus as the Davidic king to whom the entire earth will be allotted. Using words from Isaiah 42:1, Jesus is identified as the divine servant in whom the nations will put their trust. The long-awaited kingdom has advanced in a decisive phase.

---

[9]In Mt 3:17, the divine voice declares, "This is my beloved Son." The word *beloved* probably indicates the suffering ahead of Jesus as it evokes Abraham's beloved Isaac who experienced the ordeal of sacrifice. Cf. Ralph Martin, *Mark: Evangelist and Theologian* (Grand Rapids: Zondervan, 1973), 128.

After his baptism, Jesus is led by the Spirit into the wilderness where he fasts for forty days before he begins his ministry. In some ways he is reliving the experience of his people who wandered in the wilderness for forty years, Moses who fasted for forty days before being given the law on Mount Sinai, and Elijah who traveled for forty days without food and water before being given a revelation on the same mountain. But there is a logic here. Before the new Adam can begin his mastery of the creation and his announcement of the kingdom, he must meet the current occupier of the throne of the human kingdom, the Prince of Darkness. And it is here where Jesus directly encounters the ruler of this world. The crafty Serpent tempts again, not in a luxurious Garden but in an arid desert (Mt 4:1-11; cf. Gen 3). Jesus has just heard the Father's voice assuring him that he is the Son of God, and now Satan tempts him to prove it by turning stones into bread to satisfy his personal hunger, and then to demonstrate his messianic status in spectacular fashion by jumping off the temple mount and seeing if God would save him with his angels, and finally by tempting him to circumvent his difficult mission to become king of the world by simply bowing down and worshiping Satan. In each case Jesus fends off every temptation by quoting Deuteronomy. What a human being needs most, he tells the tempter, is a word from God, not bread (Deut 8:3). Similarly, he declares that one should trust God's timetable, not presume on it by acting rashly (Deut 6:16). And finally, Jesus tells Satan in no uncertain terms that God alone will be worshiped (Deut 6:13). This is how Adam will become king again.

The meaning of this encounter must be viewed against the larger canvas of Scripture. Since he, the true Joshua, is coming into occupied territory, Jesus must deal with the illegal occupier. To win this battle he must reflect the true image of God: relying on the divine word, trusting in the divine plan, and submitting to and worshiping God to receive all the kingdoms of the world.

THE KING'S INVASION

When Jesus leaves the desert after defeating and dethroning Satan, he invades the devil's domain in the northern part of Judea, Galilee of the nations, and he begins to announce the coming of the kingdom. Indeed, his message is the same as the Baptist's: "Repent for the kingdom of heaven is near" (Mt 4:17).

Matthew regards this as nothing less than a fulfillment of Isaiah's ancient prophecy of a Davidic king who will become a universal ruler:

Land of Zebulun and land of Naphtali,
the Way of the Sea, beyond the Jordan,
Galilee of the Gentiles—
the people living in darkness
have seen a great light;
on those living in the land of the shadow of death
a light has dawned. (Mt 4:15-16 NIV; cf. Is 9:1-2)

The quote is a good example of an author using one part of a text to invoke a larger context. The passage in Isaiah continues:

For to us a child is born,
to us a son is given,
and the government will be on his shoulders.
And he will be called
Wonderful Counselor, Mighty God,
Everlasting Father, Prince of Peace.
Of the greatness of his government and peace
there will be no end.
He will reign on David's throne
and over his kingdom,
establishing and upholding it
with justice and righteousness
from that time on and forever. (Is 9:6-7 NIV [Heb. 9:5-6])

Hence, Jesus begins his healing ministry amid his preaching of the good news of the kingdom. Satan's kingdom is being despoiled. Jesus demonstrates this later when he is accused of being in league with Satan after the healing of a demon-possessed man (Mt 12:22-32). When the amazed crowd exclaims that Jesus must be the messianic king, the Son of David, the religious leaders claim that his power comes from the devil himself! Jesus shows the absurdity of the accusation by stating that Satan would never cast out Satan. Then he clinches his argument by declaring, "If I, by the Spirit of God, cast out demons, then the kingdom of God has come upon you." He elaborates, "Or again, how can anyone enter a strong man's house and carry off his possessions unless he first ties up the strong man? Then he can plunder his house" (Mt 12:28-29). The kingdom of God advances because the strong man in charge of the kingdom of darkness has been bound.

This is confirmed by the reaction of demons in their encounter with Jesus. When Jesus comes to Gadara and heals demoniacs (Mt 8:28-34), their demons cry out before their exorcism: "What do you want with us, Son of God? Have you come to torture us before the time?" The assumption is a coming day of judgment when the reign of God is established on the earth. They are fraught with fear that their end has arrived prematurely. When Jesus grants their wish to be expelled into a nearby herd of swine, they exit their tortured human captives, inhabit the pigs and race headlong down over a cliff into an abyss as a foretaste of their future judgment. This is positive proof that the kingdom of God is advancing further into enemy territory. Instead of mutilating themselves and living naked among the tombs, the demoniacs are liberated, clothed, and in their right minds (cf. Mk 5:1-20). This is kingdom come.

ROYAL WORKS

It is probably best to consider the works of Jesus in this context, and then consider his words. In Matthew alone there are twenty-one miracles performed for individuals, mainly healings. There are at least nine summary statements of miracles done for crowds of desperate people, whether sick, lame, epileptic, demon-possessed, or deceased. This was certainly one of the main reasons for his large following. Not only was he a charismatic teacher, but he was also an extraordinary miracle worker.

The miracles can be divided into nature miracles and healing miracles. But as the above exorcisms show, they demonstrate the inbreaking power of the kingdom of God. People afflicted by sin and disease are forgiven and healed, highlighting the fact that the kingdom had reached a decisive phase with the arrival of Jesus. Isaiah the prophet looked forward to this new age stating: "Then the eyes of the blind will be open, the ears of the deaf will hear, the lame will leap like a ram, and the tongue of the dumb will sing" (Is 35:5-6). In fact, when an imprisoned John the Baptist was reconsidering whether Jesus was the coming king or not, whose presence would usher in the new world order, Jesus sent back word via his disciples: "The blind receive sight, the lame walk, those who have leprosy are cleansed, the deaf hear, the dead are raised, and the good news is proclaimed to the poor" (Mt 11:5 NIV). Jesus allays John's doubts by telling him that the kingdom's arrival is even better than Isaiah ever dreamed.

The summary statements in Matthew demonstrate conclusively that these are proof of the kingdom's invasion into the world (Mt 4:23; 9:35).

By far the majority of the miracles are healings, while there are some nature miracles (Mt 8:23-28; 14:15-21; 14:22-33; 15:32-39; 17:27; 21:18-22). Almost all are positive, with only one being negative—the cursing of a fig tree (Mt 21:18-22). While the miracles show the compassion of Christ in helping the needy and the helpless, their fundamental intent is eschato-logical—they are signs of the inbreaking of the kingdom. They are intent on restoring the brokenness of creation. Death and disease are the result of the fall and the curse of creation. Jesus came to reverse the curse, and everywhere he goes he is doing this. In Isaiah's classic description of the return from exile, the prophet declares:

> Behold your God will come with vengeance, the recompense of God will surely come and he will save you. Then the eyes of the blind will be opened as will the ears of the deaf . . . for waters will burst forth in the desert and streams in the desert. . . . There will be a highway and a road called the highway of holiness, . . . and the unclean will not walk on it and fools will not wander there, nor lions and wild beasts. . . . But the redeemed of Yahweh will return and come singing to Zion and everlasting joy will be on their heads! (Is 35:4-10)

Similar language is found in other passages, such as Isaiah 65:17-25 and Isaiah 61:1-2, where Yahweh's servant makes the proclamation of the year of Jubilee.

In the longest citation of Israel's Scriptures in Matthew, Jesus is regarded as Yahweh's royal servant who heals the sick and the destitute and desires no acclaim. He is a different type of king bringing about a new world order—one in which even the Gentiles will hope (Mt 12:16-21; cf. Is 42:1-4)! Thus, when this king heals the sick, he does more than heal them; like the royal servant he absorbs the evil associated with the sickness:

When evening came, many who were demon-possessed were brought to him, and he drove out the spirits with a word and healed all the sick. This was to fulfill what was spoken through the prophet Isaiah:

> "He took up our infirmities
>   and bore our diseases." (Mt 8:16-17 NIV; cf. Is 53:4)

This anticipates his greatest act of saving people from their sins: the cross is intimately connected with the kingdom. Several features lead to this conclusion. On the way to Jerusalem, just before he and his disciples arrive, Jesus must educate his disciples who are expecting a certain type of kingdom, one that dazzles with power, and will spectacularly throw off the yoke of Rome (Mt 20:20-28). Some of them wish to be able to sit at his right and left hand in the new kingdom. Jesus gives them a quick lesson: different values are at work in his kingdom than the kingdoms of the world, where the driving force is upward mobility, where people push, shove, and step on others to climb to the top. People move in the opposite direction in his kingdom. Downward mobility is the norm, and Jesus is the great example. The "Son of Man did not come to be served but to serve and give his life as a ransom for many" (Mt 20:28). Here Jesus combines two texts from the Old Testament: (1) the heavenly Son of Man from Daniel 7 to whom all the kingdoms of the world are given, and (2) the suffering royal servant in Isaiah 53 who suffered in the place of many sinners so that they could be righteous (Dan 7:13-14; Is 53, esp. Is 53:12).

This is all confirmed at the Passover seder with his disciples, their last meal together. The Passover was the liberating act that brought about complete freedom from Egyptian slavery. In every Egyptian home there was death: the firstborn male died. But in Israelite homes a firstborn lamb or goat died instead of a person because the blood of the lamb was splattered on the doorposts and lintels, signaling to the angelic destroyer that a substitute had been slain in the place of a person. Thus, when Jesus signals for his disciples to drink from the cup of wine at the Passover, he says: "This is my blood of the covenant, which is poured out for many for the forgiveness of sins" (Mt 26:28 NIV). This is the definitive interpretation of his coming death on the Roman cross.

The fact that this is inextricably tied with Daniel 7 is shown by Jesus' trial where he confesses that he is the Son of Man who is coming in his glory (Mt 26:64). The subsequent crucifixion and horrendous suffering culminating in divine abandonment occurs not for his own sins but for those of the world. This is absolutely necessary for the establishment of the kingdom. Jesus cites the beginning of Psalm 22 ("My God, My God, why have you forsaken me?"), expressing the ultimate intensity of pain and anguish (Mt 27:46). Yet his cry from Psalm 22 implies the rest of the psalm, particularly its concluding thrill of triumphant victory and thanksgiving that God's kingdom has been firmly founded:

> All the ends of the earth
>> will remember and turn to the LORD,
> and all the families of the nations
>> will bow down before him,
> for dominion belongs to the LORD
>> and he rules over the nations. (Ps 22:27-28)

Thus, after the resurrection, Jesus' exaltation is complete, as he declares to his followers that he has received all authority in heaven and on earth. He is Daniel's Son of Man, and he commands his disciples (the saints of the Most High) to go to all the nations as his representatives, teaching them everything he has commanded them (Mt 28:18-20). The cross and the kingdom are crucially linked as forgiveness is offered and obedience is the result. A new world has dawned with a new Ruler.

ROYAL WORDS

As some of the above illustrations show, throughout Matthew's Gospel Jesus' words confirm his view of the kingdom. Arguably the most well-known discourse of Jesus in Matthew is the Sermon on the Mount, which probably distills the essence of everything he commanded (Mt 5–7). When viewed independently of the kingdom of God, it becomes a simple source of ethical preaching and exhortation. In its context, however, as the first major teaching of Jesus following a summary of his miraculous works, it is a virtual announcement of the constitution of the kingdom, of a new way of living in the world under a new King. As Moses gave Israel its Torah from Mount Sinai when the nation was constituted as a priestly kingdom, Jesus ascends a mountain and brings his Torah to his people.

Throughout his new Torah, the word *basileia* ("kingdom") appears eight times in significant contexts (Mt 5:3, 10, 19 [twice], 20; 6:10, 33; 7:21). The entire structure of the discourse frames this central idea. The initial Beatitudes are kingdom blessings, both present and future (Mt 5:3-10).[10] The first and last stress the present reality of the kingdom; the six in between, its future reality; and they all dramatically demonstrate that the kingdom is the opposite of all past and present kingdoms in the world. Citizens of this kingdom are those who are poor in Spirit—those who recognize their need for God, those mourning over loss, the meek and humble, those hungering and thirsting for God's rule in the world, the merciful, the pure in heart, the peacemakers, and those persecuted for the sake of righteousness. Those living out these qualities in the world will preserve it from corruption and shine in the darkness (Mt 5:13-16).

Jesus also shows how different this kingdom is from that of his religious contemporaries. The righteousness required for entrance into this kingdom is far more than the external righteousness practiced and sought by so many (Mt 5:17-20). What is required is a righteousness of the heart, where anger, lust, and vengeance are transformed into reconciliation, purity, and love; where hatred for enemies gives way to love; where private prayer is more important than public devotion; where alms are given before an audience of One; where fasting occurs without fanfare; and where doing the will of God is more important than anything else (Mt 5:21–7:27).

One of the prime petitions for prayer is the coming of the kingdom on earth as it is in heaven (Mt 6:10). As one scholar correctly remarks, Jesus teaching about the kingdom of heaven "is not about people going to heaven. It is about the rule of heaven coming to earth."[11]

Throughout his message Jesus compares his teaching to the great Moses. There are six antitheses that show the comparison: "You have heard that is has been said . . . but I say unto you" (Mt 5:21-22, 27-28, 31-32, 33-34, 38-39,

---

[10]The additional blessing in Mt 5:11-12 expands on the one in Mt 5:10.
[11]Wright, *How God Became King*, 43.

43-44). Repeatedly the antitheses imply that Jesus' kingdom is aiming at a transformation of the heart not just behavior, and this, like the command not to covet in the Ten Commandments, can only be enforced by God, not by human beings. Thus, it is not enough to forbid the external act of murder; one must deal with the anger and hatred that leads to it. It is not enough to prohibit the act of adultery; one must rid oneself of an adulterous heart. What is happening here is that Jesus aims at bringing to fulfillment the message of the prophets regarding the new covenant as a kingdom reality (Jer 31:31-34; Ezek 36:24-27). The law must be transcribed on the heart rather than on tablets of stone. A heart of stone must be exchanged for a heart of flesh. God's Spirit must inhabit the heart and bring about different desires.

To this end Jesus chooses his disciples deliberately to represent the calling out of a new Israel (Mt 10:1-6). "The call of the twelve [apostles] said, in language far easier to read than Greek or Aramaic, that this was where YHWH was at last restoring his people, Israel."[12] The exile was over, and God was setting up a new and decisive stage in his kingdom. They were sent out to announce the same message as Jesus: the kingdom of heaven is near (Mt 10:7).

Jesus' proclamation of the kingdom was in a distinct genre—it took the form of parables, that is, little picture narratives illustrating his kingdom mission, comparisons taken from daily life to illuminate spiritual realities.[13] They were intended to prod people to think, to burrow deep down into their minds, obscuring the message to the thoughtless, but enlightening the thoughtful. Matthew states that the use of parables was Jesus' main method of teaching about the kingdom (Mt 10:34-35). The presentation of seven of them in Matthew 13 is Matthew's way of distilling his teaching ministry.

The parables in Matthew 13 occur in three pairs climaxed by a seventh. The first pair deals with sowing and planting, and the gradual nature of the kingdom's growth (Mt 13:1-30, 36-43). The second pair presents the success of the kingdom despite small beginnings (Mt 13:31-35). The third pair describes the surprising, inestimable worth of the kingdom to all its recipients

---

[12]N. T. Wright, *Jesus and the Victory of God* (Minneapolis: Fortress Press, 1996), 431.

[13]One of the essential meanings of the Hebrew word *māšāl*, which the Greek word *parabolē* ("parable") often translates in the Septuagint, is a comparison with the meaning "to be like."

(Mt 13:44-46). The final parable reveals the separation that will take place at the final judgment (Mt 13:47-50).

It is worth taking a closer look at this text, which functions almost as a summary statement of Jesus' message about the kingdom, and in many ways embodies George Ladd's description of Jesus' message: "The mystery of the Kingdom is the coming of the Kingdom into history in advance of its apocalyptic manifestation. It is in short fulfillment without consummation."[14]

In the first pair of parables about sowing seed, the seed is the message of the kingdom (Mt 13:3-9). The kingdom is being planted, but there are different effects. Sometimes the word does not even penetrate the soil, but it is picked up by birds. Occasionally it lands on rocky soil and the growing plant cannot put down deep roots and eventually dies. At other times the word is sown among weeds and after springing up its life is choked out. Finally, when the word falls on good ground, it brings forth a great harvest, some thirty, some sixty, some one hundred times what is sown.

The point of the parable becomes transparent after Jesus' explanation (Mt 13:18-23). The kingdom of God will not come with shock and awe, as the Old Testament generally expected, but with the gradual nature of a farmer planting seed. Immediate disinterest is a sign of satanic opposition—the hard ground. Instant interest but eventual indifference is the result of either persecution (rocky ground) or the distractions of the age (weed-infested ground). But prolonged interest and fruitfulness is the result of the seed being sown in good soil. The right soil is the key so that is why Jesus often adds the important words about attentive listening to the end of his teaching: "Those who have ears to hear, let them hear!" (Mt 11:15; 13:9, 43). And although a harvest is guaranteed, there is a considerable *delay* between the planting of the seed and that harvest.

In the next parable about the sowing of the tares alongside the wheat, the growth of each alongside one another will be a feature to the end of the age (Mt 13:24-29). The tare or weeds represent "the people of the evil one," whereas the wheat signifies the people of the kingdom. Pulling up the tares, that is, the immediate elimination of evil, would inadvertently endanger the wheat/

---

[14]George Eldon Ladd, *The Presence of the Future: The Eschatology of Biblical Realism* (Grand Rapids, MI: Eerdmans, 1974), 222.

righteous. The consummation of the kingdom is delayed, enabling the kingdom to grow alongside evil.

Parables about planting lead into parables about success. Although the third parable continues the planting theme, it emphasizes the amazing growth of the kingdom: a tiny seed that eventually grows into a great tree, in which all the birds gather on its boughs (Mt 13:31-32). This represents the kingdom in its small beginnings growing into the largest tree. This parable's complement, the metaphor of a woman kneading a little leaven into a large mass of dough, makes the same point (Mt 13:33). The leaven eventually permeates the entire batch. From small beginnings the kingdom will gradually permeate the entire world.

In his third pair of parables, Jesus points out the surprising value of the kingdom and its cost to individuals. First, the kingdom is like a treasure found in a field, which someone discovers and, realizing its value, goes and sells everything to purchase the field, to gain the treasure (Mt 13:44). Or it is like a pearl merchant who discovers in his business dealings one pearl of great price, and then sells everything to acquire it (Mt 13:45-46). Jesus is teaching that nothing compares to the value of the kingdom. Selling all one's possessions is the wisest decision one could ever make.

The seventh parable functions as a climax (Mt 13:47-50). The hearer is transported to the end of history for the final judgment. The kingdom is like a net cast into the waters by fishermen searching for a great catch. After a while they haul in the nets and bring in the fish, the good and edible and the bad and inedible. The fish are then separated, the good kept and the bad tossed away. This parable speaks of the present reality of Christ's disciples casting out their gospel net of the kingdom, but the focus swiftly shifts to the end, and the final judgment when the righteous are separated from the wicked.

All of this is serious business. The final apocalypse is coming but the kingdom is present now, and one must realize that present responses entail eternal consequences. Thus, Matthew, in presenting this paradigm of Jesus' teaching ministry, stresses the different responses to the kingdom, the gradual nature of kingdom growth growing alongside a kingdom of evil, its success despite small beginnings, the inestimable value of the kingdom as well as its cost, and finally the separation of the righteous and the wicked at the end of the world.

After the last parable, Jesus offers a saying about how a scribe well versed in the kingdom can bring out from his storehouse treasures old and new (Mt 13:52). This is a reflection on the previous parables to show the continuity and discontinuity between Jesus' understanding of the kingdom and that of his contemporaries. Their basic understanding was a one-time sudden intervention at the end of time when the world would be put to rights. For the most part this is what a natural reading of the Old Testament suggests. The prophets largely focused on the final, visible stage of the kingdom. Jesus as the Master Scribe does not disagree with this (the old treasure), but he shows with his parables a new element: the kingdom has an invisible beginning and a gradual growth before its consummation. This also elucidates those texts in the Old Testament about the salvation of the nations.[15]

DISCUSSION QUESTIONS

1. Why do you think Matthew is the ideal segue from the Old Testament to the New?

2. Why do you think there is a gradual growth in the kingdom as opposed to an instant arrival?

---

[15]In other words, this is how salvation can take place. See the perceptive study by G. K. Beale and Benjamin L. Gladd, *Hidden and Now Revealed: A Biblical Theology of Mystery* (Downers Grove, IL: IVP Academic, 2014), 74-75.

Chapter Fifteen

THE CENTER OF THE BIBLICAL STORYLINE, PART 2

THE GOSPELS OF MARK, LUKE, AND JOHN

WITH MATTHEW AS THE IDEAL SEGUE into the New Testament, I wish simply to supplement its picture with some kingdom aspects of each of the other Gospels.

MARK: HIGHLIGHT REELS

The Gospel of Mark launches immediately into Jesus' ministry, opening (and closing) on the point that he is God's Son (Mk 1:1; 15:39). This Gospel has an air of immediacy: it as if the writer cannot wait to begin. He starts with John the Baptist's announcement of the kingdom in the desert. He does not linger over the temptation story but condenses it and keeps it moving from one scene to another. The hallmark of this Gospel is the word *euthys* ("immediately"). Mark uses the term forty-two times, and his narrative is more like a series of "highlight reels" from an action movie.[1] Jesus is a man of action more than a man of words, performing miracles and wonders.

---

[1] I owe this term to describe the action-packed narrative of Mark to my student, Jonathan Steeves.

At the beginning, demons recognize Jesus as "the Holy One of God" (Mk 1:24). At the end, a pagan Roman Centurion at the crucifixion realizes the same truth: "Truly this man was the Son of God" (Mk 15:39). Throughout, Jesus forbids the disclosure of his identity, to keep it a secret, so that the nature of his kingship would not be misunderstood. But the real turning point in Mark is Peter's declaration of Jesus as the Messiah (Mk 8:27-30). Peter can perceive his messianic identity through divine enlightenment, but he relies on his own reason to object vehemently to the prediction of Jesus' imminent death. Jesus sharply rebukes him because of his failure to understand the messianic mission (Mk 8:31-33). For Peter messianic identity means majestic authority, but for Jesus it first means suffering and death. Jesus has a more accurate and comprehensive understanding of Israel's Scriptures. Persecution must be the path of every follower of Jesus, at least to some degree (Mk 8:34-37).

In terms of the structure of this Gospel, Martin Kahler is probably correct to see it "as a passion narrative with an extended introduction," as almost one-half of the book narrates Jesus' last week in Jerusalem.[2] He is not only the triumphant Son of God who works miracles (Mk 1-8), he is the suffering Servant of God, who gives his life as a ransom for many (Mk 9-16). Again, Mark links kingdom and cross. This evokes language from Isaiah 52:13-53:12, where Isaiah's high and exalted servant descends to the depths of horrific death. He comes as Israel's king, but he has a different understanding of kingship entirely, with a different understanding of Israel's need. Israel's main problem is not deliverance from a human oppressor but from spiritual enslavement.

After a gradual revelation of his mission, Jesus now enters Jerusalem riding on a colt (Mk 11:1-11), a deliberate echo of the messianic king in Zechariah riding into the city proclaiming peace to the nations (Zech 9:9-10). The Zechariah passage itself is an intentional allusion to Jacob's prophecy of a ruler from the tribe of Judah who will rule the nations (Gen 49:8-12). Thus, the people cry, "Blessed is the coming kingdom of our Father, David!" (Mk 11:10).

---

[2]Martin Kahler, *The So-Called Historical Jesus and the Historic Biblical Christ*, trans. Carl Braaten (Philadelphia: Fortress, 1964), 80n11.

Everything is related to the kingdom in this section. Jesus clears the temple of merchandise, for the King's palace has been violated (Mk 11:15-19). He curses a fig tree because it is not producing fruit, indicting Israel for not producing the fruit of justice and righteousness (Mk 11:12-14, 20-25). To those trying to trap him into siding with either the Roman Empire or the Jewish nation by asking him if taxes should be paid to Caesar or not, Jesus answers in kingdom language (Mk 12:13-17). Image indicates ownership, so a coin with Caesar's image belongs to Caesar. But this raises the more important question as to whose image is on each human being. A much greater payment—one's entire self—is owed to God. Similarly, a poor widow belongs to the kingdom because she gives her all (Mk 12:41-44). Moreover, to follow the law of love for God and love for neighbor brings one close to the kingdom (Mk 12:29-34, esp. Mk 12:34).

Consequently, it is not accidental that as Mark builds to his climax, Jesus' identity is finally publicly revealed. He is Israel's king, and he is enthroned by being crucified, lifted onto a cross (Mk 15:21-41). It is in this act of the nethermost possible service of suffering in the place of sinners that he is exalted. And it is a Roman soldier who witnesses his death with the exclamation, "Truly this man was the Son of God" (Mk 15:39). Thus, the Gospel of Mark returns where it all began: "The beginning of the Good News about Jesus the Messiah, the Son of God." But oh, what a difference between the beginning and the end!

LUKE: KINGDOM MANIFESTO

The Gospel of Luke assumes other circulating accounts of the life of Jesus and is written to reassure a recent Christian of the certainty of the things that he has believed. The author had examined these other texts and systematically presents his own study, together with a sequel, the book of Acts (Lk 1:1-4; Acts 1:1-3). As many scholars indicate, Luke has a strong interest in the universal mission of Christ, not just as a Messiah for the Jewish people, but also for the Gentiles. He also has an inordinate interest in God's concern for the marginalized: the least, the last, and the lost.[3]

[3]Ben Witherington III, *Invitation to the New Testament: First Things* (Oxford: Oxford University Press, 2017), 112-15.

Kingdom rumblings begin with the miraculous birth narratives of John the Baptist and Jesus, which echo the extraordinary births in the patriarchal narratives (Lk 1:5-80). The aged Elizabeth and Zechariah have a child, John, the herald of God's kingdom, and the announcement of the birth of his cousin to the virgin Mary escalates the miraculous by repeating the words given to a doubtful Abraham and Sarah: nothing is impossible with God (Lk 1:37).[4]

Another unique feature of Luke is the use of speeches at critical junctures in his Gospel to announce the kingdom. Mary's Magnificat (Lk 1:46-55) echoes Hannah's song (1 Sam 2:1-10), which viewed the birth of her son, Samuel, as reversing the status quo of historical inevitability with the divine inbreaking of God's kingdom. Zechariah prophesies that his son will usher in the promised Davidic kingdom (Lk 1:67-79).

While the word *basileia* ("kingdom") is nowhere used in Mary's song, the concept is everywhere: it is a kingdom manifesto. Recalling its Old Testament counterpart, she sees the irruption into history of a new divine government where the proud are humbled and the humble exalted, where the rich starve and the poor are filled. Her son's birth means a new reading of history. The upside-down world of power and oppression will be made right side up in mercy and justice because of the fulfillment of the covenant made with Abraham!

Zechariah's antiphonal response views the birth of his son in a similar light:

Praise be to the Lord, the God of Israel,
> because he has come to his people and redeemed them.
He has raised up a horn of salvation for us
> in the house of his servant David . . .
> to remember his holy covenant,
> the oath he swore to our father Abraham:
to rescue us from the hand of our enemies,
> and to enable us to serve him without fear
> in holiness and righteousness before him all our days.
>> (Lk 1:68-69, 72-75)

---

[4]Note the two passages: *mē adynatei para tō theō rhēma* (Gen 18:14 LXX); *hoti ouk adynatēsei para tou theou pan rhēma* (Lk 1:37).

Zechariah's poem complements Mary's with the focus on the deliverer, the horn of salvation raised up in the Davidic house, to bring about deliverance from enemies, forgiveness of sins, the end of darkness, the empowerment to pursue righteousness, and John as the forerunner of the king's return to Zion, in fulfillment of the Abrahamic covenant.

At the actual birth of Jesus, an angel, joined by an innumerable company— not just the few who announced miraculous births in Israel's Scriptures, announces the birth of all births, not in the luxurious halls of power, but on the forlorn hills of the little Judean town of Bethlehem to poor shepherds (Lk 2:8-15). And this announcement is good news for the world. And when the infant is presented at the temple for circumcision, an old prophet pronounces a blessing on the child described as God's salvation for all peoples (Lk 2:22-38).

After his baptism, but before the temptation in the wilderness, Luke inserts his genealogy of Jesus (Lk 3:23-38). This genealogy receives a very different placement than the one that introduces Matthew's Gospel. Luke's strategy is to show that the lineage of this King is traced back beyond David and Abraham, to the first king, Adam, who was a son of God.

> By calling Adam son of God [Luke] makes a link between the baptism and God's purpose in creation. Man was designed for that close filial relationship to God which was exemplified in Jesus, and which Jesus was to share with those who became his disciples.[5]

Jesus is returning as the true King Adam, the one the original Adam was intended to be.

The announcement of Jubilee. After his temptation in the wilderness, Luke presents Jesus returning to his hometown, to begin his ministry. This episode explains his future rejection by his own people and his embrace of a more universal audience. As Jesus reads from Isaiah in the synagogue, he specifically connects his mission with that of the one prophesied in the text:

> The Spirit of the Lord is on me,
>   because he has anointed me
>   to proclaim good news to the poor.

---

[5]G. B. Caird, cited in James R. Edwards, *The Gospel According to Luke*, ed. D. A. Carson, The Pillar New Testament Commentary (Grand Rapids, MI: Eerdmans, 2015), 124.

> He has sent me to proclaim freedom for the prisoners
>> and recovery of sight for the blind,
> to set the oppressed free,
>> to proclaim the year of the Lord's favor. (Lk 4:18-19 NIV; cf. Is 61:1-2)

In context, Jesus has just been anointed by the Spirit, and he has, by his defeat of Satan in the wilderness, gained access to Satan's "prison house" to proclaim good news to the poor, liberate the prisoners, give sight to the blind, and set the oppressed free. These words also hark back to the earlier poems about exalting the poor and humble (Lk 1:52) and shining light on those who live in darkness and in the shadow of death (Lk 1:79). But Jesus is also, as it were, taking the ram's horn and announcing the long-awaited ultimate Jubilee—the seventh seven is here![6]

When Jesus' announcement is met with radical rejection in his hometown, he uses the Scriptures to show that this is no surprise. A prophet is without honor in his own town (Lk 4:24), as shown by Elijah ministering to a Phoenician widow instead of many Israelite ones (1 Kings 17:8-24; Lk 4:25-26). Elisha heals a Syrian leper instead of curing Israelites afflicted with the same disease (2 Kings 5; Lk 4:27). The message is not lost on Luke's audience: the Jewish rejection of Jesus means the salvation of the Gentiles.

As Jesus leaves Nazareth, he preaches the message of the kingdom with words as well as exorcisms and other miracles (Lk 4:31-42). The nature of his ministry, while physical and material, has a profound spiritual and universal dimension. Indeed, throughout his ministry Jesus liberates few physical prisoners, but his good news leads to a revolution in forgiveness and reconciliation and the creation of a new community, a kingdom community.

Kingdom mission. The kingdom is impossible to miss in a few other key texts. Two missionary commissions stand out in the Gospel, the first commission for the twelve disciples followed by one for the seventy-two. Jesus gives the Twelve the authority to drive out demons, to cure diseases, to proclaim the kingdom of God, and to heal the sick (Lk 9:1-6). Later he sends out the seventy-two with a similar mission. They are to heal the sick and proclaim that the kingdom has drawn near (Lk 10:1-23). When they return, Jesus

---

[6]Note especially the link between Is 61:1 and Lev 25:10.

rejoices because he has seen the kingdom make a great advance in the enemy's domain: "I saw Satan falling like lightning from heaven. I have given you authority to trample on snakes and scorpions and to overcome all the power of the enemy; nothing will harm you" (Lk 10:18-19 NIV). But he warns his disciples that their significance does not lie in their defeat of Satan, but in their citizenship in the kingdom, that is, their names are written in heaven (Lk 10:20). Later Jesus explains his own exorcisms with similar language: they testify to the presence of the kingdom (Lk 11:20).

In Jesus' final missionary commission after his resurrection, his disciples are to be sent out to the world, not just to the nation of Israel. "Repentance and forgiveness for sins will be preached in his name to all nations" (Lk 24:47). But before this universal mission takes place, the Holy Spirit will come and empower his disciples.

Jesus holds together the presence of the kingdom and its future consummation without any difficulty. When asked by Pharisees when God's kingdom would come, he remarks that it is already present in their midst, but they have been unable to observe it. On the other hand, he remarks to his disciples in the same literary context that the kingdom will come with shock and awe, like the flood in Noah's day or like the judgment at Sodom (Lk 17:20-37). The kingdom is clearly present, but its full realization awaits the future, when the good news of the kingdom has reached the far corners of the world.

JOHN: SIGNS AND GLORY

John's Gospel has been recognized as fundamentally different from the previous Synoptic Gospels. There seems to be more theologizing in John. And instead of the rapid movement from place to place, John features long discourses. Instead of one journey from Galilee to Jerusalem there are three. Instead of the plethora of miracles that Jesus performs as signals of the inbreaking kingdom of God, there are only seven, and they function mainly as signs of the kingdom's presence in the world.[7] If people miss their signatory value, they miss their main point. Instead of one moment of transfiguration before some intimate disciples, the whole of Jesus' life is viewed as a

---

[7]Witherington, *Invitation to the New Testament*, 132-56.

transfiguration, of God setting up his tabernacling presence in the world. In fact, the book can be neatly divided into the following thematic sections after an initial prologue (Jn 1:1-18), which culminates in the statement that Jesus Christ is the exegesis of God: the book of seven signs revealing God's glory (Jn 1:19-12:50), and the book of glory revealing the ultimate sign of the cross and resurrection (Jn 13:1-20:31). A concluding epilogue has the resurrected Christ reinstating a disciple, indicating the sign by which he will glorify God (Jn 21:1-25). This book is about the exaltation of Jesus as the King of the universe.

Instead of beginning the Gospel with the baptism of Jesus, or his birth, or John the Baptist's birth, John begins back in eternity past, to indicate the ultimate origin of the gospel. "In the beginning was the Word . . ." (Jn 1:1) immediately connects the reader with Genesis 1. Instead of constantly referring to the kingdom of God, John refers to eternal life, which is both a present and future reality. As some scholars have observed, if the Synoptics consider what seems to be on the surface of Jesus' ministry, John provides more depth perception. It is not as if history is unimportant, but rather history is plumbed for its meaning.[8]

Kingdom confusion clarified. The first reference to the kingdom is found in John 3 and it refers to its present reality, which cannot be seen by the spiritually blind. Nicodemus, a Jewish leader, comes to Jesus by night to interview him about his teachings (Jn 3:1-14). He realizes that Jesus must be a deeply spiritual man, because no one can accomplish what he has done without the divine presence. Jesus tells him that unless he is born from above, he will not even be able to see the kingdom of God. In other words, it is not enough for Nicodemus to be a leader among the Pharisees with orthodox theology. He will not even be able to see the kingdom unless he has a spiritual rebirth. As the conversation continues, Nicodemus asks Jesus to explain this mystery, since it is impossible to enter again into his mother's womb. Jesus explains again that it is impossible to enter the kingdom of God unless he is born by water and the Spirit, since flesh gives birth to flesh and spirit to spirit. This is a direct reference to Ezekiel 36 where the prophet describes a spiritual

---

[8]N. T. Wright and Michael Bird, *The New Testament in Its World: An Introduction to the History, Literature, and Theology of the First Christians* (London: SPCK, 2019), 648-52.

revival of the exiles in which they will be sprinkled by clean water, cleansed from their sins, and given a new spirit and heart, that they may walk in God's ways and live under his rule (Ezek 36:24-27). This indicates that the kingdom is a present reality, but visible only to those with new eyes resulting from a spiritual rebirth. John intensifies here what Jesus said in the Synoptics, that one must become like a child to enter the kingdom (Mk 10:13-16).

The next explicit mention of the kingdom in John points to this present, spiritual reality. When Pilate interrogates Jesus, asking whether he is the king of the Jews, Jesus answers that his kingdom is not of this world, that is, not a kingdom wielding material power such as armies, police, and armaments. If it were, Jesus says, his servants would fight to prevent his arrest (Jn 18:36).

The "exaltation" of the King. The irony in the book of John is that Jesus takes up residence as king in the most humiliating, shameful, and degrading way possible. He is "raised to the heights" on the cross. This is directly related to the idea of kingship. Throughout the book there are seven "hour" sayings that show the temporal course of Jesus' life (Jn 2:4; 7:30; 8:20; 12:23, 27; 13:1; 17:1). Everything is headed for the revelation of glory on the cross. At critical moments John makes the point that this hour has not yet arrived and therefore Jesus cannot reveal his full glory or be taken captive by authorities (Jn 2:4; 7:30; 8:20). But finally in John 12, after Jesus enters Jerusalem on a donkey, being hailed as the Messiah, and later meeting Gentiles, he states, "Now the hour has come when the Son of Man is to be glorified" (Jn 12:23). He employs a metaphor to illustrate his approaching death: unless a grain of wheat falls into the ground and dies, it will not be able to generate a plant (Jn 12:24). It is with this death, that the ruler of another kingdom is decisively defeated (Jn 12:31-33).

The hour of exaltation arrives in climactic demonstration as Jesus' pain-racked body is lifted from the earth. Here is Israel's king, the suffering Messiah. By this atoning death, he provides forgiveness and healing for the world.

Paradoxically, Jesus crowned with thorns as king and lifted to the highest place of "honor" indicates that his miracles are not just arbitrary acts of power, but signs disclosing the reality of the kingdom. In fact, when Pilate presents Jesus to the Jews after his interrogation and before his crucifixion, he ironically declares, "Behold the Man!" (Jn 19:5). But for John there is a completely different meaning: here is God's original intention for humanity, the new Adam, the messianic King! Look and see the King![9]

Several of the seven miraculous signs in the book point to this exaltation. Indeed, when he turns the water into wine at the wedding at Cana, the idea of the later Communion meal, where Jesus represents his blood with wine, cannot be far from John's mind (Jn 2:1-11). When Jesus feeds the five thousand, he later says that he is the Bread of Life who gives life to the world (Jn 6:5-15, 25-35, 48-50). The Communion meal brought about by his death on the cross is foreshadowed, particularly, in his statement that the one who eats his flesh and drinks his blood experiences life (Jn 6:51-59).

Some of the seven signs intensify the opposition to Jesus that would lead to his death (Jn 5:1-18). Indeed, the seventh sign is the resurrection of Lazarus from the dead (Jn 11), the preeminent signal of the new age, but this sign also seals his fate on the cross: "So from that day on they [the religious authorities] plotted to take his life" (Jn 11:53 NIV).

An eighth sign, not mentioned explicitly, but there for all to see, is the resurrection of Jesus himself from the dead, a forceful exclamation of the arrival of the new age (Jn 20).

End time in the middle of history. Jesus' miracles are signs of the end time in the middle of history. His answer to Martha at the graveside of Lazarus confirms this. When Jesus says that he can raise the recently deceased Lazarus from the grave, Martha assents by saying that she knows he can raise him up at the last day. To which Jesus replies, "I am the resurrection and the life [right now], he that believes in me, though he were dead, yet shall he live [I will raise him up at the last day], but he that believes in me [now] will never die!" (Jn 11:24-25). And to show that this is not just left to the last day, Jesus confirms it with Lazarus's resurrection! The end of history has invaded the middle of history.

With Jesus' own resurrection the new creation has arrived. After the resurrection, he meets his disciples and breathes on them the Holy Spirit (Jn 20:19-23). This is a direct echo of the breathing into Adam the breath of life at the old creation, and the breathing into the army of exilic corpses the

[9]Alan Richardson, *The Gospel According to St. John: Introduction and Commentary* (London: SCM Press, 1959), 197.

Spirit in Ezekiel 37. The new creation has come. What is to be the distinctive message of those who will bring new life into people in the new creation? The announcement of forgiveness, amnesty. God is sending out his new humanity with a desire to save all humanity with the stunning news that by believing in Jesus Christ they can have eternal life—they can enter the kingdom (Jn 20:31)!

John's Gospel has been regarded as only being interested in realized eschatology. The last chapter, however, makes the point that his eschatology is also future. John 21 may well have been added after John died, as "a secondary epilogue after an original conclusion (Jn. 20:31), with a final editorial comment."[10] It recounts how Jesus commissioned Peter to be the shepherd of the early church. The chapter features Peter as the paradigm of the forgiven sinner, destined to be a martyr for Jesus (Jn 21:18-19). But Peter's question about the apostle John—which probably assumes for the reader the death of John or its imminence—and Jesus' answer indicate Jesus' future return. When Peter asks about the fate of the apostle whom Jesus loved, Jesus remarks, "If I wish that he should remain until I come, don't worry, you follow me!" (Jn 21:22). Jesus is clearly implying his second coming. Furthermore, the saying had currency in the early church, for many thought that this event would occur within John's lifetime, but this view is corrected by the author, as he explicitly remarks that this had been a false deduction (Jn 21:23).

DISCUSSION QUESTIONS

1. What do you think is the value of having four Gospels instead of one?

2. In John 21, the early church had deduced that Jesus would return within the apostle John's lifetime. What can you learn from this false deduction?

---

[10]Wright and Bird, *New Testament in Its World*, 659-60. See further, 660n66.

Chapter Sixteen

KINGDOM EXPANSION AND COMMUNITY

ACTS AND THE LETTER COLLECTIONS

THE ACTS OF THE APOSTLES extends the narrative of the Gospels past the death and resurrection of Jesus into the early Christian community. The resurrected and enthroned Jesus pours out his Spirit from on high into his disciples to extend the kingdom, first in Judea, then Samaria, then to the uttermost parts of the world (Acts 1:8). The letters of the apostles instruct the young churches in kingdom life and behavior as they wait for the new heavens and new earth.

THE KING EXPANDS HIS KINGDOM (ACTS 1:1–8:3)

The book of Acts begins with Jesus and his disciples speaking about the kingdom of God and ends with Paul preaching about the kingdom, and everywhere in between is about the kingdom (Acts 1:3, 6-8; 28:23, 31). When the first disciples gather after the resurrection, Jesus' main discourse is about the kingdom. They are specifically told to wait in Jerusalem for the gift of the Father, the baptism of the Holy Spirit. Concerned about the kingdom, they wonder if the kingdom of Israel will now be completely restored. Jesus deflects the question but says they will receive the power of the Holy Spirit and as a result become witnesses in Jerusalem, in all Judea, and Samaria, and unto the ends of the earth (Acts 1:4-8). In other words, they are looking for a restored *Israel*, but Jesus is looking for a restored *world*! This is a direct fulfillment of the prophetic words in Israel's Scriptures about the word of Yahweh going out from Jerusalem to the nations, the expansion of the Servant's task not only to restore the tribes of Israel but to bring salvation to the ends of the earth (Is 2:3; 49:6; Mic 4:2-3)! Then Jesus ascends to the heavens. The disciples, looking up at the sky, are told by two men dressed in white that he will someday descend from the heavens to inherit the kingdom in its fullness (Acts 1:9-10). His ascension does not mean simple departure, but enthronement and hence the ushering in of a new age. This is shown by his outpouring of the Spirit at Pentecost, when the linguistic confusion and chaos of the tower of Babel episode is reversed, as Jews from all over the then known world hear about the mighty acts of God in their own language (Acts 2:1-40).

The reversal of Babel. Genesis 10:1–11:9 is the backstory of Pentecost, where the scattering of the seventy nations over the earth was the result of the judgment of the tower of Babel. The building of a city and tower extending to the heavens as a monument to human arrogance created a false unity. The judgment of this towering symbol of pride, which defined itself as a gateway to the heavens, was the confusion of tongues that led to the division of humanity into many language groups. The miracle of tongues—speaking in a language unknown to the speaker—to all the various language groups gathered at Pentecost in Jerusalem, reverses Babel. All the people now hear the mighty acts of God in their own language. The speakers have all been baptized by the fire of the Holy Spirit, a clear fulfillment of John the Baptist's prophecy about the Coming One who would bring in the kingdom of God (Mt 3:1-3). One hundred and twenty disciples have tongues of fire on their heads as they receive this gift. They are not consumed by the flames but empowered. Instead of God speaking from one burning bush to send his servant on a mission to save his people, there are now 120 announcing a message of salvation to one and all.[1] Peter leaves no one in doubt that this is the sign of the last days. The new age has dawned as revelation is poured out on the old and young, male and female, irrespective of social class (Acts 2:17-21). The resurrection of Christ is the fulfillment of Scripture (Joel 2:28-32 [Heb. 3:1-5]), and now the ascension, says Peter, means that Christ is enthroned at the right hand of the Father and has poured out the Holy Spirit (Acts 2:33-34). The great day of the Lord has come, and people can now have their sins forgiven and a new relationship with God.

The consequence is a mass conversion and a new society where people eat together and share their possessions. There is no needy among them because of the generosity. They are a new family bound together by the apostle's teaching and the Holy Spirit. They are experiencing the kingdom of God (Acts 2:42-47; 4:32-35). Yet the kingdom has not arrived in all its fullness. Jesus will remain on his throne until the time for the restoration of all things (Acts 3:21).

A new king. The apostolic preaching provokes persecution from the Jewish leaders, but the nascent church is not deterred. They cite Psalm 2, which views the persecution arising by the installation of the recently anointed King who will someday rule over the earth (Acts 4:23-31). The assumption of this citation is that God's Holy Servant, Jesus, is God's Anointed Ruler, and the larger context indicates that he will one day inherit the entire world as his domain. The contrast between the present and the future is seen in the martyrdom of Stephen, who is stoned to death for his witness to Jesus. Before he dies, he sees Jesus standing on the right hand of the Father interceding for his servant on earth (Acts 7:55-8:1).

THE PROMISE FULFILLED (ACTS 8:4-13:41)

A new King now reigns on the throne of the universe. The message goes out to Samaria (Acts 8:4-25), to Africa through the Ethiopian eunuch (Acts 8:26-40), and finally through the conversion of Saul to the Gentiles, when he is struck down by the resurrected Christ on the way to Damascus to persecute Christians (Acts 9:1-31). When Saul and Barnabas participate

---

[1] I owe this image to a sermon by Timothy Keller, "Acts 2:1-13: The Descent of the Spirit" (November 25, 2012), https://gospelinlife.com/downloads/the-descent-of-the-spirit-6180/.

on their first mission to Asia, they travel first to the local synagogues, seeking to prove from the Jewish Scriptures that Jesus of Nazareth is the Messiah, the long-expected King foretold by the prophets (Acts 13:13-41). They show that at his resurrection Jesus fulfilled Psalm 2:7; that he fulfilled promises to David made in Isaiah 55:3; and that the ultimate meaning of Psalm 16:10 points to one of David's descendants, whom God was going to raise up from death to be king over the nations.

After planting churches, Saul and Barnabas return to visit the churches reminding them that "we must experience many hardships before we enter the kingdom of God" (Acts 14:22). Thus, there is both a present and future dimension of the kingdom in evidence. The churches exist now in the world as colonies of the kingdom (Phil 3:20-21), and are experiencing persecution, but the restoration of all things awaits the future (Acts 3:21).

KINGDOM GROWTH AND OPPOSITION (ACTS 15-28)

The Jerusalem Council in Acts 15 provides an insight into the present dimension of the kingdom. The council was called because of a controversy in the early church over the mission to the Gentiles, where many Jewish distinctives had been relaxed by Paul's mission, such as circumcision and dietary laws. The council concluded with an official declaration that the Gentile mission should proceed without the necessity of practicing these regulations since it is a direct fulfillment of the prophecy of Amos regarding the restoration of David's kingdom:

> After this I will return
>   and rebuild the fallen tent of David.
> From its ruins I will rebuild it
>   and raise it up again,
> so that the rest of mankind may seek the Lord,
>   as well as all the Gentiles whom I have claimed as my own.
> Thus says the Lord who is doing this,
>   as he made known from long ago. (Acts 15:16-18; cf. Amos 9:11-12 LXX)

The truth of this growing kingdom is not lost on the opponents of the early Christians, as they draw the right conclusions from the preaching. At Thessalonica Paul preached the message of Jesus as the Christ, the Messiah, from

the Jewish Scriptures. This brought the charge leveled at the Christians that
they had turned the world upside down, declaring that Jesus, not Caesar, was
the real king of the world (Acts 17:6-7).

At Athens Paul proclaims the importance of present repentance and a
final day of judgment presided over by God's appointed judge, whom he has
installed by his resurrection from the grave (Acts 17:31-32). At Ephesus Paul
preaches in the synagogue, arguing with his Jewish compatriots about the
truth of the kingdom of God (Acts 19:8). On his departure he describes his
time with Ephesian believers as one of urging Jews and Greeks to turn to
God and believe in the Lord Jesus (Acts 20:17-38). His mission has been to
"bear witness of the good news of God's grace" (Acts 20:24), which he further
describes as the "preaching of the kingdom" (Acts 20:25) and as the "whole
will of God" (Acts 20:26). Later, when imprisoned on trumped-up charges,
Paul declares his testimony before King Agrippa, explaining that the enthroned Jesus explicitly told him "to open their eyes [the Gentiles] and turn
them from darkness to the light and from the dominion of Satan to God, so
that through their faith in me they will experience the forgiveness of sins"
(Acts 26:18). What is this but kingdom language? Satan is a rival king, and
Jesus has come to dethrone him and liberate his captives.

In the conclusion of Acts the message of the kingdom has spread from
Jerusalem to Judea, to Samaria, to the very center of the Gentile world in
Rome. There under house arrest Paul witnesses to his fellow Jews, "testifying
to the kingdom of God and trying to persuade them about Jesus, arguing
with them from the Law of Moses and the Prophets" (Acts 28:23). When the
message is not accepted, Paul describes the kingdom as "this salvation" and
states that it has now been sent to the Gentiles. Thus, the book of Acts ends
with these words:

> For two whole years Paul stayed in his own rented house and welcomed all
> who came to visit him [under house arrest], proclaiming the kingdom of
> God and the truth about the Lord Jesus Christ with complete freedom and
> without hindrance from anyone. (Acts 28:30-31)

As the first half of the First Testament closed with Jehoiachin's release from
prison as a sign that God's kingdom project for the world had been revived,

so the first half of the Second Testament closes with another prisoner, Paul, this time under house arrest, preaching the kingdom of God. Paul is under no illusions that the seed of the Serpent is being crushed as he notes in the conclusion of his theological treatise to the Romans: "The God of peace will soon crush Satan under your feet" (Rom 16:20).

THE LETTER COLLECTIONS: KINGDOM LIFE AND HOPE

The letters of Paul and other apostles follow Acts, and there was the question whether the kingdom of God was as prominent in their theology as it was in their preaching. Some scholars had argued that Paul's theology presents a type of static state-like quality instead of the kingdom. Jesus is not a king in his theology, whereas king and kingdom are reserved for the Father. Instead of kingdom, Paul speaks of a country, a household, a family, a body, and so on.[2] However, the canonical structure of the New Testament, with Acts and the letter collections in close relationship, argues that the apostles found in Acts are the same as those linked to the letters. While the explicit references to the kingdom of God are not that prominent in the Pauline and Catholic Letter collections, it is surely because the concept of the kingdom is assumed, both as a present reality and a future hope.

PAUL'S LETTERS: A KINGDOM MESSAGE FOR THE WORLD

In general terms, the divergence between the Gospels and Paul in terms of kingdom terminology seems quite striking. For example, there are 105 occurrences of the term *kingdom* in the Synoptics and fourteen in Paul. Yet, it cannot be overlooked that there are thirteen references to the Holy Spirit in the Synoptics, and 110 occurrences in Paul. But, as James Dunn has astutely observed about these statistics, Jesus' kingdom focus has been effectively replaced by Paul's Spirit focus, because the kingdom has come in power![3] Pentecost is now a reality.

---

[2]F. J. Foakes-Jackson, "The Kingdom of God in Acts, and the 'City of God,'" *Harvard Theological Review* 12 (1919): 193-200.

[3]James Dunn, "Kingdom and Spirit," *Expository Times* 82 (1970) 36-40. I am indebted to Reuben Bredenhof and his insightful essay on "The Kingdom of God in Jesus and Paul" for alerting me to Dunn's article and its significance: www.academia.edu/45055938/The_Kingdom_of_God _in_Jesus_and_Paul.

Specifically, Romans, which begins the Pauline collection (probably because of its size), is the most systematic of Paul's letters in terms of his theology. Paul begins his letter to the Romans with the customary identity that he is a servant and apostle of Jesus Christ, chosen to preach the good news promised long ago in the Prophets. He is thus an emissary of the kingdom of God. He then announces that his king, Jesus, is a Davidic royal descendant according to his human nature but empowered to be the Son of God through his resurrection by the Holy Spirit. The purpose of Paul's apostleship is to lead a mission in which the nations would learn the obedience that comes through faith in Jesus Christ the king (Rom 1:3-6). If it means anything, this signifies that the nations can submit to the rule of Christ, by means of faith in the Messiah, and what he has done for the world. Paul closes his letter on the same note in his benediction that all the Gentiles might come to the obedience of faith (Rom 15:18). This surely means submission to the rule of Christ.

Throughout the letter Paul describes the human condition in the world as one where the Gentiles live as slaves in bondage to sin in a kingdom of darkness. Using the language of Genesis 1–3, Paul describes how humanity exchanged the truth of God for a lie by worshiping and serving the creature instead of the Creator (Rom 1:18-32). The Jewish situation was not much better. God provided a clearer revelation to them through the Torah, but the Torah was more of a diagnostic tool than a remedy, not only revealing sin but increasing its awareness (Rom 2:17-29). So, the seed of David, Christ, invaded the kingdom of darkness. Christ was judged in the place of a sinful humanity, and by means of faith he became a substitute for the believer, who can now have peace with God and be freed from bondage, serving a new ruler rather than sin (Rom 3–5).

Paul uses different analogies to describe what has happened. The first Adam sinned and introduced sin and death into the human race, but the second Adam obeyed God and introduced light and life into the world (Rom 5:12-21). The human condition apart from divine grace is in an insoluble dilemma: no one is capable of doing good and pleasing God. But now at the end of the ages, in the appearance of Christ, his atoning work on the cross and his resurrection have resulted in the gift of the Holy Spirit into the hearts of believers who now have been given a new nature by which they cry out to their new Master, "Abba Father!" (Rom 8). They realize a new way of being human, where they love God and love their neighbors as themselves, which sums up the law (Rom 12–13). In this way, they defeat evil with love rather than vengeance, they overcome evil with good, as they wait for the kingdom to come in all its fullness. They live under a new rule as they wait for the return of Christ.

Paul envisions this divine rule as not only contemporaneous with the rule of sin and death, but also being consummated in the future. Thus, while calling the Roman Christians not to be so concerned with their personal rights about eating and drinking, he reminds them of what characterizes the kingdom of God of which they are a part:

> For the kingdom of God is not a matter of eating and drinking, but of righteousness, peace and joy in the Holy Spirit, because anyone who serves Christ in this way is pleasing to God and receives human approval. (Rom 14:17-18 NIV)

He also speaks of the purpose of Christ's coming not only being to serve the Jews but so that the Gentiles should also praise God. Paul is interested in mission because "the Root of Jesse will spring up, one who will arise to rule over the nations; in him the Gentiles will hope" (Rom 15:12 NIV; cf. Is 11:1-10; 42:4 [LXX]). Thus, Paul has become a type of priest. By preaching Christ, he would bring the offering of Gentile praise, sanctified by the Spirit, to the divine throne (Rom 15:16). This is plainly a future reality when the kingdom will be completely realized.

This present and future tension runs through the Pauline collection. Thus, the Corinthian believers were once blinded by the god of this age, but now they have been enlightened by the word of God and the preaching of the gospel (2 Cor 4:4). By his resurrection Christ has become the king of a new kingdom, and he now reigns over the world and will reign until he subdues all his enemies in the future, including the last enemy—death. When this happens, he will hand the kingdom over to God the Father, and God will be all in all (1 Cor 15:20-28). Christians are reminded to avoid taking each other to court in front of pagans for one day they will judge the world, and wrongdoers will have no part in the future kingdom of God (1 Cor 6:6-10).

In Galatians Paul states that Christians have been rescued from the present evil age (Gal 1:4). The present evil age refers to a world controlled by a worldly point of view: *kata sarka* ("according to the flesh"). But the life of the kingdom is a life oriented by the Spirit of God, *kata pneuma* ("according to the Spirit"), characterized by particular fruit, namely: love, joy, and peace (Gal 5:16-26). Yet there is a future reality as well in which people who live *kata sarka* will not inherit the kingdom of God (Gal 5:21).

In Ephesians Paul states that Christ's resurrection has become a "game changer" as he has taken up a position above all principalities and powers, not only in the present but in the future (Eph 1). Thus, the resurrected and enthroned Christ resurrects the spiritually dead who have been under the domain of Satan. They have been translated from a kingdom of darkness where Satan and the flesh rule, to the kingdom of God's dear Son where the Spirit rules (Eph 2:1-10). This is a present reality, but at the same time they are warned that "no immoral, impure or greedy person has any inheritance in the kingdom of Christ and God" (Eph 5:5).

In the virtually identical Colossians, Paul describes a present and future reality in the same breath. He states that Christians have been granted a share in the inheritance of God's holy people in the kingdom of light (future), for "he has rescued us from the dominion of darkness and brought us into the kingdom of the Son he loves (present), in whom we have redemption and the forgiveness of sins" (Col 1:12-14). For practical living this means that the Spirit of Christ should rule in them, bringing about peace and love, so that they are being remade into God's image (Col 3:10-12). Thus, Paul's fellow coworkers, Aristarchus, Mark, and Justus, are "coworkers in the kingdom of God" (Col 4:10-11). Remarkably in this "throwaway" line, Paul sees his mission as kingdom building.

To the Thessalonian Christians Paul encourages them to be found worthy of the kingdom of God as they suffer persecution (2 Thess 1:5). In the Pastoral Epistles, Paul makes the claim that God will rescue him from every evil attack and bring him safely into the heavenly kingdom (2 Tim 4:18). In Titus Paul combines both the present and the future, reminding believers to remember "the grace of God that has appeared and offers salvation to all, teaching us to say no to ungodliness and worldly passions and to live self-controlled lives in this present age, waiting for the blessed hope" (Titus 2:11-13). Thus, they need to live the future now, that is, to practice a kingdom lifestyle while waiting for the kingdom.

HEBREWS AND THE CATHOLIC COLLECTION

The letter to the Hebrews and the Catholic letters mainly focus on the kingdom of God in future tense. The Hebrews are told that they are receiving an unshakable kingdom, and should persevere to the end, above all things being faithful to the God who has given them precious promises about the future (Heb 12:28). In James, the congregations are exhorted not to show partiality to the rich, remembering that the poor are rich in faith and will inherit the kingdom promised by God to those who love him (Jas 2:5). Peter speaks of a rich inheritance for believers kept in heaven to be revealed at the last time (1 Pet 1:1-5). Believers who persevere in pursuing sanctification will receive "a rich welcome in the eternal kingdom of our Lord and Savior, Jesus Christ" (2 Pet 1:10). Peter also cites the Levitical command to be holy while Christians wait for the second coming of Christ (1 Peter 1:13-16; cf. Lev 11:44-45; 19:2). John describes the entire world as under the control of the evil one. This probably represents his understanding of the world as a kingdom that is completely opposed to the kingdom of God: the world, the flesh, and the devil (1 Jn 2:15-17; 5:19).

Nevertheless, there are important dimensions of the present kingdom of God in these letters. In Hebrews, Jesus reigns very much in the present. As a result of his atoning work for sin, he sits "on the right hand of the Majesty in heaven" (Heb 1:3). There he has received the divine throne forever, and his scepter of justice is the scepter of his kingdom (Heb 1:8; cf. Ps 45:6). No one else in heaven has been given such a royal position, and it is given until all his enemies are subdued (Heb 1:13; cf. Ps 110:1).

Jesus now holds the position for which human beings were originally made, to rule over creation with everything placed under their feet. But because of sin, that rulership was abdicated, as it is presently obvious that human beings are not in control of the world. But it is also evident that Jesus, who tasted death for every human being, is now crowned with that glory and honor, and will lead many to future glory. Thus, by his death and resurrection he breaks the power of death and the devil over humanity and has promised a glorious future (Heb 2:5-18). Because Christ tasted death, his present followers have now tasted the powers of the age to come (Heb 6:5)!

While Peter calls his congregations exiles and foreigners, he describes their identity as a holy nation, a royal priesthood, whose purpose is to "declare the praises of him who called you out of darkness into his wonderful light" (1 Pet 2:9 NIV). The kingdom of light is very much present in the darkness even as they wait for the final abolition of darkness "on the day God visits us" (1 Pet 2:12).

In 1 John, Christ has appeared to destroy the works of the devil (1 Jn 3:8) so that every believer would pass from a kingdom of death into one of life. Each one is now a child of God, whose identity will be revealed at the second coming (1 Jn 3:1-3).

DISCUSSION QUESTIONS

1. Why do you think the church grew so fast in such a hostile culture?

2. What can you learn from these books to help your church thrive, not just survive, as an outpost of the kingdom in a hostile secular culture?

Chapter Seventeen

GRAND FINALE AND KINGDOM COME

REVELATION AND THE PRESENT

THE BOOK OF REVELATION is a fitting conclusion to the Christian Bible as mentioned at the beginning of this study. Many of the key themes in the Bible are intensified.[1] Its opening salutation immediately focuses on kingship. Grace and peace are extended to the congregations from the one who sits on the throne "and from Jesus Christ, who is the faithful witness, the firstborn from the dead, and the ruler of the kings of the earth" (Rev 1:5 NIV). And almost immediately the congregations are reminded of their identity: "To him who loves us and has freed us from our sins by his blood, and has made us to be a kingdom and priests to serve his God and Father—to him be glory and power forever and ever! Amen" (Rev 1:5-6 NIV). A prophecy immediately follows (Rev 1:7), combining two prophecies about kingship, Daniel 7:13(-14) and Zechariah 12:10. Both of these are used to indicate that Christ is returning to set up his kingdom on the earth. To reinforce the picture,

---

[1]Barbara A. Isbell, *The Past Is Yet to Come: Exodus Typology in Revelation* (Dallas: Fontes Press, 2022).

John receives an astonishing vision of the resurrected Jesus, described in rich imagery found in Israel's Scriptures (Is 11:4; 49:2; Ezek 1:24-28; Dan 7:9; 10:4-6). Jesus is truly in charge, the First and the Last, the one who holds the keys of death and Hades.

To beleaguered and suffering churches in Asia Minor, the imprisoned John shows them that the kingdoms of this world, with all their pomp and splendor, are savage beasts underneath it all, and that the resurrected and enthroned Jesus will reign until all his enemies are underfoot.

Lampstands represent the seven different churches in Asia Minor. They are lights shining in a dark world (Rev 1:19-3:22). They are kingdom outposts, and the reigning Christ holds them high, as his mission is to shine the light of his kingdom in the dark world of the ancient Roman Empire. In each of the exhortations to the various churches, promises and rewards are presented for being faithful, and some of them have Edenic and royal features. The church at Ephesus can receive the reward of eating from the tree of life in Eden (Rev 2:7). To the church at Thyatira faithfulness means being given authority over the nations, similar to the way Christ has been given authority (Rev 2:27-28). The faithful Laodiceans are promised the right to sit down on the throne of Christ to rule (Rev 3:21). Through their faithful witness, they are conquering the kingdom of darkness, and in a certain sense their light does the same thing as they "reign" with Christ. But they also wait for a future glorious reign where they will be seated on the throne with Christ.

THE THRONE ROOM

In Revelation 4–5, John himself is given a front row seat in the divine throne room in heaven, where God sits on his dais surrounded by twenty-four elders sitting on thrones. Their main task it seems is to leave their thrones, cast down their crowns before the divine throne, and bow and kneel in adoration and worship (Rev 4:10). Angelic creatures representing all creation continually sing the trisagion from Isaiah's time in honor of the King seated on the throne: "Holy, holy, holy is the Lord God Almighty" (Rev 4:8 NIV; cf. Is 6:3). It seems that the time envisioned by the prophetic words of the seraphim in Isaiah's vision, that the whole world will be filled with the glory of God, will soon be realized.

But a crisis emerges as the King holds a sealed document that no one is found worthy to open among all the myriads of heaven and earth. Why is this a crisis? It seems as if this document contains the historical process, the future, and this is of prime concern to all the churches in Revelation, as well as to all creation. The situation on earth seems chaotic as the churches deal with martyrdoms, persecution, heresy, corruption, affluence, sexual immorality, and religious assimilation (Rev 2–3). Can anyone understand the future? Is control an illusion? Israel's Scriptures, with their grand prophetic vision, are like a sealed book. But John's vision patiently demonstrates that the future is in good hands, because one who is a lion and a lamb from the tribe of Judah, the root of David, comes forward; he can control the future and give enlightenment and direction to these desperate churches (Rev 5:5-14).

This figure is not only a lion of Judah and a root from David, but also a slain lamb with incredible power—seven horns—and omniscience—seven eyes—and he takes the scroll indicating the vision of the future in God's revelation. When he grasps the scroll firmly in hand, a cry of worship from the angelic beings and the elders bursts forth. They praise him for his sacrifice in redeeming people from every tribe and nation, to make them to be a kingdom of priests to reign on the earth (Rev 5:9-10). Caesar is not in control; Christ is. Human beings redeemed by him will reign on the earth, just as they were intended from the beginning!

CHRIST'S RULE IN HISTORY

When Christ breaks open the seven seals, he shows who really controls history despite the war, famine, plagues, persecutions, and earthquakes (Rev 6–7). It is the lion from the tribe of Judah, the root of David, the lamb that was slain. When these seals are broken by Christ and the book is finally opened, a great multitude from every tribe and nation sings God's praise around the throne of God and the lamb. God's kingdom is finally present; death, famine, plague, and natural disasters are under his control and are signs of the end.

The subsequent series of judgments—seven trumpets, seven signs, and seven bowls of wrath—bear a striking similarity to the seven seals as the sequences repeat the content of judgment with increasing intensity. At the end of the blast of the trumpets, voices declared the universal dominion of the kingdom: "The kingdom of the world has become the kingdom of our Lord and of his Messiah, and he will reign forever and ever" (Rev 11:15 NIV). At the close of the seven signs, one like the Son of Man is seated on a cloud wearing a crown and having a sharp sickle. He comes to exercise final judgment on the earth (Rev 14:14-20). After the outpouring of the seven bowls of wrath, the judgment is final and there follows the great battle of Armageddon in which Christ, riding a white horse, defeats all the forces of evil. His name is written as "King of kings and Lord of lords." All the kings of the earth and all the evil spiritual forces are dethroned and destroyed (Rev 19).

If one considers this recursion, these judgments are radical escalations of the images of Israel's liberation from tyranny and slavery in Egypt at the beginning of the Bible. They also provide the background of the liberation of planet earth from the kingdom of this world at the end of the Bible, a final and complete exodus.[2] Last, there is a wonderful picture of a restored heaven and earth, where the divine throne sits in the center and the entire world transforms into an Eden-like paradise (Rev 21–22). The King has returned to his rightful place as the Lord of creation. Christ sits on the throne. Those whom he has redeemed will serve him, see his face, and have his name written on their foreheads like the high priest in the temple. And they will reign forever and ever (Rev 22:1-4). Theocracy and democracy will be in perfect harmony.

In this return of the kingdom, it is now much more glorious. There is now no sun or moon, because God will be the light. There is no chaotic sea, for the shalom of God will reign everywhere. The river in the Garden of Eden now flows through the street from the city, its fountainhead flowing from beneath the throne of God. Trees of life—not just one—line each side of the river, continually bearing fruit for the healing of the nations. There is no temple, because God is the temple. The new Jerusalem is one gigantic holy of holies, which suggests that holiness pervades everything because God will be all in all.

---

[2]Barbara Isbell makes this very point in a remarkable study: *Past Is Yet to Come*.

But probably the greatest difference between the end and the beginning is the awareness of the fact that the great Creator of heaven and earth (the Lion), loved humanity so much that he became a human being, was born, lived, and died a horrific death, so that he might reunite them and bring them into his family (the Lamb). This is virtually impossible to comprehend. Behold, what manner of love is this that we should be called the children of God (1 Jn 3:1)!

THE PRESENT: HOW SHALL WE THEN LIVE?

How is it possible for contemporary Christians to relate to this biblical teaching of the kingdom of God and its seeming imminence in the New Testament, in the light of the fact that two thousand years later Christ has still not come? There have been several responses. One response holds that Christ was simply wrong. According to this view, the kingdom for him was totally future, all apocalyptic. But when it did not happen, according to the most famous proponent of this view, in a last-ditch effort, Jesus sought to bring history to an end by dying on the cross, but instead he was crushed by the "wheel of the world" and his mangled body was the result.[3] But the church still believed in the imminence of his coming, and many passages in the New Testament seem to make this claim. This view of the kingdom is all future and is an underrealized eschatology. When this view is held by orthodox Christians, it can often lead to an anxious concern for the future, an immobilization in the present for social concerns, and the postponement of kingdom ethics until the consummation.

On the other hand, another response believes in an overrealized eschatology—an all-present kingdom. The kingdom has come, and the church must work in concert with the Spirit for social justice and the improvement of society, bringing about a heaven on earth. This was the view of thinkers in the Social Gospel movement near the beginning of the twentieth century.[4] There is no anxiety about waiting for the kingdom because it is already here. The rest is up to the church to realize it fully.

---

[3]Albert Schweitzer, *The Quest of the Historical Jesus: A Critical Study of Its Progress from Reimarus to Wrede*, trans. W. Montgomery, 2nd ed. (London: Adam and Charles Black, 1911), 516.

[4]Walter Rauschenbusch, *A Theology for the Social Gospel* (New York: Macmillan and Co., 1922).

EMBRACING AN INAUGURATED ESCHATOLOGY

From the teaching of Christ and the early church, and as scholars like George Ladd and this study affirm, there are elements of truth in both responses: the kingdom has come but it is also future. In the pertinent words of one of Ladd's books, in the Bible and the kingdom we have "the presence of the future."[5] Thus, there is the helpful phrase *inaugurated eschatology*. What the Old Testament seemed to picture as one major coming has been split into two phases. The kingdom has come, but it is a slow process that has begun and will eventually be consummated with shock and awe. Thus, both its imminence and distance can be explained. Some of the images that Paul uses regarding the gift of the Spirit and the resurrection of Christ and his people show the importance of both nearness and distance, and demonstrate the necessary adjustments required to understand the one general coming in two phases. Therefore, the gift of the Spirit is a down payment in the present of the full measure of the Spirit at the end of time (2 Cor 1:22; 5:5; Eph 1:13-14). The experience of having an existential spiritual renewal in the present makes one long for a complete renewal in the future. The image of the first fruits and the later full harvest explains the difference between the resurrection of Christ in the middle of history with the general resurrection of believers at the end (1 Cor 15:20-28). They are indivisible much like the Son of Man and the saints of the Most High in Daniel 7, but in the former case they are temporally separated. But once the first has happened, it automatically sets in motion the expectation of the full harvest.

Jesus made it clear that the kingdom was both already and not yet. The sowing parables illustrate both (Mt 13). Sowing the seed begins an "already" process without an immediately perceivable result. The harvest will come but it does "not yet" occur until long after the sowing. Similarly, the tares are sown among the wheat indicating that evil and good will coexist until the harvest. The mustard seed metaphor also indicates the long process between the planting of the smallest seed and its growth to the largest tree.

---

[5]George Eldon Ladd, *The Presence of the Future: The Eschatology of Biblical Realism*, rev. ed. (Grand Rapids, MI: Eerdmans, 1974).

Moreover, the last five parables of Jesus in Matthew 24:36–25:46, which immediately follow his teaching about the future, all emphasize important facets about the kingdom to come. They are all prefaced by his declaration that the timing of his second coming is not even known to him, only to his Father (Mt 24:36-41). This point must never be forgotten in all teaching about the kingdom. The first pair of parables deal with the unexpected early arrival of the kingdom and the importance of being alert. The example of the deluge during Noah's time is the background for this set. It came unexpectedly when no one was prepared. Deftly Jesus segues to the first parable of the owner of the house who ought to be prepared for the coming of a thief, by always being alert (Mt 24:42-44). The second parable presents the image of a wise servant placed in charge of his master's household while the master is away (Mt 24:45-51). Thinking that his master will delay his return, the servant exploits his position, abusing those under his care and living immorally. In such a situation, the master's early arrival shocks the servant, who is judged severely.

The second set of parables underline the delay of the Kingdom. In the first one, the parable of the ten virgins and the bridegroom (Mt 25:1-13), the wedding is imminent, and the virgins were to wait for the bridegroom to arrive and accompany him at night with their lamps to the wedding to meet his bride. But the bridegroom delayed his coming and five of the virgins were not prepared for his arrival because they had not purchased enough oil for their lights to continue to burn. When the bridegroom finally came, they could not accompany him to the wedding. If it is realized that light symbolizes good works, the point is crystal clear: keep shining until Jesus returns even if it is much later than you think (Mt 5:14-16). The second parable makes the same point (Mt 25:14-30). Before the master departs on a long journey, he distributes various amounts of wealth to three different servants: five bags of gold to one, two sacks to another, and one to a third servant. In the meantime, the first two servants use the wealth to make more while the last servant simply buries the wealth to protect and preserve it. When the master finally returns, he rewards the servants who increased his wealth and judges the one who did nothing. Though the second coming be delayed, one must use all the resources one has been given to add to the kingdom.

In the final parable of the sheep and the goats, Jesus gives a sobering image of final judgment (Mt 25:31-46). When he returns, destinies will be determined by how people treated the "least of these my brothers and sisters": the hungry, the thirsty, the stranger, the naked, the sick, and the imprisoned. The sheep, those who helped such marginalized believers, helped Jesus himself and thus will inherit the kingdom in all its fullness. The goats, those who did not, will experience eternal punishment. It is that simple. This last parable stresses both the kingdom to come and the kingdom now. The kingdom will come in all its glory in the epiphany of the Son of Man at the end of history. But he is also present right now in disguise in the least of his brothers and sisters.

The contemporary church is often enthralled by a celebrity culture in which dazzling speakers are paraded at conferences, and megachurches with their charismatic pastors are all the rage. The culture at large is mirrored where the grandiose event is celebrated, the huge donations are announced, and the awards of achievement are presented before millions. The headline news on our screens makes us aware of every movement of newsmakers, both good and bad, and we are lost in information overload. We are left wondering with Dorothy Day, the Catholic social reformer, about the experience of futility this engenders: "One of the greatest evils of the day is the sense of futility. [People say:] What good does it do? What is the sense of this small effort?"[6] Jesus, the final judge, makes us aware in this last parable of the newsfeed of the kingdom. The headlines of the kingdom are upside-down headlines. Someone fed the hungry, someone gave a drink to the thirsty, someone welcomed a stranger, someone clothed the naked, someone healed the sick, someone visited a prisoner, someone. . . .

All these parables point out the importance of being ready and prepared for the consummation of the kingdom, what John Donne (ca. 1572–1631) called "the world's last night,"[7] and that means living out the presence of the inauguration of the kingdom in daily life. Whether the consummation arrives early or late, readiness is required. If what you are doing is interrupted, so be it: "no matter; you were at your post when the inspection came."[8] And

---

[6]Dorothy Day, "Vocation to Prison," in *The Catholic Worker* 24, September 1957, 6.
[7]John Donne, "What if this present were the world's last night?" (1609/1611).
[8]C. S. Lewis, *The World's Last Night and Other Essays* (New York: Harcourt, Brace & World, 1952), 112.

come it will. In the end, what shall it profit people if they gain the whole world but lose their souls at the inspection.

A German theologian, Oscar Cullman, once used an analogy from World War II to indicate the gap between the first and the second comings of Jesus.[9] Two particular days were important in liberating Europe from Nazi oppression: D-Day (June 6, 1944), the invasion of Europe; and VE-day (May 8, 1945), the end of the war. On D-day the Allied forces successfully landed on the beaches of France after horrific fighting and were able slowly to move east to Germany. In a sense, this meant that the war was over, because Germany was now fighting a war on two fronts, with western Allies and eastern ones invading their territories. But Hitler and his armies continued to fight until the bitter end. More western troops were killed in those eleven months than in the previous five years. The continuation of the war for those months was due to the stubbornness, delusion, and evil of Germany's leader, Adolf Hitler.

Cullman used these two days to mark the inauguration of the kingdom (D-day) and the consummation of the kingdom (VE-day). The first day stands for the first coming of Christ and what he accomplished for his people with his work on the cross for their salvation, while the second day stands for his second coming in glory and judgment, when the kingdom is consummated. The question may be asked rightly: Why is there such an immense gap between the first and second coming? It is not because of stubbornness, delusion, and evil. It is because "the Lord is not slow in keeping his promise, as some understand slowness. Instead he is patient with you, not wanting anyone to perish, but everyone to come to repentance" (2 Pet 3:9 NIV).

The goodness and the love of God are the reason for delay. His patience means salvation. The necessary consequence: "So then, dear friends, since you are looking forward to this, make every effort to be found spotless, blameless and at peace with him" (2 Pet 3:14 NIV). Or as one of my former professors once said about this passage: "In light of the gracious delay, we all have another day to be more holy!"[10]

---

[9]Oscar Cullmann, *Christ and Time: The Primitive Christian Conception of Time and History*, trans. Floyd V. Filson, 3rd ed. (Philadelphia: Westminster Press, 1975), 84-87.
[10]The professor was D. Clair Davis.

DISCUSSION QUESTIONS

1. Read Matthew 23:23. How do you think a knowledge of the entire biblical story can help you avoid Jesus' condemnation here?

2. What are some ways you can embrace God's rule in your own life and in the life of your church?

GENERAL INDEX

SCRIPTURE INDEX

ALSO IN THE ESBT SERIES

Exodus Old and New
978-0-8308-5539-1

Rebels and Exiles
978-0-8308-5541-4

The Path of Faith
978-0-8308-5537-7

God Dwells Among Us
978-0-8308-5535-3

Face to Face with God
978-0-8308-4295-7

The Hope of Life After Death
978-0-8308-5531-5